WE SEE IT ALL

WE SEE
IT ALL

Liberty and Justice in an
Age of Perpetual Surveillance

JON FASMAN

PUBLICAFFAIRS

New York

PublicAffairs
Hachette Book Group
1290 Avenue of the Americas, New York, NY 10104
www.publicaffairsbooks.com
@Public_Affairs

Printed in the United States of America

First Edition: January 2021

Published by PublicAffairs, an imprint of Perseus Books, LLC, a subsidiary of Hachette Book Group, Inc. The PublicAffairs name and logo is a trademark of the Hachette Book Group.

The Hachette Speakers Bureau provides a wide range of authors for speaking events. To find out more, go to www.hachettespeakersbureau.com or call (866) 376-6591.

The publisher is not responsible for websites (or their content) that are not owned by the publisher.

Library of Congress Cataloging-in-Publication Data
Names: Fasman, Jon, author.
Title: We see it all : liberty and justice in an age of perpetual
    surveillance / Jon Fasman.
Description: First edition. | New York : PublicAffairs, 2021. | Includes
    bibliographical references and index.
Identifiers: LCCN 2020035296 | ISBN 9781541730670 (hardcover) | ISBN
    9781541730687 (epub)
Subjects: LCSH: Electronic surveillance—Social aspects. | Electronic
    surveillance—Moral and ethical aspects. | Security systems—Social
    aspects. | Security systems—Moral and ethical aspects. | Public safety.
    | Civil rights.
Classification: LCC HM846.F37 2021 | DDC 323.44/82—dc23
LC record available at https://lccn.loc.gov/2020035296

ISBNs: 978-1-5417-3067-0 (hardcover), 978-1-5417-3068-7 (ebook)

LSC-C

Printing 1, 2020

IN MEMORIAM
GEORGE ATWELL KRIMSKY
AND
SIDNEY METZGER

What the War on Drugs has done for police militarization, the War on Terror is now doing for police intelligence gathering, and the privacy of millions of Americans is at risk.

—**Adam Bates,** CATO INSTITUTE

CONTENTS

PREFACE

ON THE WEST SIDE OF CHICAGO AVENUE BETWEEN THIRTY-SEVENTH AND Thirty-Eighth Streets in South Minneapolis, there sits a long, low brick building housing a few small businesses. The building's south side faces a patch of asphalt that in ordinary times could serve as a small parking lot; aside from two rows of glass-block windows near the top, the south side is solid brick. When I saw it, on a balmy July day, the building had been painted purple, with bluish clouds on top and vibrant yellow sunflowers below. Between the flowers and the clouds, in swooping block letters, was painted, "You Changed the World, George."

That building sits down the street from the Cup Foods store, where on May 25, 2020, a Minneapolis police officer slowly choked George Floyd to death, in broad daylight and in full view of spectators and their cellphone cameras, as three of his fellow officers looked on. Millions of people saw the horrific video of the incident, which went viral on May 27.

I'm writing this sentence on the afternoon of July 12, just a couple of hours after my visit to the intersection now known as "George Floyd Square," so I don't know whether or how the weeks of protests that followed Floyd's murder affected, or perhaps even determined, the presidential election—still months ahead as I write, but in the past as you read. Nor do I know what lasting reforms they will have wrought in American policing. But on this warm afternoon, the muralist seems to have gotten it right: George Floyd did change the world.

A couple of doors down from the purple building, I saw a boarded-up shopfront window covered in signs calling to "Defund & Dismantle the Police." A row of flowers hanging on a clothes-line framed a piece of laminated paper urging people to "creatively imagine a world <u>without</u> police." On a bus shelter a few blocks away, a sign showed a balance, with a police car weighing down a school, a hospital, a bus, and houses, and asked, "Why are we fighting over crumbs for the things we need? #DefundMPD."

Minneapolis's city council pledged to abolish the city's police de-partment, and while as I write that hasn't happened, that they even passed such a measure at all shows how much the ground has shifted. Politicians, particularly Democrats, used to be terrified of appearing soft on crime. City politicians never wanted to get on the wrong side of the police and their unions. Now many otherwise left-wing, pro-union activists and politicians cast police unions as impediments to reform, and openly discuss curtailing their collective-bargaining power.

Two things link all of these developments. First, they involve a long-overdue rethinking of the rules around American policing. I don't agree with all of them. I would rather see a world with good, well-regulated police than no police, for instance, and in my view, the city council acted precipitously in vowing to abolish the Minne-apolis Police Department without a full consideration of what comes next. But as a society, we have asked the police to do too much. To the extent that "defund the police" means "redirect some share of the police budget to social service workers better equipped to handle many of the problems that, by default, police handle today," I'm all for it. To the extent that it means "wantonly reduce police budgets for political reasons," I'm against it. Vindictive, grandstanding policy is almost always bad policy.

Second, the protests escalated and spread across the world only after I submitted the manuscript for this book, on May 30, 2020. Hence this preface.

It's true that the protests did not directly concern surveillance technology, the main subject of my book. But George Floyd's apprehension and murder were recorded on security and cellphone cameras—both of which I discuss in these pages. During the protests that followed, cellphone cameras captured police officers assaulting unarmed, peaceful protesters and driving SUVs through crowds. In many instances, they shot rounds of nonlethal rubber bullets at journalists (nonlethal just means they don't kill you; they still injured numerous people, some permanently, simply for engaging in First Amendment–protected activity). Thomas Lane, one of the four officers present at Floyd's death, bolstered his motion to have his aiding and abetting charges tossed with transcripts from officers' body-worn camera (bodycam) footage.

The eighty-two pages of the transcript make for horrific reading. Those transcripts showed that Floyd was, as he said, "scared as fuck," pleading with officers, "Please, don't shoot me." He told officers that he couldn't breathe fifty-one times, at one point saying, "I'll probably just die this way." Without bodycams and cellphone cameras, Floyd's death may have gone unnoticed by the wider world.

That points to an important benefit to camera footage that I perhaps paid too little attention to in my chapter on the topic. I was mainly concerned with the question of whether being filmed—by bodycams or cellphones—improves officer behavior, principally as measured by use-of-force and other civilian complaints. On that question, the social science is ambiguous: some studies have found that outfitting officers with bodycams results in fewer use-of-force complaints; others have found that doing so produces no noticeable changes.

But an immediate, universal, and objectively observable reduction in use-of-force complaints is neither the sole benefit of bodycams nor the only measure by which to judge them. In conjunction with social media, they also publicize bad behavior, and in so doing galvanize social and political pressure to stop it.

This may ultimately be how bodycams drive change: not because police chiefs and other senior officers review footage and decide to change policy, or even because individual officers change their behavior because they know they are being filmed (though of course many might), but because millions of people see something unjust and gruesome, and take to the streets to make sure it doesn't happen to someone else. Had I delivered my manuscript just a few weeks later, I would have more strongly emphasized this point.

I would also have written more about police use of bulk location data and social media monitoring to surveil protesters. On June 24, Lee Fang reported in *The Intercept*—which does particularly good work on surveillance tech—that the FBI "modified an agreement" with Venntel, a firm that aggregates and sells cellphone location data, and "signed an expedited agreement to extend its relationship with Dataminr," an AI firm that monitors social media.

Just over two weeks later, Sam Biddle, also writing in *The Intercept*, reported that "Dataminr relayed tweets and other social media content about the George Floyd and Black Lives Matter protests directly to police, apparently across the country"—despite Twitter's terms of service ostensibly prohibiting "the use of Twitter data and the Twitter APIs by any entity for surveillance purposes, or in any other way that would be inconsistent with our users' reasonable expectations of privacy. Period." Among the tweets about which Dataminr alerted the Minneapolis Police Department was one that read simply, "Peaceful protest at Lake & Lyndale."

A Dataminr spokesperson told *The Intercept* that "alerts on an intersection being blocked are news alerts, not monitoring protests or surveillance." That distinction seems fuzzy and artificial. The real distinction between "news alerts" and surveillance, it seems to me, is who gets alerted. When I cover a protest, for instance, I'll talk to people, ask their names and other identifying information, but they are at no risk of state-run violence or further intrusive monitoring from me. That's not true when a police officer does the same thing (not to mention that people can more easily refuse to speak to me, or tell me to get lost, than they can a police officer).

It may not be reasonable to expect privacy for tweets, which are of course public, but it also seems reasonable to expect that if a company says it won't allow third parties to exploit its data for surveillance purposes, then it won't allow a company's AI to monitor social media feeds on a scale impossible for humans, or to forward the tweets of peaceful protesters—people engaged in activities protected by the First Amendment—to police.

I was gratified to see, in the wake of the protests, that IBM stopped selling facial-recognition products, and that Amazon put a one-year moratorium on police use of its facial-recognition technology. Amazon hoped its moratorium might "give Congress enough time to implement appropriate rules" around the technology. Having covered Congress for the past few years, I have to admit that Amazon's hope seems wildly misplaced, though I hope a new Congress and administration prove me wrong. IBM also called for "a national dialogue on whether and how facial recognition technology should be employed by domestic law enforcement agencies."

A couple of weeks after these firms announced their decisions, Detroit's police chief admitted during a public meeting that the facial-recognition software his department was using misidentified subjects "96% of the time." This was a striking revelation, and it bolstered the case for police departments to reject this uniquely dangerous technology. It also bolstered the case for everyone concerned about civil liberties to vigorously protest it. I do not think I overhype its dangers in this book—to my mind it represents a bigger threat to our privacies and liberties than any other technology I discuss—but I did underestimate how responsive tech firms that sell it would be. Activists, take note!

In early June, when the protests were at their peak, I wrote a long piece on police reform for *The Economist*. In the course of my reporting, I spoke to Barry Friedman, who runs New York University's Policing Project. His favored reform was simple: better regulation. "It's remarkable," he told me, "that most states don't have clear laws on use of force. Instead, every agency has its own use-of-force policy. The same is true with surveillance technology. It's remarkable that we just leave it to the police themselves."

In no other aspect of life would we even consider that approach. We don't tell banks, "Just figure out how you want to run things;

I'm sure it will all work out." (Yes, thank you, I remember 2008, and I agree that America is often too lax when it comes to enforcing the rules of finance. But at least they exist.) Regulating the police, however, requires confrontation. That does not mean it should be done with hostility or anger, but people will have to push politicians to set rules and penalties for an entity that has long been left to regulate itself.

Before George Floyd's murder, that seemed a heavy lift for most of America. Oakland did it early and well, as you'll read in the book's last chapter, and some other cities in the Bay Area followed suit. A few other places, mainly coastal or college towns, passed some sort of surveillance-oversight legislation. But the protests—and more importantly, politicians' responsiveness to them, both rhetorically and in policy changes—suggest that I underestimated Americans' readiness for police reform and regulation. I hope it's not a passing fancy.

PROLOGUE

"A perfect architecture of control"

SOMETIMES THE FUTURE REVEALS ITSELF AS THE PRESENT.

On February 10, 2020, I flew from New York to Las Vegas. The Democratic primary campaign had begun in earnest. As *The Economist*'s Washington correspondent and a co-host of our new American politics podcast, *Checks and Balance*, I was on the road nearly every week from just after New Year's Day until Covid-19 shut everything down. I had been in New Hampshire the previous week and Iowa before that, and I was about to spend three days in Nevada, followed by five in South Carolina—after a brief stop at home to do some laundry and make sure my wife and kids still recognized me and hadn't changed the locks.

Delta's cross-country and international flights both leave from the same terminal at JFK. Nearly all the gates had a placard advertising Delta's facial-recognition boarding—blue, tall, and thin, with an outline of a face captured by the four corners of a digital camera's viewfinder. "ONE LOOK AND YOU'RE ON," it blared above the picture. A banner just below read, "You can now board your flight using Delta Biometrics, a new way to more seamlessly navigate the airport." And, in tiny type at the bottom, down at foot level: "Boarding using facial recognition technology is optional. Please see an agent with any questions or for alternative procedures. Visit delta.com to view our Privacy Policy."

About eight months earlier I had flown to Quito through Delta's biometric terminal in Atlanta. Facial recognition was a strange novelty: the cameras weren't working; most people boarding my flight, including me, walked right past them and had their tickets checked by a flight attendant. But apparently it worked well enough—or soon would work well enough—for Delta to roll it out more aggressively. I had noticed facial-recognition gates in Minneapolis and Detroit; in late 2019, Delta announced it would install them in Salt Lake City. Some 93 percent of customers boarded without issue, Delta said in a press release, and 72 percent preferred it to standard boarding.

Signs of Delta's ambition can be found in the banner text below the picture, which mentions not just boarding, but the ability to "more seamlessly navigate the airport." And indeed, Delta's press release touted its "curb-to-gate facial recognition": you can use your face to check in for your flight, check luggage, go through security, and board your plane. It's all very convenient. If you've traveled internationally, the airlines already have your passport picture on file—either in their own database or accessible in one built by Customs and Border Protection.

My feeling about this program is clear: I opt out, and I hope, after reading this book, that you will too. Facial recognition imperils our civil liberties. Volunteering to use it normalizes it. The more you choose to use it, the more it will be used in ways and places that you do not choose. Whenever you have the option to avoid using it, you should take that option; you should do everything you can to slow facial recognition's spread.

After I posted a picture of Delta's placard online, a friend commented that at least Delta gave passengers the choice: he had flown Singapore Airlines to Tokyo and was required to board using facial recognition. That was relatively new: until July 2017, I was based in Singapore for *The Economist* and flew Singapore Airlines several times each month. They did not then use facial recognition. Future as present.

◍

When I landed in Las Vegas, I found messages from several friends asking me what I thought of that day's episode of *The Daily*, the *New York Times*'s daily news podcast. I hadn't heard it, but on their advice I listened as I drove between meetings. It was the audio version of a terrific, terrifying story that Kashmir Hill had broken a couple of weeks earlier.[1] Hill has been reporting on tech and privacy for about a decade; she is a perceptive, thoughtful, and engaging writer and a terrific reporter—one of the rare few whose stories tend to get better as they get longer.

This particular piece concerned a company called Clearview AI that had developed a facial-recognition app. When a user snaps and uploads a picture of anyone they see, the app tells them who that person is, thanks to Clearview's database of more than three billion images scraped from the public domain, including Facebook, YouTube, and other widely used sites. That's more than seven times as big as the FBI's facial-recognition database.

To put it another way, if you are an American, there is a one in two chance that you're in an FBI-accessible database. If you are a person in a first-world country, you're probably in Clearview's. Anyone who has Clearview's app on their phone can learn in just a few seconds who you are, and with a little sleuthing they can find out much more: your address, employer, friends, family members, and any other information about you that may be online.

As I write, hundreds of law enforcement agencies use it, as do some private companies (Clearview declined to say which ones). Some of Clearview's investors—and their friends—have used it as well: John Catsimatidis, a grocery-store magnate, happened to see his daughter on a date with someone he didn't recognize.[2] He asked a waiter to take the guy's picture, which he then ran through Clearview. Within seconds, the app told him who his daughter was eating dinner with—a venture capitalist from San Francisco. Catsimatidis also used it in his stores to identify ice-cream thieves. ("People were stealing our Haagen-Dazs," he complained. "It was a big problem.")

Police love it; they say it helps them identify suspects quickly. But that convenience alone should not determine a product's worth or legality. There are many things—such as indefinite detention without charge and repealing habeas corpus—incompatible with a free and open society that would make the job of law enforcement easier.

And while police are the main customers now, nothing is stopping Clearview from selling its app to anyone who wants to buy it. Indeed, the founder of a firm that was one of Clearview's earliest investors seems resigned to this possibility. He told Hill, "I've come to the conclusion that because information constantly increases, there's never going to be privacy. . . . Laws have to determine what's legal, but you can't ban technology. Sure, that might lead to a dystopian future or something, but you can't ban it." If backing a technology that produces "a dystopian future or something" for everyone on earth makes him richer, then bring on the dystopian future.

Facebook and other social media sites ban others from scraping their images; Clearview did it anyway. Eric Schmidt, Google's former chairman, said in 2011 that facial recognition was "the only technology that Google has built and, after looking at it, we decided to stop," because it could be used "in a very bad way."[3]

Clearview's founder, Hoan Ton-That, displayed no such qualms. On *The Daily*, he did not sound evil; he sounded smug, callow, and indifferent. When Hill asked him about the implications of creating technology that "would herald the end of public anonymity," she wrote, he "seemed taken aback": "I'll have to think about that," he replied. One would have hoped he had done so before he invented his nightmare app.

Today, too much of our privacy, and too many of our civil liberties, depend on the whims of people like Ton-That. I'm sure that Mark Zuckerberg did not sit in his dorm room at Harvard dreaming of building a platform to help Russia undermine American democracy, but that's what he did. He more likely dreamt of building something great, and world-changing—of being successful, of making his mark on the world. He did all that too. And today, he has a fiduciary responsibility to his investors to maximize their returns. He has no such obligation to the rest of us. If our civil liberties imperil the profits of tech entrepreneurs and firms that sell surveillance technology, they are free to choose the profits every time.

That is not because they are bad people. After all, even the CEOs of crunchy, green companies probably also care more about maximizing returns than about strangers' civil liberties. But Clearview AI's technology, and the panoptic powers of modern surveillance technology more broadly, when combined with low-cost and permanent digital storage—particularly in an era of resurgent authoritarianism and institutional weakness in developed countries—imperil our democracy in a way that we've never before seen. To put it another way: our liberty isn't threatened by people buying more ethically produced yogurt or BPA-free water bottles; it is by people buying more of what Clearview is selling.

It is our responsibility to speak up for ourselves, our civil liberties, and the sort of world we want to see. Is it one in which any stranger can snap a picture of us and know everything about us? If not, it is up to us to prevent that world from emerging. In the coming chapters, I hope to show you why and how.

This book grew out of a series of articles I reported and wrote for *The Economist* in the first half of 2018 about how technology is changing the justice system—in particular, police work, prisons, and sentencing.[4] I chose to focus on police and tech because police are perhaps the most tangible and familiar representatives of state power. If I told you that the National Security Agency, or the Chinese government, had surveillance technology that could overhear and store every conversation we had on our cellphones, or track all of our movements, you might be outraged, but you would probably not be surprised. I hope it would both outrage and shock you, however, to learn that every police department has that ability, with virtually no oversight about how it's used. By writing about the police, I am really writing about state power.

When I was reporting, facial recognition was still largely theoretical to most people—it was not part of their lived experience. Some police departments had launched modest trial programs. A few small ones used it for limited purposes—Washington County, Oregon, began using it in 2017 to identify suspects. Today it's in airport terminals. Even if Clearview were to fold tomorrow, another firm would probably do what they are doing.

Some critics argue the technology is unreliable, and it is— particularly, in America and Europe, for people of color. But that's not really the point. Yes, facial recognition is dangerous when it's unreliable, because it risks getting innocent people arrested. But it's dangerous when it's reliable, too, because it lets governments track us in public anytime. And it *is* getting more and more reliable.

License plate readers can track our cars, and they can go on as many police cars and city-owned light and telephone poles as political whim and budgets will allow. Devices that mimic cellphone towers, tricking our phones into revealing who we've called, what we've texted, and what websites we've searched, can now fit in the trunk of a car.

The architecture and infrastructure of a surveillance state are here. We've seen what it looks like in China, which now has more state-owned surveillance cameras than America has people. It has used its capacity to repress free speech and expression, monitor dissidents, and keep more than a million Muslims in modern-day concentration camps—and, when not locked up, under permanent, crushing surveillance.

The single most incisive and unsettling question I heard in the year I spent reporting for this book came from Catherine Crump, a law professor at the University of California, Berkeley, who directs the school's Samuelson Law, Technology and Public Policy Clinic and codirects the Berkeley Center for Law and Technology. "We can now have a perfect architecture of control," she told me—as China does. "What democratic practices do we need to not become China?" This book is a modest effort to answer that question.

1

TECHNOLOGY AND DEMOCRACY

How much state surveillance and control are you
willing to tolerate in the name of public safety?

I'M IN THE FRONT SEAT OF A POLICE SUV. BEHIND THE WHEEL IS A
precinct supervisor, the profoundly good-natured Lieutenant Leo
Carrillo, born and raised Down Neck, in Newark's historically Portu-
guese Ironbound district. Twenty years a Newark cop, his knowledge
of the city is encyclopedic. Mark DiIonno is in the back. DiIonno is
the police department's public information officer, but before that he
spent twenty-six years writing for the *Newark Star-Ledger*. He's tough,
smart, and streetwise, with a gruff and warm manner and a solid turn
of phrase. Those qualities together give him the enviable impression
of having sprung fully formed from a Damon Runyon story.

We've been driving around for about four hours, with every corner
rattling free a raft of stories and memories from both men: here's the
pizza parlor where Willie Johnson was shot; there's the corner where
a mother went down to buy milk for her three kids and got clipped in
a running gun battle; my parents used to take us shopping here, now
it's a warehouse that has seen better days; Hawk's Lounge is boarded
up—looks like they're renovating it—it used to be pretty rough.

It's late Friday afternoon, a week before the summer solstice, and
Newark is preening. New Jersey's biggest city has a lousy reputation.

Unless you're lucky enough to know the city well, you probably think of it, if you think of it at all, as a punchline or an object of sympathy. Perhaps it conjures up a similar set of associations as Detroit or Youngstown: violence, postindustrial decay, and abandonment. Newark is Rust Belt in spirit, economy, and circumstance, if not location: it deindustrialized along with other northeastern manufacturing towns, and nothing has really replaced the industry that left.

But what nobody ever tells you, and you can't understand until you put in some time here, is how beautiful it can be—especially on one of those June afternoons so long and mild that you decide to put aside, even just temporarily, all of your quarrels with God and your fellow man and bask in the liquid gold. The art deco buildings downtown look like they've been bathed in honey. You wouldn't want to skip through the overgrown vacant lots without a hazmat suit and thick-soled boots, but from across the street they really do look like little squares of sylvan paradise, with all the weeds in flower and bees droning lazily above.

Driving past Weequahic Park—a three-hundred-acre expanse in the city's south ward, designed by the sons of the man who designed New York's Central Park—we hear young kids laughing and playing tag. The surrounding area is tidy and cozy, a suburb built in the days of streetcars and modest incomes: two-story homes separated from each other by little strips of lawn, a car in every driveway.

Philip Roth grew up here (his family's house, on Summit Avenue, has a plaque in front of it), in this neighborhood of midcentury American promise. It's a modest, charming house a few miles west of the park. Roth maintained a romantic connection to Newark, if not an actual one, throughout his career. By far his best comment about New Jersey and literary ambition came from *The Counterlife*: "While dialing home from the restaurant, Henry remembered that after the lecture, during the question period, Nathan had been asked by a student if he wrote 'in quest of immortality.' He could hear Nathan laughing and giving the answer—it was as close to his dead brother as he'd come all day. 'If you're from New Jersey,' Nathan had said, 'and you write thirty books, and you win the Nobel Prize, and you live to be white-haired and ninety-five, it's highly unlikely but not impossible that after your death they'll decide to name a rest stop for you on the Jersey Turnpike. And so, long after you're gone, you may indeed be remembered, but mostly by small children, in the backs of cars, when they lean forward and tell their parents, "Stop, please, stop at Zuckerman—I have to pee." For a New Jersey novelist that's as much immortality as it's realistic to hope for.'"[1]

Groups of older kids are out on the side streets, beginning their weekends on the stoops and sidewalks, shouting and flirting and puffing out their chests the way teenagers do everywhere, caught in that awkward lope between tag in the park and adult life. At one corner we stop as a father—tall, proud, and gleamingly bald—picks up a toddler under one arm and offers the other hand to his son to cross the street. He throws a nod and a smile to someone he knows across the way. Cookout sounds and smells waft on the evening air. Just an ordinary summer evening: so long it feels eternal, so perfect it can only be fleeting.

As we pass the empty Seth Boyden Homes—low-rise brick buildings, now abandoned and boarded up—Lieutenant Carrillo's smartphone chirps. An app tells him that seven shots were fired about a minute ago, a few blocks from where we are. Carrillo taps the icon on his phone's screen, which brings up a map that shows the intersection where the app believes the shots were fired, along with an audio clip: seven shots in quick succession—two, a brief pause, then three, another pause, then two again. It doesn't sound like a gun battle, or two shooters: the shots all have the same pitch and frequency; they sound like they all came from the same gun, fired from roughly the same place.

The app is called Shotspotter, and as of December 2019, police departments in over one hundred cities across America were using it.[2] The premise is fairly simple: across these cities, arrays of mounted acoustic sensors are trained to recognize gunfire and alert police in real time. In Newark, the sensors look like white diamonds; they are usually mounted on traffic lights. When they recognize something that sounds like a gunshot, they triangulate its location on a city map, then alert Shotspotter's acoustic analysts, who confirm that the sensors detected gunshots, and not a metal door slamming or a large truck backfiring. Then an alert goes out to police: how many shots fired, from how many guns, and where.

Carrillo grows alert, flipping the scanner to the precinct's channel as he drives, lights flaring and siren bleeping at every intersection. So far nothing from dispatch, but as we get closer to the scene, cruisers approach from every direction.

The app says the shots came from inside an immense cemetery that backs up onto a high school. The cemetery is locked and surrounded by a tall chain-link fence, topped with three rows of rusty barbed wire. By the time we stop, seven other police cars are parked alongside the cemetery's edge. A couple of officers stand on the high ground behind the school, scanning the cemetery to see if anyone is running. Others patrol the perimeters.

On one hand, there was nothing unusual about this scene: police got a call about a shooting; they went to the scene and tried to find the shooter. But one thing about it was extraordinary, and would have been unthinkable just a decade ago. The dozen or so officers on the scene came not because their dispatcher or lieutenant told them where to go, but because their phones did.

Perhaps it should not be surprising that the police are sometimes led by their phones. After all, the rest of us are. But the day before I went out with Lieutenant Carrillo, I spent some time with his boss, Anthony Ambrose, Newark's public safety director. (Newark's mayor, Ras Baraka, merged the city's police, fire, and emergency management operations; Ambrose runs the consolidated entity.)

Big, bald, and broad, with an old-school Jersey accent, Ambrose is perfectly cast in his role. He joined the Newark Police Department in 1986, when, he explained, "the only thing that may have been computerized was how you got gas in your car." Police recorded their activity on a log sheet with a pen. Dispatchers wrote down assignments on index cards that were filed and kept for three years. Officers stuck thumbtacks into a wall map where crimes occurred, then colored the tack's head: red for homicide, black for robbery, and so on.

Ambrose recounted these details with wry affection, but without nostalgia. The shift toward digital information and storage, he said, "makes [policing] easier. . . . Computers are great for record keeping, plotting crime, using your automatic vehicle locator." In the old days, he added, amassing a file on a homicide victim—including not just name, address, and age, but also any arrests, convictions, and police stops, and known associates and family members—could take the better part of two days. Now all of that information is available with a click on an officer's tablet or in-car laptop.

And yet, he said, "most of our cops . . . they end up working for the computer. There's no proactive policing." GPS systems track where officers go, and computerized dispatch tracks what they do and how long it takes to do it. With every minute and movement tracked, recorded, and judged, officers are less likely to spend unstructured time walking their beats and getting to know people in the communities they patrol.

The impact of forgoing that practice is hard to track; there is no metric for un-had conversations. But it is worth at least considering what gets lost when an institution lives and dies by the numbers. The stop-and-frisk policy of the New York Police Department (NYPD)—reformed after a judge ruled that the way the department carried it out was unconstitutional—was driven at least in part by the desire to appear statistically productive.[3] That is not an argument against technology, of course—just an awareness of its limits in this area.

There are other limits worth considering, too. There is much to praise about Shotspotter. Too often, gunshots go unreported. Perhaps they happen on a vacant lot, and nobody hears them. Or if people hear them, everyone assumes someone else will call. Maybe people who heard the gunshot have learned not to trust the police, and so don't call. They may fear retaliation. But nobody wants to live in an area plagued by gun violence. If Shotspotter can help catch shooters who would otherwise not have been caught, that is all to the good, right?

But consider, more broadly, what it means to have police directed not by a commanding officer, or by a call from a concerned citizen, but by a private company using proprietary technology. If a citizen were to ask one of those officers scanning the cemetery why they were there, he would have to say the phone sent him. What does that mean for accountability, and for law enforcement autonomy? Perhaps the citizens of all ninety of the cities where Shotspotter is used are fine outsourcing some dispatching decisions from police officers themselves to an opaque gunshot-detection algorithm offered by a for-profit company. But perhaps that is not what they want—and if not, they deserve a say.

☜

Or consider another piece of technology aimed at solving unreported crimes: the monitoring service offered by Ross McNutt's Persistent Surveillance Systems. This technology was born on the battlefields of Iraq as a way to catch people planting the improvised explosive devices that killed American troops.

McNutt, who headed the Air Force Center for Rapid Product Development, put cameras on drones and flew them over the city of Fallujah to record what they saw. If you're in your twenties or early thirties, you may have no particular associations with the Iraqi city of Fallujah. But those of us who remember the start of America's catastrophic invasion of Iraq after the attacks of September 11, 2001, also remember the violent fights for control of that city.

"We could watch a bomb go off," McNutt explained to me, "follow the people who set it, and go back in time to see where they came from. . . . We helped significantly to bring peace and stability to Fallujah."

When McNutt retired, he decided to use that technology to try to solve murders in America. Most go unsolved, often for the reasons I mentioned above. McNutt figured that eyes in the sky would let police see more. Police would no longer be dependent on citizens to alert them to violent crimes. It would give them a time machine: they could see a killing, and then rewind the video to see where the shooters came from.

Would you want a technology like that flying over your city? Would you want it flying over your neighborhood? What if it wasn't over your neighborhood, but over another one across town—one that you avoid because of its high crime rate? Who gets to decide which communities the drones fly over? How do you weigh the wishes of people in neighborhoods with high levels of reported crime, which would presumably receive the most intense surveillance, against those of the rest of the city?

How rigorous are the rules governing how the footage can be used, seen, and stored? And is this really a precedent we want to set? McNutt's footage now just renders people as indistinguishable little dots, but what happens when the cameras get better—or when the drones fly lower, and we're not just dots but recognizable people? What happens when a city gets a police chief with a well-hidden vindictive streak, who wants to keep an eye on his critics? Can police use those drones to monitor and record a protest against police brutality, in the name of public safety, and then turn the time machine on protesters, to see whether they may have done anything warranting arrest?

We can boil all these questions down into a fundamental one, which you should bear in mind as you read this book: How much state surveillance are you willing to tolerate for improved public safety?

These are not easy questions, and they are not going to get any easier.

◉

"We believe we can remove the repeat offenders early in their career," McNutt told me. "By stopping someone after they shoot their first person rather than their tenth person, you can save a lot of people. We reduce crime by solving otherwise unsolvable crimes. . . . And by solving those otherwise unsolvable crimes, we're showing that the system works, that if you commit major crimes here you'll get caught and convicted. That's where deterrence kicks in."

Who could disagree with any of that? Catching shooters who otherwise would have evaded justice, strengthening faith in the criminal justice system's efficacy, deterring people from committing further crimes—those are goals that everyone can support.

But can they support those goals at any cost? Persistent Surveillance's drones can circle above a huge swath of a city, watching and recording everyone, even those—mostly those, statistically—not suspected of committing any crime.

Now, for the moment, this sounds worse than it actually is. As I explain later in this book, the resolution of the company's cameras is extremely low, so people look like little dots. You can't tell what they look like, what they're wearing or holding, or what color hair or skin they have. But camera technology is constantly improving. Even if McNutt's company maintains a principled fidelity to low-resolution imagery, nothing is stopping another company from mounting high-resolution cameras on drones and setting them aloft above a city.

Persistent Surveillance, McNutt told me, responds to reported crimes, meaning that when they hear that a shooting has happened in an area under surveillance, they focus on that—they're not looking for jaywalkers. But again, another company could. This technology can be used to target crime, but it could also be used to see who goes to abortion providers. Or Alcoholics Anonymous meetings. Or churches, synagogues, and mosques—and how often. It could follow people home from a demonstration. You could argue that the police could just as easily follow someone around in public. But you would notice a police car if it was following you for days. This technology is invisible and undetectable.

The Baltimore Police Department (BPD) used Persistent Surveillance for much of 2016. It was a privately funded trial—paid for by John and Laura Arnold, two philanthropists from Texas who have funded a range of criminal justice innovations. The department did not have to go through—or even inform—the city council, so it did not. The program only came to light after *Bloomberg Businessweek* wrote a story about it, prompting a spokesman for the BPD to explain that a surveillance program that nobody knew about was somehow not "a secret surveillance program."[4]

During the trial run, the BPD reported that it retained images gathered by Persistent Surveillance for only forty-five days unless they were related to an ongoing case. But later that year, Baltimore's police chief told the city's Office of Public Defenders that "all images recorded/captured during the pilot program have been saved and archived and are therefore available, regardless of whether the images were provided to BPD for use in investigations."[5] This contradiction highlights another recurring theme of this book: usage policies are crucial, but without independent auditing and real penalties for failing to abide by them, they aren't worth much.

McNutt talked to me at length about his commitment to assuaging people's privacy concerns, about the audit trail that exists for the footage—which means that if an officer sneaks onto the system to peep at an ex-girlfriend's house, they'll know. I believe he is genuinely concerned about public safety and privacy. But in evaluating technology's potential harms, the intent of a company's founder only goes so far—which is not really all that far.

McNutt also talked about his conversations with the American Civil Liberties Union (ACLU). To his credit, he attempted to plead his case to the group at their headquarters in Washington, DC, arguing that the low-resolution images presented no threat to privacy. It did not go well. According to the article in *Bloomberg Businessweek*, Jay Stanley, a privacy expert and policy analyst with the ACLU, "felt as if he were witnessing America's privacy-vs-security debate move into uncharted waters." Stanley said to himself, "This is where the rubber hits the road. The technology has finally arrived, and Big Brother . . . is finally here."

Some would argue that McNutt is also a citizen, and would no more want to be subject to intrusive surveillance than you or I would. But financial motivations, the temptations of success, and fiduciary responsibilities to shareholders can do strange things to principles. As tinkerers from Victor Frankenstein onward can attest, creations can take on lives of their own, often quite different from those envisioned by their creators. Jack Dorsey probably did not set out to make Twitter a website for people to spread misinformation and spit bile at each other—but that is the website he created.

Obviously, Baltimore's experiment with Persistent Surveillance was poorly handled. Police departments should not deploy active surveillance systems like this one and not tell anyone. But controversy notwithstanding, the drones did good work, and as I'll explain later, they will fly again. In around three hundred hours of flight time, they captured twenty-three shootings on film, five of them fatal. Our phones track our locations; cookies let advertisers know our web-browsing habits; police on foot and in cars can see us as we go about our day. The drones are filming city streets, not the insides of our houses; they watch us in public, not private. Is it really that big a deal to appear as an indistinguishable dot on some drone footage, if the drones catch shooters and killers who would otherwise not be caught?

Or consider what was happening as I worked my way through the copyedited manuscript of this book—the last chance an author has to make significant changes. It was mid-May 2020, and, like the rest of the East Coast, I had been locked down at home for a little over two months. Nearly 90,000 Americans had died of Covid-19—more than a quarter of them in my home state of New York.

America and South Korea confirmed their first cases of Covid-19 on the same day—but at the time of my writing, just 260 people had died of it in South Korea. America's population is a bit over six times South Korea's, but it saw more than 330 times as many of its people killed. That is attributable in large measure to South Korea's extensive human and app-based contact tracing, which involves levels of government intrusiveness, monitoring, and information gathering that many Americans simply would not tolerate. Even the suggestion to wear masks in public was too much for some.

Curiously, attitudes toward surveillance did not seem consistent or partisan: opposition to shut-down orders—and, presumably, to mandated contact-tracing app-downloading—was far more prevalent on the right than on the left, as is sympathy for the police. I spoke with numerous people on the left who are uneasy with police surveillance but pined for the sort of active health monitoring that South Korea used to corral the spread of Covid-19. For the record, I did not pine, exactly, for that sort of surveillance. But if a contact-tracing app were available—and if I had confidence that its data would go only to state and local health departments, and would not be accessible to law enforcement under any circumstances—I would have downloaded it. If it becomes available between the time I'm writing this and when you're reading it, I will download it—and then I'll delete it as soon as I'm vaccinated.

Some collection of personal data is essential for contact tracing, and contact tracing is essential to stop the unchecked spread of Covid-19. But there is a world of difference between voluntarily providing limited personal information for public-health purposes—and to public-health authorities—and the sort of creeping, invisible, police-driven surveillance I discuss in this book. Accepting the former, which is limited in scope and purpose, does not require accepting the limitless latter. If anything, rejecting surveillance creep becomes even more important in the face of pandemic-driven surveillance.

I began digging into these questions about surveillance and policing, as I explained in the prologue, in early 2018, when I reported a series of articles about how technology is changing justice systems around the world. That series started with the same premise as this book: technology is radically changing policing, and we have not fully come to grips with the extent or implication of those changes. In one sense, that statement is banal: technology is changing virtually every aspect of our lives. This revolution is still young, and we haven't fully come to grips with any of it.

But policing is unique. Police are the most visible representatives of state power. Their job is to keep us safe; to do so they are empowered to surveil, interrogate, beat, imprison, and kill. How they exercise their power can have lethal consequences, and the police are intimidating—by design.

I have been out on patrol with police officers in Newark, Los Angeles, Atlanta, and Washington, DC, as well as in High Point, North Carolina, and in Newport News, Virginia. I've spoken with officers from a good dozen more departments, and I've met scores of police officers. I have laughed with them, argued with them, gone out drinking with them, and learned from them.

Still, whenever I see a police car parked by the side of the highway, or coming up in my rearview mirror, I get nervous—and for the record, I'm a middle-aged white man who has never been arrested. I feel a sudden spike in adrenaline—the sweaty palms, the metallic taste in the mouth. Several years back, while driving my family home from Florida to Atlanta, where we then lived, I was pulled over by an officer in a tiny town in south Georgia for driving a few miles over the speed limit. (Many Atlantans believe that south Georgia police officers ticket cars with Dekalb or Fulton County plates—i.e., from Atlanta—with particular ferocity.) I was shaking—and I knew I hadn't done anything more than mild speeding.

Police are also familiar. If I told you that, say, the National Security Agency (NSA) could listen in on our phone calls and track our movements, you would probably gnash your teeth and shrug. But "NSA" conjures up images of endless rows of computer monitors in a remote office park. Police are more identifiable, ordinary, even routine. You can put faces to police officers in ways that you probably cannot for NSA agents.

Yet police have access to much of the same street-level surveillance capacity as the NSA, with relatively little oversight. In America and other liberal democracies, the complex interlocking web of privacy laws and expectations have not yet caught up to the observational and retentive powers available to most police departments.

For instance, police cannot tap your phones to listen to your conversations without a warrant. But in most jurisdictions, your metadata—the non-call content of your phone use, including who you called, when, and for how long; your SMS messages and web-browsing data; and your location information—carries much less protection, even though, in aggregate, it provides far more information than police could glean from overhearing a few conversations: where you have been, who you talked to, what you looked for online.

Under the law, all of this is public information, because you have shared it with your telephone service provider. The "third-party doctrine" holds that voluntarily surrendering information to a third party—such as a bank or a telecom provider—negates any reasonable expectation of privacy.[6] So police can obtain your financial records from your bank, for instance, without a warrant. Courts have begun to take a more skeptical view of that principle, but it remains operative even today, when for cellphone and online communications, it makes no sense.

Or consider social media postings. These are, of course, public, to varying degrees, depending on the service and your settings—but far more public than, say, a diary or folded sheet of paper that you lock in your bedside table. It makes sense that the police should want to use suspects' posts in an investigation.

An officer for one East Coast department shook his head ruefully as he told me just how often people post videos of themselves committing crimes, or pictures of themselves with the proceeds of their crimes. My favorite of this sadly extensive genre of stories comes from Kentucky, where a young man posted a picture of himself giving the middle finger with one hand while with the other he siphoned gas from a police car (he spent a night in jail).

And yet governments have used tools that scrape data (often invisibly and without the user's informed consent) from social media posts on an immense scale. They reap not just the contents of the posts and users' IDs but also their IP and email addresses, telephone numbers, location data, and social media history.

In early 2019, the ACLU sued the federal government for failing to respond to Freedom of Information Act (FOIA) requests regarding its social media monitoring of immigrants and visa applicants.[7] That July, the FBI solicited proposals for a tool that would let the agency track people by location and use keyword monitoring in real time. I would guess that most people understand that police can follow them around in public without a warrant, but are still uneasy at the sort of massive, warrantless monitoring offered by Persistent Surveillance; in the same way, I would guess that most also understand that social media posts are public, and therefore fair game for police to use in an investigation, but are still uneasy at this sort of warrantless, intensive, secretive monitoring on a massive scale.

In the course of writing this book, I have heard police officers and privacy activists gripe about each other extensively. Police often think that activists are naive, annoying, and reflexively anti-police; activists often think that police are deceptive and bent on control. In fact, they need each other. Activists, like everyone else, need police to maintain public safety; police need activists to hold them to account.

To a large extent, as reluctant as both sides might be to admit it, they benefit from each other's work.

A small ideological note here: I have spoken with and read the work of both police authorities and abolitionists. The latter believe, if I understand and can compress their central argument correctly, that society would be better served without police, with communities setting their own standards for criminal behavior and enforcing them collectively. I sympathize with that view but do not share it. I believe that societies need both police and civilian oversight of police; if you think otherwise, I hope you will still find the sort of activism and oversight that I endorse in this book beneficial.

Police officers will tell you—have told me—that they do not do what the privacy activists fear. They do not monitor or compile files on innocent people. They are not interested in peeking into people's bedroom windows or keeping tabs on what political rallies they attend. But, of course, law enforcement has done all those things, and emergent forms of technology give them the power to do all of them—and more—with minimal cost and effort.

Police should have access to technology they deem necessary to do their jobs, but they should also explain to the people they serve why they need it and how they want to use it. They should set rigorous usage policies, with independent auditing, public-reporting requirements, and penalties for failing to follow them. I believe in rigorous civilian oversight of police, not because police are bad people, but because our civil liberties should not be dependent on the state's whims and preferences, or on our ability to prevent the coming of another J. Edgar Hoover. Citizens deserve a say in how they are policed.

The overwhelming majority of both police and privacy activists have the safety and well-being of their community at heart. That is not to say they want the same thing all the time. I'm sure, for instance, that most police would prefer minimal oversight, and most activists would like maximal. But get them in the same room instead of in front of TV cameras, talking to rather than at each other, and they can quickly iron out 90 percent of their disagreements. Slowly, honestly, and laboriously, they can almost always reach a workable compromise on the remaining 10 percent. I know this to be true because I have seen where and how it works, and I will take you there.

◉

In this book I've tried to create a framework for how citizens should think about emergent forms of surveillance technology. I've applied the framework to police practices, but the issues go way beyond policing. Is an open, liberal society possible if we can be tracked and recorded everywhere we go? Do we have a right to a degree of public anonymity—to expect that we won't be tracked and monitored if we're not suspected of committing any crimes? What is the state permitted to know about us? How, and with what degree of oversight, can they glean that knowledge? Jeremy Bentham conceived of a prison designed in such a way that a single guard could see every inmate from his post. His "Panopticon" was never built, but in essence, we all now live in a panopticon. What should we do about it? This book will look deeply into the sorts of technology that are giving rise to these questions.

The book starts by examining automatic license plate readers (ALPRs)—cameras that are being mounted on an increasing number of police cars as well as at fixed points and on private vehicles. When these devices sit atop police cars, they automatically capture images of each license plate the car passes. They let police easily find cars suspected of being used in crimes: so far, so good. But of course they also capture license plates of cars not suspected of involvement in crimes. In effect, they let police amass a granular record of everywhere you drive: whom you visit and when, how long you stay there, and where you go next.

These devices track your movements in public; nobody is peering through your window shades or listening to your phone calls. But if a police officer were standing on your street all day every day, writing down the names of every passing license plate, day after day, week after week, you would notice. And your local police department would have to decide that assigning officers to this task, for twenty-four hours each day, was a worthwhile use of resources. ALPRs accomplish the same thing effortlessly, invisibly, and cheaply.

The license plate images often wind up in databases shared by multiple police forces and supplemented by privately held ALPR companies. Who should have the right to access that database, and when? What sort of security safeguards does the database need? What happens in the event of a data breach? More importantly, do we have the right to have our data deleted, or must we simply accept that police now amass records of everywhere we go, that they can then keep forever?

The book then looks at body cameras and cellphone cameras, which give police and citizens new ways of looking at each other. Bodycams have been touted as a tool to promote transparency: instead of two conflicting verbal accounts of a contested police-citizen encounter, adjudicators can rely on video evidence. But who decides when to turn on the camera? What does it really show—and what does it leave out? What happens to the footage? Who gets to see it, how long is it stored, and with what safeguards? Who decides when to delete it? And how can it be used? These are not academic questions: What happens when you walk past a police officer on your way to a protest, and the officer is wearing a bodycam equipped with a facial-recognition app?

The next chapter discusses drones, which give police eyes in the skies. Few technologies have a larger upside. They can fly over fires without risking a helicopter pilot's life and health. Equip them with a heat-sensitive camera, and they are peerless at finding people lost in the wilderness in winter. But they can also subject a city to, as you've read above, perpetual surveillance. And they can easily be weaponized.

I then consider electronic monitoring, a technology familiar to most people as ankle monitors. This technology offers immense promise as an alternative to incarceration, either post-conviction or (more politically plausible) for people awaiting trial: it's better that they stay at home, maintaining ties with their families, perhaps with permission to travel to work each day, than sit in a criminogenic jail for months.

But even as a pretrial alternative to jail, it subjects people not yet convicted of crimes to constant, burdensome state surveillance.

The book examines facial recognition, which poses perhaps a more dire and lasting threat than any other technology I discuss. When I began my research, facial recognition still had a pie-in-the-sky aspect to it, at least for the general public. Today it is in use at airports and by police departments; it is part of China's architecture of control and repression. A growing number of places have banned it. Initially that struck me as alarmist; now it seems like good sense.

I go on to describe the algorithms used in policing, which purport to predict where and when crime will occur, as well as those used in sentencing, which try to forecast how big a risk of reoffending a suspect poses. Backers of the former use say it helps them better allocate patrol forces. Backers of the latter say it removes human bias from sentencing and pretrial detention: a judge prejudiced, consciously or not, against defendants of a certain ethnicity will no longer be able to act on that prejudice.

But these algorithms operate opaquely, and they rest on data amassed over decades, by individuals with all their biases. Far from eliminating bias, they risk calcifying it in the name of science and objectivity, thus making it harder to combat.

The book looks into encryption and the tools that can defeat it, rendering privacy protections useless. Governments and police often argue that they need a "back door" to encrypted communications services like WhatsApp and Signal: the "bad guys" shouldn't be able to keep their communications secret. But weakening privacy protections for suspects weakens them for all of us.

And when should police be able to use these tools? When should they be able to use Stingrays, which capture the metadata of all phones in a given area? Police may trot out those tools to eavesdrop on someone they have good reason to eavesdrop on, but what happens to the rest of our data caught up in that dragnet?

I also explore what can happen when all of these technologies are combined and put in the hands of a government with scant regard for its citizens' civil liberties. I was unable to report from China, for reasons I will explain later, so I went to Ecuador to look into that country's Chinese-built emergency management system, which centralizes feeds from thousands of cameras across the country. It improves the responses of police, fire departments, and ambulances to emergencies, but it is also an effective central monitoring system: it lets the government spy on almost anyone, anytime, almost anywhere in public.

And finally, I report on what citizens have done in one city, Oakland, California, to safeguard their civil liberties and forge a more productive relationship with their city's police. Their example, I hope, is the heart of the book.

Some may accuse me of scare tactics in how I write about these technologies. Guilty. You should be scared. But I do not only want to scare you. I want to scare you into taking action—into using the democracy available to you in the most effective way possible. The surveillance state is here, and it is up to us to stop it.

Ultimately, this book is less about technology than it is about democracy—I am less interested in how various pieces of surveillance tech function than in the risks they pose to citizens of open, liberal democracies. The risk in writing a tech book is that it will be quickly outdated, overtaken by news and new technology. But I trust my thesis is proof against that fate, at least for some time. I want to provide citizens with the heuristics, framework, and tools necessary to come to grips with surveillance technology in whatever form it takes for the foreseeable future.

As you read, I hope you bear in mind three metrics for evaluating emergent forms of technology.

First, consider where each new technology places *responsibility* for decision-making. If a security agent pulls you out of line at the airport for a secondary search before you board the plane, you know who made that decision, and you can ask why. If a machine using facial recognition does the same, then who, ultimately, has decided you should be subject to additional screening?

If, over a period of years, the facial-recognition machines at Major City X airport are found to select a disproportionate number of nonwhite people for secondary screening, whose fault is that? The airlines using the system? The agents who follow the machines' recommendations? The programmers who created the algorithm powering the system? Can they all point fingers at each other? If a passenger believes she was unfairly treated, to whom does she turn for redress?

Can the airlines and agents just blame the algorithm? And if so, what happens then? Tech firms often consider their algorithms trade secrets, and worry that revealing them would put them at a competitive disadvantage, or let criminals game the system. The latter has always struck me as deeply implausible: show me the mugger or car thief who decides to shift hunting grounds because he knows, day to day, which neighborhoods his local police department's predictive-policing algorithm has flagged for extra attention.

How much do citizens have the right to know about algorithms that decide their fate? In my view, they have the right to know a whole lot, but many tech firms disagree, and so far no mechanism has yet forced them to open their books.

Second, consider what each emergent form of technology means for our *privacy rights and expectations.* What information does it gather, and how; how is it stored, and who can see it; who can make a decision to use the technology, and with what degree of oversight?

Stingrays are devices that mimic cellphone towers, tricking all the phones in an area into connecting to them rather than the actual towers. Stingrays can then determine each phone's unique subscriber number, and hence its owner, as well as its location, the numbers each phone calls, the numbers that call them, and how long the two phones remain in contact. They also intercept text messages and data usage, such as the websites each phone visits. Police have used these devices without a warrant—which they would need if they wanted to examine your browsing history on your laptop or look inside your mailbox.

The data from automatic license plate readers includes the times and locations of the pictures. Many police departments upload these images to shared databases, where they reside next to images captured by other police departments as well as by private actors, such as repo men. State, federal, and local police from across the country may be able to see everywhere your car has been for the past several years.

Outside of the few cities with public transportation extensive and reliable enough to let people live without cars, these images paint a granular portrait of people's lives: where they go, when, and how long they stay. They show where someone worships, who they visit, where they shop, what doctors they see. Some agencies store these images for years, and they can remain on the shared databases for years as well. Police do not need warrants to take the pictures—they are, after all, capturing images in public view, where you have little or no expectation of privacy—nor do they always need to have any particular reason to access these databases.

A 2016 study from Georgetown Law Center found that more than half of all American adults have their faces stored in facial-recognition databases accessible to law enforcement.[8] By now the share may well be higher, and at the same time, the number of law enforcement agencies that can access a given database is growing. Cameras enabled with facial-recognition technology are increasingly common, allowing unmatched tracking capacity.

In August 2019, the *New York Times* reported that New York City has a DNA database with 82,473 profiles.[9] Some come from people convicted of crimes, but others are from those merely arrested or questioned. Police officers offered a twelve-year-old boy, whom they were questioning, a soda, then pulled his DNA from his straw and put it in their database. They've done the same with water bottles and cigarettes that suspects used and discarded. The practice is not unusual: at least thirty states have similar databases, comprising profiles similarly collected, often from people without their consent.

New York state law mandates that a person be convicted before his DNA can be entered in the state database. But no such law governs cities. Does that make sense? What should the law require when it comes to governments amassing genetic databases? What sort of control should we have over our own genetics and biometrics—over when the state can capture such data, who can see it, and for what purpose? Currently, we effectively have none.

Technology moves faster than the law. That is a descriptive statement, but comes fairly close to also being normative. The law should not be capricious; innovation should not be ponderous. Today, however, the threats to privacy far outstrip the antiquated guidelines set by jurisprudence developed in the landline and postal-service era.

We need to think about what privacy means in an age of perpetual surveillance. We need to think much harder than we have about what constitutes a reasonable expectation of privacy, particularly in public spaces. For instance, I doubt you would object to being captured on video by a CCTV camera that a store has trained on its front door as you quickly walked past it on your way to work. But what if that camera were suddenly to train itself upon you as you passed—as did the next one, and the ones across the street, and those on the next block, and so forth? Each of those cameras would fundamentally do the same thing as the first one: capture your image while you were in a public space. But scale and purpose make this objectionable in a way that a single, occasional camera is not.

Finally, consider how each new form of technology imperils—or can be used to enhance—*equity*.

Start with algorithms used in predictive policing, which, again, forecast where crimes are likely to be committed, and pretrial risk-assessment tools, which determine whether someone gets released or detained to await trial. Among these algorithms' promises is that they can eliminate, or at least help to reduce, systemic bias. Instead of having, say, a veteran police captain, who may have formed, consciously or not, biased judgments about a particular racial group, assigning officers to patrol a neighborhood where that group is over-represented—or a judge, who may have formed similar biases during decades on the bench, deciding the fate of a member of that same group—the department and the court would use data-driven analyses to make better, less biased decisions.

PredPol, one of the leading predictive-policing firms, proclaims that its algorithm only uses "the three most objective data points . . . crime type, crime location, crime date and time."[10] Shotspotter Missions (known as HunchLab before Shotspotter bought it), a PredPol rival, notes that its algorithm "does not use personally identifiable information to create its predictions." Instead it uses historical crime data in an area, calls for service in the area, the time and day (crime tends to rise in the evening and on weekends), "upcoming events" (such as concerts or sporting events, which might dump large crowds of possibly intoxicated people on the same street at the same time), and "environmental factors" (such as the density of bars and clubs in a neighborhood).[11]

But historical crime data is not an objective record of all the crimes committed in a city. It is a record of all the crimes the police record. If certain neighborhoods, often poor and majority-minority, are overpoliced, and certain laws have been enforced in a biased way—such as African Americans being arrested for marijuana-related crimes nine times as often as whites, despite similar rates of use—then using that data in an algorithm will perpetuate those biases under the guise of objectivity.

Arrest patterns born from racial bias are used to determine where to send police to find further crimes. In her outstanding book *Weapons of Math Destruction*, Cathy O'Neil calls this "a pernicious feedback loop" in which "the policing itself spawns new data, which justifies more policing." It echoes the famous streetlight effect—in which a drunkard looks for his lost keys beneath a streetlight not because he thinks he lost them there, but because that's where the light is. But now it's about crime and race, not a drunkard's lost keys.

Or consider facial recognition's well-known problem identifying darker-skinned people. In 2018, the ACLU built a database out of twenty-five thousand publicly available arrest photos using Rekognition, Amazon's publicly available facial-recognition tool. The researchers then ran all the sitting members of Congress through that database, which misidentified twenty-eight of them as criminals. Fully 40 percent of those twenty-eight were people of color.[12] That was embarrassing for Amazon, but in the real world that sort of misidentification could have fatal consequences.

So what does a concerned citizen do? Should we push for national and statewide bans on facial recognition, criminal justice algorithms, and other emergent technologies because they disproportionately imperil the civil liberties of people of color? That would be worth-while as far as it goes, but it probably doesn't go all that far: bans may pass in more liberal cities and states, but that leaves people—partic-ularly people of color—elsewhere unprotected. And the problem is not the technology. The problem is unaddressed racial bias in the criminal justice system that risks being exacerbated if we pretend that technology can magically become race-neutral when the practices and data that feed it never have been.

Built into any humane system of laws is a contradiction. On one hand, we want laws to be enforced fairly and objectively. It offends our sense of justice when one person gets away with something for which another is punished. On the other hand, we want some space for disobedience. Jaywalking is a crime, but should everyone get a ticket every time they cross any street away from a crosswalk? That would be fair, but it would also be inhumane. We want to be able to ignore some rules at our own risk, provided doing so does not risk harm to others, and we want a measure of understanding when we break them—a warning, occasionally, when a policeman pulls us over for speeding, rather than a ticket.

These emergent forms of technology, which gather and store more information about more people with less effort than at any time in human history, imperil precisely that space for disobedience. They risk creating a society in which everything can be seen and punished, and nothing is forgotten. I do not want to live in that world, and I doubt you do, either. It is up to us to prevent its emergence.

How do we do that? Here is how we start: we use our free-speech rights to make a public case against the unfettered use of surveillance technology. We use our associational rights to find and organize other people who feel the same. And we use our states' and cities' public-meetings laws to show up at city council and county board meetings, demanding that our cities, towns, and states, and eventually the fed-eral government, explain precisely what technology they want to use, why they want to use it, and how. We demand that they write usage policies before opening the first box of whatever new gadget they want to buy. We demand that they regularly and publicly report on what they've used, when they used it, and why. And we demand that measures be put in place to protect our data: to store it responsibly, to ensure that only those with a legitimate reason to see it can access it, and to delete it—particularly if we have not been charged with or suspected of a crime—as quickly as possible.

That task may seem daunting. Many people—in particular, many middle-class white people, who for the most part have not had the same fraught relationship with the police as communities of color—are used to treating the police with deference, and are unaccustomed to asking them hard questions. Not many of us go to city council or county board meetings. I get it—we're busy, and it's hard to make time in the evenings for meetings about permits, zoning laws, and parking police. Perhaps we see them as parochial, and prefer paying attention to national news, and giving our time and activism to bigger causes. But most police forces are locally controlled and governed, and hence respond to local politics and concerns. And so the first step in reining in the surveillance state is showing up.

Pressing for transparent usage policies—and more importantly, for the police to explain why they need the next shiny new toy or genius crime-prevention software before buying it—will have effects beyond just the near-term safeguarding of our civil liberties. It helps counter what one activist I interviewed astutely called "techno-determinism"—the idea that if something is invented, then it has to be used, and that to object to its usage, in whatever way law enforcement authorities say they want to use it, is to be a Luddite indifferent to public safety. It reminds tech firms, elected officials, and perhaps, most importantly, ourselves and each other, that we still live in a democracy, where we get to decide how we're governed.

Paradoxically, pressing for these sorts of policies can help improve police-community relations. That may seem counterintuitive. But insisting on policy changes does not have to be snarling and antagonistic; it can be done firmly but politely, through established democratic channels. In Oakland, a privacy commission attached to the city council gives citizens a way to voice their concerns to police before problems start to fester. In effect, it's a way of allowing the community and the police to create a solid, respectful working relationship.

This may strike some readers as Pollyannaish. Perhaps you believe that the police in your community cannot be trusted. Perhaps you're a police officer, and you believe that citizens can never understand your job. But a democracy cannot function if citizens who disagree turn their backs on each other. And if we do not speak out—if we simply allow the state to amass and store more and more of the increasing amounts of data we generate—we will, through inaction, hasten the arrival of the permanent surveillance state. The only thing that prevents liberal countries from becoming China is their democratic practices. Those practices are like a muscle: they atrophy through disuse. But atrophy can be reversed. It's time to start flexing.

2

EXPANDING THE PLATFORM

"Facebook and WhatsApp are spying on us anyway,"
he said, holding up his phone. "Privacy is dead."

IT'S 9:30 ON A MONDAY MORNING, AND A MAN IS JAYWALKING THROUGH
heavy traffic at the intersection of Broad and Court Streets in downtown Newark. He steps into traffic, bobbing and weaving as a couple
of cars slow to avoid hitting him, before reaching the opposite corner
unscathed.

Three blocks north, at the intersection of Broad and Lafayette,
foot traffic on the sidewalks is heavy. A silver SUV stops to discharge a
passenger at a food cart under a yellow and blue umbrella. At Broad
and Market, two men stand under the awning of a phone repair shop,
talking and drinking coffee.

I am watching these unremarkable vignettes of city life from my
desk, almost forty miles north of downtown Newark. Signing on to the
Newark Police Department's Citizen Virtual Patrol (CVP)—which anyone can do with their Google, Facebook, Twitter, or email accounts—
lets me view the feeds of 126 city-owned CCTV cameras from my
laptop. The CVP is available online. I don't think it should be, so I'm
not going to provide the link, but you can find it easily enough.

I can monitor eleven intersections on Broad Street, from its northern terminus one block east of the Rutgers University Newark campus

right down to where it stops at the train tracks and McCarter Highway. Central Avenue, Market Street, Martin Luther King Jr. Avenue, Kinney Street, Bergen Street, Elizabeth Avenue, and South Orange Avenue—all major thoroughfares in Newark—have multiple CVP-accessible cameras. From the comfort of your room you could, if you wished, and if the cameras were pointed the right way, track the progress of pedestrians as they walked down any of these streets. You might be able to see who they stopped to talk to, what stores they went into, whether they used their phones, what they were wearing.

The idea behind CVP is to let people report crimes from behind a virtual veil, so they don't have to risk the stigma—and the possibility of harm—that come from being a public witness. If they see something amiss, the Newark Police Department encourages them to report it, either by calling 911 if they are inside the city limits or calling the police department directly if they are not.

Anthony Ambrose, Newark's public safety director, told NJ.com, a news website in his state, that "60% of crimes in Newark are solved using video surveillance" (though of course that does not necessarily mean through the city's own cameras—police can also obtain CCTV footage from residents and businesses, either with the camera owner's permission or via subpoena).[1]

During a conversation in his spacious, wood-paneled office, Ambrose contended to me that viewing the camera footage from a laptop is functionally no different from looking out the right window. The cameras show public streets and intersections where people can already be seen, and thus where they have a lower expectation of privacy than they do in their own homes.

Amol Sinha, executive director of the ACLU's New Jersey chapter, argued that it's nothing at all like looking out a window. He calls it "surveillance on a massive scale," adding, "There's a limited expectation of privacy in public spaces, but nobody expects that your every footstep will be recorded and captured by cameras that can be viewed by anybody in the world." He also notes that the cameras do show places where people have higher privacy expectations, like the yards and curtilages of people's homes. And they reveal personal information: if they show you leaving your home with a couple of suitcases, and then no activity for a couple of days, viewers can surmise that you've gone on vacation and your house is empty.

Automatic license plate readers (ALPRs) come with a similar set of arguments and concerns. On the one hand, they record information that a person on the street could record using a notepad and a pen. They do not record in private places; nor do they retain images of people's faces. These cameras capture images of license plates along with geospatial information and then store that information in a database. They can be stationary or mounted on police cruisers. In either case, the numbers can also be run through a database of license plates that police have previously flagged, turning a tedious task prone to human error into an automatic one.

But if a police officer walked up and down your street every day, writing down everybody's license plate numbers, where the corresponding vehicles were parked, and at what time, you would notice, and you would probably feel it was overreach. You might start to ask questions about why the license plate numbers of cars on your street were of such interest to the police, and why the police had decided to devote staff time to this task rather than to others. What use would the department be making of the information? And so forth.

With ALPRs, however, you have to look for them to notice them (usually they are small, flat, rectangular cameras mounted on a police cruiser's roof or trunk). They do not tire or need meal and bathroom breaks. They are always watching. They render the visible invisible. They save police forces from having to make a choice about staffing, and whether capturing license plate information is worth the time and money it would otherwise take. And they let police store that information as long as they want and share it with whomever they want.

They also let companies amass that information from multiple agencies into databases that they can charge police forces to access. Between public officials (i.e., police officers) gathering the data and accessing it is a company collecting public funds. There is, of course, nothing wrong with spending taxpayers' money on essential goods and services from private companies. Police forces buy cars and guns from private companies that make those things better and more cheaply than a state-run enterprise could.

But information is not a good like any other. It's our personal data, sitting on a database managed by someone who is not accountable to us. Yes, we do that all the time with our financial and health information—but really, do we want to do any more of that than we have to? What happens, for instance, when a company that stores all of a force's digital evidence decides to raise its fees beyond what that force can afford? Who gets blamed for a breach, and what are the remedies? How comfortable is a community—how comfortable should a community be—with letting a private company store, and in many cases sell, sensitive police information? Who else has access to it? How strong are the firewalls?

Through scale, ALPRs and systems like Newark's CVP turn something that is perfectly innocent in a single iteration—writing down a license plate number or looking through a window at the street scene below—into something far less palatable. When I look at a camera feed from the CVP, I can't see anything that a citizen on that street can't see. I've flicked through all 126 cameras on offer, and none of them peered into bedrooms, apartments, or stores. But if I wanted to, I could see all the feeds at once, giving me a vista of the city that no ordinary window could provide. And if I had an ex living on Bergen or Broad Street and I wanted to stalk her without being seen—to keep track of when she left and came home (and who she left and came home with)—CVP could help me do it.

Some worry that with more people watching the cameras that film areas overwhelmingly inhabited by black and brown people, more black and brown people will have the police called on them for little more than a citizen's suspicion. And, as a boring middle-aged guy who does nothing worse than jaywalk and occasionally throw away a hunk of plastic or aluminum that I know in my guilty heart I ought to recycle, I still would not want the city security camera at the end of my block posting an online stream of me taking my kids to school, or dropping a trash bag in the Dumpster while wearing Crocs, cargo shorts, and one of my many barbecue-stained T-shirts older than my children.

But what weight should concerns like these carry? Should courts make distinctions between massive, automated surveillance and the manual, pen-and-pad type? Should we simply get used to a world in which the state can film us, without our consent, and post the camera's feed online, so that anyone anywhere can watch us going about our daily business?

London, one of the most heavily surveilled cities on earth, is a fitting place to examine these questions in detail, analyzing what information the police collect, whether this reduces crime, and if so, at what cost to privacy.

I met Mick Neville for tea one rainy afternoon in early spring at the Union Jack Club, which offers accommodation, dining, and other clubby amenities for noncommissioned officers and veterans of the British armed forces, just across from the entrance to the Waterloo rail station. The trip from *The Economist*'s offices, then near Green Park, took less time than I expected, so I arrived a bit early. Neville, a veteran of both the army and the Metropolitan Police Service, was bang on time. He is broad-shouldered and gray-haired, looking exactly as you would imagine a police and military veteran who haunts the Union Jack Club to look. He is also wryly good-humored: At one point in our conversation, he told me, "We've given America the rule of law and Magna Carta. You've given us baseball caps and hot dogs."

Neville headed the CCTV division of the Metropolitan Police (roughly London's equivalent of the NYPD—it's more commonly known by the name of its headquarters, Scotland Yard) and now runs a consultancy focused on helping business and law enforcement make the best use of CCTV and other images.

For all that London gets called the most heavily surveilled city in the world, finding an accurate count of its cameras is surprisingly difficult. That's because most of them, as in the United States, are privately owned. The most frequently cited figure—mainly from private-industry studies—is around one camera for every fourteen people in London, or perhaps one for every eleven. They are not evenly distributed: the Waterloo, King's Cross, and Oxford Circus tube stations each have over three hundred cameras (King's Cross has more than four hundred). According to Caught on Camera, which designs and installs CCTV systems, the average Londoner is caught on camera more than three hundred times each day.

Around 95 percent of those cameras, according to Neville, are in private hands. That does not put them out of police reach: after a crime, police can and usually do canvass local businesses to ask if they can use the footage their cameras recorded. They can also apply for a warrant to examine the footage, though most people comply with a request. Tony Porter, Britain's independent surveillance camera commissioner (an informative and advisory role; he has no enforcement power), said that after a crime, "99 percent of the population will hand imagery over to the police because that is in everybody's interest." American police have told me more or less the same thing.

Mindful of such goodwill, hundreds of American police departments have formed "partnerships" with Ring, an Amazon subsidiary that makes video doorbells. Ring markets its products as the backbone of a "new neighborhood watch," which has a safe, homey sound, until you stop and think about what it actually means: streets in which everyone is spying on everyone else, all the time, and granting police access to that footage without warrants.

Ring owners have shared footage of people—not thieves, just deliverymen and other ordinary people—unaware they were being filmed while they were just doing their jobs or going about their day. Installing a Ring device enrolls users in Neighbors, its social media app, where you can share footage and receive alerts for reported crimes and other public safety events in a five-mile radius of your home. It lets users post videos of people they deem "suspicious," which can amount to racial profiling. The Electronic Frontier Foundation found that Ring's app sends information that can personally identify users to analytic and marketing firms.[2]

Some police departments have paid for Ring installation for individual homeowners in exchange for a requirement that users surrender footage on demand. (Amazon bared its teeth at this arrangement: "Ring does not support programs that require . . . footage from Ring devices be shared as a condition for receiving a donated device," said a company flack.)

Yet even in areas that do not mandate footage sharing, doing so seems somewhat less than entirely voluntary. An article in CNET, a consumer-tech news and review site, mentions that in Bloomfield,

New Jersey, if people do not respond favorably to a sharing request, police show up at requestees' homes. The article said, paraphrasing the chief, "People are a lot more cooperative when an officer is at their doorsteps."[3]

Indeed, it's difficult to say no to a police officer asking for help in an investigation. Perhaps you think that's a good thing—that it should be hard for a citizen to decline to help the police, because police only ask for doorbell footage when they actually need it, and they always use it in ways consistent with the law and mindful of people's civil liberties. But it doesn't always work like that. Telling the police to come back with a warrant might seem rude, but, compared to enabling a network of perpetual surveillance available to authorities on demand, rudeness seems the lesser evil.

In December 2018, the ACLU published a patent application from Ring that would pair its product with Rekognition, Amazon's facial-recognition software. The two devices would create a system, according to an ACLU attorney, Jacob Snow, that "the police can use to match the faces of people walking by a doorbell camera with a photo database of persons they deem 'suspicious.' Likewise, home-owners can also add photos of 'suspicious' people into the system and then the doorbell's facial recognition program will scan anyone passing their home. In either case, if a match occurs, the person's face can be automatically sent to law enforcement, and the police could arrive in minutes."[4]

These devices play on, and even stoke, people's fear of crime—though crime has been falling in America for decades. One can, of course, argue that if Ring prevents even a single assault, then it's worth installing. But that logic can be used to justify any incursion on our civil rights. Ring subjects public space to the tragedy of the commons: it might make you feel good to install Ring on your front door, so you can see what's going on around you from behind a locked door, but if everyone did the same we would all be subject to a massive, decentralized surveillance network designed to assuage homeowners' fears of "suspicious" people.

Police are particularly interested in Ring's Neighbors app, in which users can share and comment on doorbell-derived video. They can also receive crime alerts for their neighborhood and share texts and videos from any source. The company posts testimonials from police averring that Neighbors has helped them solve crimes. That sounds appealing enough, though it is hard to imagine a form of ubiquitous digital surveillance that would not eventually catch some sort of crime. It does not seem worth it to me. If not being subject to an eternally vigilant network of cameras every time I walk down a street means that I might occasionally have an infinitesimally higher chance of being mugged or assaulted, I'll accept that risk.

Still, if you stow your misgivings for a moment, and imagine a neighborhood entirely populated by rational, bias-free civil libertarians, it is just about possible to see Neighbors, in that specific fictional case, as a valuable crime-stopping tool—with no unintended consequences, subjecting noncriminals to only incidental surveillance, and never alerting police about someone who "just doesn't look right" because he has the wrong clothes or skin color.

But such neighborhoods (and such people) do not exist. It is much easier to imagine Neighbors reinforcing all sorts of existing biases: people of color coming in for extra scrutiny in a white upper-class suburb, for instance.

In 2009, police in Cambridge, Massachusetts, arrested Henry Louis Gates, an esteemed Harvard professor, while he was entering his own house. Gates, who is African American, returned home after a trip abroad to find the door to his house jammed. He and his driver forced it open. A neighbor in liberal Cambridge called the police to report a break-in. Gates ended up being arrested on the front porch of his own home for disorderly conduct, and Barack Obama ended up inviting both Gates and the arresting officer to the White House for a "beer summit." One can imagine how much more frequent such calls might be when they come not from just one wary neighbor with the time to watch an app and call the police, but from dozens of them watching on their phones and laptops.

Ring also circumvents the civic conversation about the costs and benefits of surveillance that could otherwise happen if police had to request more cameras through the city or county government. Then people—especially in low-crime, high-income neighborhoods—might ask whether the local crime rate justifies spending money on dozens of security cameras to line almost crime-free streets. They might ask themselves whether they want to be subject to police surveillance in public all the time.

But because Ring is private, and appeals to a sense of personal security rather than tò the collective public good, those conversations never take place. The cameras are installed and paid for by individual homeowners, each making a discrete rational decision that collectively adds to a massive, linked surveillance network, one that the state can commandeer but does not have to pay for. When you're deciding whether to install a video doorbell on your house, don't just imagine yourself sitting behind your locked door looking out. Imagine other people behind their doors staring at you, all the time.

Ubiquitous as CCTV cameras may be, Mick Neville notes that, in his experience, for investigative purposes, they are often useless. In London, he explained, police find usable CCTV images in only around 2 percent of all crimes. "That's because they don't have systems in place," he added. "There are too many formats, and too many cameras. Maybe they're working, maybe they're not. The lesson here is don't blow millions on gear with no systems in place to extract the data. It's like a quartermaster spending millions on rifles but buying no ammunition."

Tony Porter raises a similar concern: too often, cameras see too little. "Local authorities have poor management systems," he told me (although his estimate of cameras in government control is slightly larger than Neville's—around 10 percent, rather than 5 percent). "Many cameras," he continues, referring to cameras controlled by local government entities, "are in positions that might have been justified ten years ago, but subsequently the utility has expired. It's more common than you might believe that a camera is obscured by a tree or a new building."

Barring a wave of bizarre arboreal mischief, a camera staring at a tree probably has, at best, limited utility. On the other hand, a business owner may figure that a nonrecording camera may still deter some crimes. Thieves, after all, do not know that the camera above the shop entrance has been broken for years.

But CCTV cameras do not have a universally deterrent effect. They seem to have some crime-deterrent effects in some circumstances, but studies paint a conflicting and unclear picture of their efficacy, in part because it is almost impossible to find a control group—that is, two identical locations, one with and one without CCTV cameras.

The Center for Problem-Oriented Policing, a think tank at Arizona State University, argues that a CCTV network's efficacy hinges on two factors: would-be offenders must be aware of the cameras' presence, and they must believe that the risk of capture outweighs any potential benefits of the crime.[5] The former factor is often lacking, and the latter can be mitigated by a potential offender's intake of substances that cloud judgment.

That may be why CCTV cameras are generally better at preventing property crimes, which often require some planning and observation, than at preventing violent offenses, which are often spur-of-the-moment.

CCTV cameras may also displace crime rather than reducing it overall. A study from the University of California, Berkeley, found that violent crime declined near obvious CCTV cameras, but rose away from them.

Now, to an individual with a doorbell camera, that may be a distinction without a difference. Homeowners buy cameras to keep their families safe, and if having one impels someone to burgle a house two blocks away, then mission accomplished, and tough luck to everyone else. But governments make a different calculation: Do they want to spend money just to push criminals to a different area?

But the Center for Problem-Oriented Policing identifies several potential benefits to CCTV networks beyond just reducing crime. CCTV cameras tend to reduce fear of crime (although, as with the actual crime-reduction benefit, this one only accrues when people are aware of the cameras). That benefit, in turn, may increase the number of people using the surveilled area, which itself may drive down crime. Cameras can also be used for more general population management—directing medical services, for instance, or monitoring situations to determine an appropriate police response.

At the root of this nest of questions surrounding CCTV use and benefits is the same fundamental one running through this book: How much surveillance are you willing to tolerate in the name of public safety? Technologically, we have the capacity to create the perfect surveillance state—not in some distant, dystopic future, but now, today. We even have many elements of that state already in place. We aren't going to stop homeowners from installing cameras on their front doors, or business owners from installing them in their shops and restaurants. Police have ALPRs on their cars; they're not going to remove them. It's up to us to press for sensible rules around access and storage of that footage. If you have a Ring and the police ask you for footage, ask them why, and consider refusing to surrender it without a warrant. Ask your local police department how long they store ALPR data, who they share it with, and how they secure it. Insist on your right to know and to define how you're monitored, by whom, and why.

What do people want a CCTV camera network to do? Are they— are you and your community—comfortable with a network of CCTV cameras on major streets, and police-accessible Ring networks everywhere else? Should police be able to see every street, everywhere they want?

Does your answer change situationally? My answer may not, but my feelings certainly do: If I'm walking down the street minding my own business, I don't want the state to surveil me. That sentiment goes double if I'm holding up a sign at a political demonstration. On the other hand, if one of my children were harmed, I would certainly want the police to knock on every home and business with a camera, and I would want every camera owner to share their footage. But on the other (third) hand, perhaps we should not give anxious or grieving parents undue influence in crafting policy.

◉

Rishon LeZion began as an agricultural settlement along Israel's central coast, though few traces of its rural past remain. Charming in its charmlessness, warm with an appealing scruffy edge, it blends into the sprawl of greater Tel Aviv. Today it is one of Israel's bigger cities, though it retains the feel of a place you would never happen upon, and would never visit without a purpose.

I was there to see Toplines, an Israeli security firm. Its headquarters were tucked into a little strip mall, modest and unprepossessing in a way that struck me as deeply Israeli. Israel punches way above its weight in surveillance tech. Alumni of the famed Unit 8200, the peerless Israeli military unit responsible for collecting signal intelligence (essentially, cryptanalysis and listening in on the communication of enemies), have an entrepreneurial bent, and they have used their expertise to start numerous companies, including Toplines.

Among the company's offerings are automatic license plate readers, designed for individual as well as institutional use. Several employees and I packed into an executive's minivan and drove through Rishon's narrow streets. A laptop between the two front seats showed a steady stream of license plates being captured by the cameras mounted on the car's roof and sides. First a picture of the plate appeared, then just the letters and numbers in plaintext as the system filed it away.

Plate, letters, numbers, file: that is how mobile ALPRs all over the world work (there are also stationary ones, used for parking enforcement or to admit residents into private parking lots). The system usually comprises a high-speed camera with an infrared filter, or perhaps a pair of cameras, attached to a processor that translates the picture into alphanumeric characters, along with software to compare the characters to those on a list of license plates of interest to police. Attached to a police car, they can capture well over a thousand plates per minute from cars passing at high speeds. In the course of an ordinary drive, a police car equipped with one can add tens of thousands of license plates to a database.

In most systems, geospatial information accompanies the plate: where it was seen, at what time, on what date, and even what direction the car was driving when the police officer captured the plate. Some systems include photographs of the driver and any front-seat passengers. China has equipped some of its ALPRs with facial-recognition capability; Chinese police have used them to arrest people driving cars of which they are not the registered owners.

Once a police ALPR captures a plate's image, an officer can run it through a database to see if it belongs to a car reported stolen or used in a crime. A week or so after my visit to Toplines, I spent a couple of days with a large West Coast police department. I accompanied a patrol officer on his afternoon shift, and we drove around in a car outfitted with an ALPR (as well as GPS trackers to make sure he went where he was supposed to, and only for as much time as he was supposed to).

The officer had recently transferred from the auto theft section, and he had a habit left over from those days of chasing car thieves: every time we stopped at a red light, he ran the plates of the cars stopped around us. He would tap the plate number into the front-seat laptop, which would tell him if there were any warrants attached to the plate number. Over the course of several hours, he probably ran several dozen plates—all clean.

That habit may sound alarming: it sounds, at first, like stopping and searching every person who happened to land next to him at a red light. That's not quite right: he didn't stop the cars, nor did he look inside of them. It's more like scanning people's faces using an accurate facial-recognition system: objectionable not because it's inconvenient or intrusive, but because it implies the existence of an immense database of personally identifying information that police officers can use at will on people not suspected of any crime.

Criminal records exist, of course, and information about people who have been duly convicted of crimes is and should be available to the police. But who else is in that database? How did they get there, how long do they stay there, and how do they get off it? Who else can see and use the database? What can people use the list for?

These questions have made some communities nervous enough to push back against ALPR use. Delano, California, ended its ALPR use over concerns that its vendor, Vigilant Solutions, also had a contract with Immigration and Customs Enforcement (ICE); the city worried that ALPRs could be used to target people for deportations. Michigan City, Indiana, decided against using ALPRs after the city council determined that the police department had no access or data-storage policies. As Catherine Crump from Berkeley Law noted, "Most people agree that we should use ALPRs [in some cases], but . . . it's the aggregation of data, not individual pinpoints, that creates a privacy issue."

In June 2019, California's state auditor launched a probe into the use of ALPRs by four large state law enforcement agencies. Her report, released seven months later, confirmed many civil libertarians' worst fears.[6] It found that the agencies "did not always follow practices that adequately consider the individual's privacy in handling and retaining the ALPR images and associated data." None of the agencies had a privacy policy adequate under state law, none had adequate retention and data-destruction policies, and 99.9 percent of the 320 million images in the database came from vehicles unrelated to any criminal investigation. Three of the agencies used private vendors to store their data without contractual data-protection guarantees, three shared data with hundreds of other agencies around the country without determining whether those agencies had a right or need to view it, and none of them had audited access. In other words, an officer at any of the four agencies could "misuse ALPR images to stalk an individual or observe vehicles at particular locations and events, such as doctors' offices or clinics and political rallies. Despite these risks, the agencies we reviewed conduct little to no auditing of users' searches."

This is a nightmarish set of habits and practices. In all but the most public-transport-friendly cities, ALPRs can create a granular picture of a person's life. (A common defense is that ALPRs capture license plates, not people; but for police, finding out someone's name and address from a license plate is not difficult.) Think about it: If your local police followed your car around every day for a month, what would they know about you? They would know where you lived, of course, but they could find that out from your driver's license. They would also know where you worked, but for most people that, too, is often public information.

They would know where your children went to school, what time you dropped them off, and when you picked them up. They would know if you visited an abortion clinic or attended a political rally. If you go to a place of worship, they would know where and when, and they would know what doctors you visited and where you worked out; how often you stopped at liquor stores, fast-food restaurants, or marijuana dispensaries; and whether you attended Alcoholics Anonymous meetings. They could perhaps deduce whether you were faithful to your spouse, and they would know who you saw regularly—who your close friends and family were, and where they lived. They would know where you shopped, which probably means they would have a good idea of your consumption habits. That would also give them a good sense of your income level, and perhaps also your political leanings: Do you regularly go to Whole Foods or Cracker Barrel?

To approve ALPR use without adequate retention and purging policies is to permit the government to amass this sort of information, allowing the creation of detailed personal profiles of citizens who are not suspected of any crime. Police forces might argue that they do no such thing—that no officer is sitting at a desk creating these types of profiles. I suspect that for the overwhelming majority of police forces and officers, that's true. It's also not the point. The point is that they could, easily—and again, that the civil liberties of citizens in a liberal democracy deserve statutory and enforceable protection.

Questions also arise about how and where plates are collected. If police just gather up data on public streets, that is one thing: everyone has an equal chance of being ensnared. But what if they parked an ALPR-enabled car outside a mosque where a suspected terrorist once worshiped? They would then know everyone who attended Friday prayers. What if the suspected terrorist worshiped there twice, five years ago, and the cruisers still show up every Friday?

As it happens, the NYPD did collect license plate numbers from congregants at mosques. They also sent plainclothes police officers into the mosques to listen to sermons and collect data on congregants' ethnic makeup. This kind of surveillance, according to the ACLU, has taken place at mosques throughout the five boroughs, as well as in parts of Connecticut, New Jersey, and Pennsylvania.[7] During his brief 2020 presidential run, former New York City mayor Michael Bloomberg defended the intensive surveillance directed at members of a specific faith not suspected of any crime that had taken place during his watch.

Or consider the same scenario for a gun show: a cruiser recording the plate numbers of every car that attended a legal exhibition, just because it had at some point drawn a few suspected domestic terrorists. Even the International Association of Chiefs of Police acknowledged that ALPRs could have "a chilling effect on social and political activities" by recording—even incidentally—people coming and going from rallies, churches, and other sensitive locations.[8]

The standard law enforcement argument is that ALPRs are doing nothing that an ordinary police officer could not do without them. That line is solid enough, as far as it goes. ALPRs are not phone taps; they track information that people broadcast to the public, attached to their cars. An ordinary police officer could walk up and down a public street, filming and taking notes in public—both activities that the First Amendment protects.

But that argument ignores scale. The difference between one officer writing down or typing license plates into a notebook or laptop for hours on end and officers in ALPR-enabled cars hoovering up thousands of plates, unconnected to any criminal investigation, is not merely quantitative. I'm hard-pressed to think of a commanding officer who would think that assigning a patrol officer to spend hours writing down license plates from passing cars would be a good use of that officer's time and taxpayer funds.

ALPRs are a seamless, effortless way to amass a vast database of information on innocent people. Vigilant Solutions, an ALPR titan bought by Motorola in March 2018, had a database of 7 billion license plates, complete with geospatial information—most of them, presumably, belonging to people who had committed no crimes.

Using Freedom of Information Act requests, the Electronic Frontier Foundation (EFF), a digital rights watchdog group, learned that in 2016 and 2017, 173 law enforcement agencies—state, local, and federal—scanned 2.5 billion license plates, 99.5 percent of which belonged to people who were not under suspicion at the time their plates were scanned.[9]

That may seem like a high failure rate. But compared to the police department in charming Rhinebeck, New York—which, in three months in 2011, according to the New York Civil Liberties Union, scanned 164,043 plates and found only 8 of interest, a 99.99 percent failure rate—those 173 agencies are all-stars.[10]

If these scans were quickly discarded, then they would be easy to brush off. After all, on stakeouts police incidentally observe people they do not suspect of crimes while pursuing those whom they do. But when that happens, police do not, as a matter of course, retain the personal details of the people they incidentally observe. Policies governing retention and storage of ALPR data vary wildly if they exist at all. According to the National Conference of State Legislatures, just sixteen states have statutes governing ALPR use (cities and counties may, and often do, have their own policies in the absence of state laws, or have policies tighter than state laws).[11]

At the time of writing, Maine forbids ALPR data from being kept longer than twenty-one days, and California requires that it be deleted within sixty days unless it is evidence in a felony case. Colorado allows it to be kept for three years—but New Hampshire, the Live Free or Die State, requires that ALPR data be deleted within three minutes unless it leads to an arrest or citation, "or identified a vehicle that was the subject of a missing or wanted person broadcast." Penalties for violating these statutes vary: sometimes, as far as I can tell, there are none, rendering them hortatory.

In Maine, by contrast, violating the ALPR law is a Class E crime, punishable by a $1,000 fine or six months' imprisonment. Only two states, Vermont and Minnesota, require audits to determine whether police departments are following their ALPR usage policies, and just one—California—requires law enforcement to report to the legislature on how they use ALPRs.

Several states specify that ALPR data is not subject to public disclosure, which should be a relief even for people who favor maximal transparency: Who wants a nosy neighbor perusing our comings and goings, especially when the nosy neighbor may be miles away? But that does not mean that nobody outside the police department sees it.

First, breaches happen: In 2015, a journalist in Boston found the city's entire ALPR database online, including the addresses of everyone with a city parking permit, along with thousands of people suspected of being terrorists or gang leaders.[12] That same year, the EFF found live feeds from multiple stationary ALPRs accessible to anyone with a browser who knew where to look. Four years later, *Tech Crunch*, an American tech news website, found more than 150 Internet-connected ALPRs; many of the feeds were either completely exposed or protected by just a default password.[13]

Second, law enforcement agencies routinely share information. Vigilant's promotional materials boast that "joining the largest law enforcement LPR sharing network is as easy as adding a friend on your favorite social media platform." EFF found that on average, agencies shared ALPR data with 160 other agencies—though several shared with 600 or more. Many also shared data with the National Vehicle Location Service, which hundreds of other entities can access.[14] The more widely the data is shared, the greater the potential for breaching, hacking, or abuse.

Sometimes this sharing contravenes local policy. The ACLU of Northern California learned, also through a Freedom of Information Act lawsuit, that several law enforcement agencies in California—including police departments in Merced, Union City, and Upland—shared ALPR data with ICE. They argued that this practice violated the California Values Act, a 2017 state law that forbids California's state and local law enforcement agencies from using resources to investigate or arrest people for violating federal immigration law.[15] The counterargument is that simply allowing ICE to access data police departments are already collecting does not constitute an expenditure of resources. But that just highlights how easy ALPRs make it to amass a trove of personal information.

Soon after news broke that ICE had bought access to Vigilant's database, Alameda County, in Northern California, canceled a $500,000 contract with Vigilant. In June 2018, the city of Richmond, also in the Bay Area, canceled its contract with Vigilant for the same reason. The company protested that individual agencies do not have to share data with anybody they do not want to share it with, and

Richmond's police chief noted that ICE had never used ALPR data against anyone in Richmond. But what if the next chief takes a different view? What if an agency with whom Richmond shares data shares its data with ICE?

Private companies can also elect to share ALPR data with police, with little or no oversight. Shopping malls and apartment complexes often use ALPRs, as do some repo men.[16] And while, as discussed above, at least a few states have laws governing the use and retention of ALPR data collected by public agencies and employees, no such laws protect data gathered by private ALPRs. It can be stored indefinitely and shared or sold as widely as the data owners like.

Because people who fall behind on car payments are often poor—and in America, nonwhite people are likelier than whites to be poor (though overall there are more poor non-Hispanic white people than there are of any other racial category)—repossession agencies' cameras may end up disproportionately turned on people of color. The same can be true of police ALPRs. In 2015, EFF found that Oakland's police deployed ALPR-enabled cars most often to low-income neighborhoods, even though those areas did not necessarily have higher crime rates.[17]

So what are the right policies regarding ALPRs? Let's start with a wrong one. Toplines, the firm I visited in Rishon LeZion, wants to add voice and facial recognition to its ALPR cameras and offer them to private citizens to install on their cars. In exchange for insurance rate discounts, the data its cameras collect would be transmitted to a "mobile broadcast system" that police can access. The information cars transmit could help keep us all safer.

In response to my question about the privacy concerns this raised, a Toplines executive shrugged. "Facebook and WhatsApp are spying on us anyway," he said, holding up his phone. "Privacy is dead."

One of the hardest things a journalist has to do is learn how to react with equanimity when someone says something insane or offensive. I believe my training held up in Rishon, but I hope it goes without saying that I find Rishon's proposal appalling. It would create a police state in the name of marginally reduced insurance rates. Privacy may be dying, but I don't think it's quite dead yet. But every incursion deals it another blow, and at some point it won't be able to get up again. The quickest way to ensure that this executive's cynical quip becomes reality is to accept his world-weary complacency. Remember that when someone offers you a cool new gadget, or a piece of technology that nobody else has, you can always just say no.

Of course, this is an easy proposal to turn down. But what would sensible ALPR laws look like? A good starting point would be to sharply limit the amount of time police can retain ALPR scans of people not suspected of any crime. New Hampshire's three-minute rule seems sensible, though I could see the case for extending it to, say, twenty-four hours, but no longer. Police should use ALPRs to search for vehicles they have genuine cause to suspect of involvement in a crime, not to amass a database of license plates and locations that might turn out to be useful at some point in the future.

Beyond that, people have a right to know how their local police force uses ALPRs and whether their own information is in a database. If so—assuming their vehicle is not suspected of criminal involvement—they should have the right to remove it. Agencies should set clear usage policies with penalties for breaking them, especially for unlawful access. They might also ensure that their feeds are not accessible to just anyone with an Internet connection.

◉

What share of gunfire incidents result in a 911 call? What share result in a reported felony (assault with a dangerous weapon)? In America, the answers are depressingly low: 12 percent and less than 7 percent, respectively, according to a 2016 paper by Jillian B. Carr and Jennifer L. Doleac.[18] One effort to change that is being led from a nondescript office park in Newark, California—home to Shotspotter, the company cited earlier whose core product is a gunshot-detection system. I saw the product in action for the first time when I deployed with Newark's police department.

Shotspotter's acoustic sensors are placed in clusters of around twenty per square mile. They are trained to detect the sound of gunfire by triangulating the source of the sound, and, by calculating how much time the sound takes to reach the sensors, the system determines where the shots were fired.

When Shotspotter's sensors detect something they believe to be gunfire, an alert pops up on the screens of acoustic analysts in a small, dark room at Shotspotter's headquarters. When I visited the company's home office in the other Newark—in California, just down San Francisco Bay from Oakland—early on a Thursday morning, there was just a single analyst working, a good-natured, red-haired woman whom I'll call Susan. More analysts would arrive that afternoon, as the East Coast dusk began. Peak gunshot times are Thursday through Sunday evenings.

America's 327 million people own, according to a June 2018 paper from the Small Arms Survey, 393.3 million guns—around 120.5 per 100 people, more than twice as many per capita as the second most heavily armed country on earth, which is Yemen. (In total numbers, the 393.3 million guns rattling around America mean that the nation has more than five times as many guns as the country that comes in at second place, India, whose population is more than three times America's.)[19] Those guns can go off at any time. So it surprises nobody when Susan's computer pings at Shotspotter. She listens to the sound intently a couple of times, then relaxes. What the sensors thought was gunfire was in fact a truck's "jake brake"—a type of engine brake that opens an engine's exhaust valves, releasing compressed air with a meaty, jackhammer-type sound.

The sensors are trained to recognize what Sam Klepper, the Shotspotter executive who was showing me around that day, calls "loud, impulsive sounds" between 120 and 160 decibels. Jake brakes are among the most common false positives, along with helicopters, fireworks, and cars backfiring or driving over metal plates. For this reason, the company uses a mixture of artificial and human intelligence: the AI recognizes a genre of sound, the person can distinguish between a truck brake, fireworks, and gunshots.

If it had been gunfire—as it was, for instance, that Friday night in Newark, New Jersey, that I discussed in Chapter 1—Susan would have sent out an alert to the appropriate police force. It would have included the number of shots, the number of shooters or weapons (meaning whether it sounded like a single shooter or a gun battle: shots from one weapon responding to shots from another), and whether it was an automatic or high-capacity gun. It would also have included the sound file, so officers could hear the gunshots themselves. It would have shown on a map where the shooting took place. Klepper boasts that the system is accurate to within twenty-five meters, and Shotspotter contends that the entire process, from gunshot to alert on officers' cellphones, takes less than a minute.

We move from the darkened room over to a touchscreen map in the lobby, with markers showing which cities in the world have Shotspotter. Klepper zooms in on the US map, then zooms further until a circle with the number 14 appears on the grid of a moderately sized Rust Belt city, for a shooting Shotspotter caught a few days earlier. Klepper presses Play, and I hear fourteen shots in rapid succession. It sounds to me like two guns: eleven shots fired quickly from one gun (which makes it a high-capacity gun, illegal in that city), and three, lower-pitched, answering from another. Shotspotter puts the shooting in an empty lot at the end of a dead-end street. Nobody had called 911.

That is not unusual, as Carr and Doleac's work made clear. Perhaps nobody but the shooter and the victim heard the shots, and the victim is dead. Perhaps there were witnesses, but they were scared and didn't want to get involved. Or maybe everyone who heard the shots figured somebody else would call the police, and so nobody did. The shooting may have taken place in a community where people don't trust the police. It could have been a black-market gun transaction, and the buyer wanted to test-fire a clip.

When people do call, they often get the location wrong. In cities, sound bounces off of buildings and echoes down alleyways; deriving location from sound in a built environment is difficult for a person to do. Shotspotter is designed to solve those problems—to alert police to gunfire without having to wait for someone to call 911, to pinpoint the location so police know where to show up, and to let them know to be alert for automatic or high-capacity guns.

I spoke with several officers in Newark (New Jersey) who liked the technology—though, when pressed, some seemed more enamored of the idea than the results. The general sense seemed to be that it's better to know about gunfire than not to know about it, but that often the alert does not lead to an arrest, a victim, or actual evidence of gunfire. Sometimes they go to a scene and find nothing there, either because the shooter hit nobody and fled, or because it was a false alarm.

This is not unusual. In 2016, *Forbes* did a deep dive into the company's success rate and found that in more than two dozen cities, 30 to 70 percent of Shotspotter alerts produced no evidence of gunfire. The disparities are striking: in a thirty-month period in San Francisco, for instance, 4,385 Shotspotter alerts led to 2 arrests, while nearly one-third were "unfounded / unable to locate / gone on arrival." In thirty-two months in Omaha, Nebraska, 737 of 1,181 alerts were similarly classified, with just 14 leading to arrests.[20]

Some might argue that this leaves cities no worse off than the status quo, in which only a small minority of gunfire incidents lead to an arrest anyway, or even to police being notified. But deployments take time and resources, and Shotspotter is not cheap: typically, it costs between $65,000 and $90,000 per square mile per year, along with a "one-time Service Initiation fee" of $10,000 per square mile.[21] This cost can force cities into an uncomfortable choice: pay to cover a wide area, and eat up a chunk of the police budget, or try to save by forecasting the hotspots, and risk choosing the wrong places or covering too small an area.

Still, the company is doing well enough to have bought Hunch-Lab, a predictive-policing firm, in October 2018 with cash on hand. Klepper called HunchLab's predictive modeling "a natural extension of gunshot detection." HunchLab's customers, he said, could use "patterns of gunfire incidents to plan where patrol resources should be in the future," calling it "a semi-sophisticated way of crime forecasting." In his view, Shotspotter is fundamentally reactive, while predictive policing is, at least theoretically, proactive.

Shotspotter's extension into predictive analytics is part of a larger and subtler story having to do with the back-end technological transformation of policing and the platforming of police technologies. Few government entities take in more information than the police. But that information is often siloed and poorly organized, which means it does not get used as effectively and efficiently as it should be. So in addition to companies offering products that give police more and new information—such as where guns were fired, or video evidence of what happened on a policeman's shift—they build platforms to organize the information they take in.

Shotspotter bought a company that makes predictive programs that help police act on information that its gunshot detectors gather. Axon and Panasonic offer both bodycams and evidence-management systems—again, technology both to gather information and to organize it. Motorola, which also makes bodycams, bought Vigilant in January 2019, and also offers a digital-evidence management platform. The acquisition of HunchLab lets Shotspotter offer not just gunshot detection but also a way to integrate that information into a predictive-policing program.

Klepper is an enthusiastic and effective spokesman for his company, with an infectious zeal and a politician's ability to remain on message. It is difficult not to share his enthusiasm when he talks about possible future iterations of Shotspotter: one that links to a mounted point-turn-zoom camera, for instance, which pivots to the location and starts snapping pictures as soon as it hears an alert, and another that uses a drone rather than a camera (neither is yet on the market— they are still theoretical).

But how much of a measurable difference does Shotspotter really make? Chicago seems to like it, having expanded its coverage area to more than a hundred square miles from just three in 2012, and the number of shooting victims and incidents declined markedly from 2016 to 2018. Shotspotter sent out a press release filled with praise for the system from Chicago's police chief, Eddie Johnson. Certainly, it has alerted police to shootings they otherwise would have missed; sometimes, arrests and gun confiscations have followed.

It has also expanded its coverage in other cities at the same time that homicides and shootings have declined. But just as many factors contribute to a rise in violence, many contribute to a decline, and teasing out in a more than anecdotal fashion precisely which factor is most responsible is difficult, if not impossible (there is, alas, no control group for reality).

Shotspotter's promotional material boasts that "there has never been a single city where Shotspotter did not technically work," citing "detecting, locating and alerting on illegal gunfire." But some cities have canceled their Shotspotter contracts—notably Fall River, Massachusetts, which decided that paying $120,000 for a service that worked, according to the city's police chief, less than half the time—and missed a seven-shot downtown homicide—was not a good use of public funds.

Shotspotter acknowledges that some cities "did not have a positive experience," for which it blames "suboptimal deployment strategies and poor practices." These include "too small a deployment area"—an answer that borders on parody (Don't like our product? Buy more!). The firm refers to its product as "a critical component of any comprehensive gun violence reduction strategy," just like bacon and sugary cereal can be "part of a nutritious breakfast," if the rest of that breakfast includes statins and a truckload of bran. I say that facetiously—I do not mean to call Shotspotter useless, only to encourage people not to mistake sales pitches for evidence.

I want to make two final points about Shotspotter before moving on, both of which apply to the police-tech world more generally. The first concerns salesmanship, in a sense. Imagine you head the police department in a moderately sized city with enough shootings to get the mayor shouting down the phone at you regularly. Your current policing strategies aren't working. People in poor, minority communities—the ones most plagued by gun violence—do not trust the police, for reasons that long predate your arrival. You're working to improve those relationships, but those efforts take time. And meanwhile, you need to do something: people are dying, and every time you see the mayor he looks like he's deciding what the most humiliating way to fire you might be.

So somewhere in the middle of your fifth straight month of heartburn and sleep measured in minutes rather than hours, the city dispatches you to one of those policing conferences where department brass, academics, and vendors drink, gossip, and attend the occasional workshop.

A vendor buttonholes you: Hey, we've got this great product to help you solve crimes. It does something nothing else on the market does—detects gunshots, say, or catalogs bodycam videos, or crunches decades' worth of crime data to tell you where to put your forces. Maybe they offer it to you for free; maybe it costs the equivalent of a handful of new hires and some new office equipment next year. New York, Los Angeles, and Chicago are all thinking about signing up, but no other city your size: we're offering it to you first. What do you do?

Do you say no thanks—everything's fine in our city? Or do you start thinking about how saying yes would make you look proactive and cutting-edge? The familiar strategies—the ones you came up with, and the ones you've borrowed from friends in other cities— aren't working. Maybe this will.

If it sounds as though I'm mocking this theoretical chief, or deriding him for being technologically unsophisticated or falling into a salesman's hand, that is absolutely not my intent. Running a police department is a difficult, pressure-filled, often thankless job. The press criticizes you; the mayor barks at you; your deputies all know they could do a better job than you. Here comes a company willing to give you something for nothing. I don't know what I would do in that situation.

But I hope I would not be too blind and eager for good results to consider two things. First, nothing comes free. If a company offers a police department some service gratis, then pay attention to who owns and can use the data it generates or collects. Consider whether the company has the same obligation to citizens whose information it gathers as it would to a paying customer. Perhaps a department is willing to play guinea pig in exchange for some possibly useful tech. If so, it should announce what it is doing and own the consequences of that decision going in.

The second point is simpler. The question—for police departments and for concerned citizens paying attention to how their local department works—is not just whether the technology on offer might help reduce crime, but whether, on balance, it would help more than other equivalent expenditures. If the goal is a safer city for all inhabitants, does it make more sense to spend money on tech, or on schools, mental health services, and housing? Obviously, it's not going to be entirely one or the other, but keeping tech spending in perspective, and evaluating it against non-tech spending, is essential. Do not be dazzled by the promise of the new.

My last point is another thought experiment. Every so often, in Newark, New Jersey, or in Oakland, Chicago, or Washington, DC, I would speak to an activist or just an ordinary citizen—bartender, cab driver, person next to me on a train—who believed that Shotspotter could record people's conversations. I heard this belief expressed on both coasts and in between, from old people and young, men and women, of many different ethnicities. It was not a majority view, but neither was it snake-eyes rare.

Shotspotter insists that the technology cannot do that. So does every police officer familiar with Shotspotter with whom I have spoken. People do not sound like fireworks or engine brakes; they do not have loud, impulsive conversations at 120 or 160 decibels, which is what the sensors are trained to recognize; and no sound stays on the Shotspotter system for more than seventy-two hours. I am aware of no charges brought anywhere based on Shotspotter-intercepted conversations. If reviewing hours of bodycam video taxes a department's resources, what would monitoring every conversation in listening distance of a Shotspotter sensor do?

Now, either Shotspotter and every policeman who uses the technology are lying—and we have on our hands a conspiracy spanning ninety cities, thousands of police officers, and hundreds of employees of a public company, all acting in concert to protect "evidence" of dubious (at best) probative value—or Shotspotter does not recognize or record human conversation.

But before you roll your eyes at yet another conspiracy theory, imagine yourself back in the moderately sized city with lots of shootings and poisoned police-community relations—only this time, you're not the chief. You're an ordinary nonwhite working person from a down-at-heel part of town.

For as long as you've been alive, police have stopped you, and a lot of people you know who look like you, without probable cause. They have spoken to you disrespectfully, rifled through your pockets without permission, maybe written you up for a ticky-tack violation and a hefty fine. Maybe they've laid hands on someone you love. Things have been better recently, you have to admit—it seems like the department is either making a real effort or under federal monitoring. But the things that happened—they happened for years, for decades. Everyone you know who looks like you has a story about a frightening or upsetting interaction with law enforcement.

So when you see a group of officers massed on a corner, lights flashing, hands on holsters, on the hunt, and you ask one what happened, and he points to one of those little white diamonds next to the traffic light, and tells you that those things call the police when they hear gunshots, are you going to just take that explanation at face value? Or are you going to think that maybe—in light of what you and your loved ones have been through—the police aren't being entirely straight with you? *Isn't eavesdropping illegal?* you wonder. But then, the police didn't seem too concerned about the letter of the law when they pulled you over and rifled through your car without a warrant that time.

Every piece of surveillance technology a government introduces has the potential to worsen or improve relations with the community they serve, and the result often depends on how transparent they are. To citizens—to me, certainly—there is an immense difference between, on one hand, acoustic sensors just appearing one day on the street, and, on the other, police going through the admittedly annoying, burdensome process of holding months of public forums to explain what those sensors are, what they can and cannot do, and why they are there. The latter is clearly better. How a city explains the tech it uses is at least as important as the tech itself.

3

WATCHING EACH OTHER

"It is the Interest, and ought to be
the Ambition, of all honest Magistrates, to have
their Deeds openly examined, and publicly scann'd."

THE MAN SITTING ACROSS THE TABLE TELLS ME HE'S BEEN TASED SEVEN
times. He's tall, hale, and well dressed, with thick, graying hair,
heavy-lidded eyes, and an enthusiastic, open demeanor. We are in
a WeWork office in Times Square, not a police station or a mental
hospital. To my knowledge, the man has no criminal record; nor does
he strike me as a masochist or a thrill-seeker. His name is Rick Smith,
and he gets Tased for the same reason a baker eats bread. He runs a
company that is coming to define how police and citizens keep eyes
on each other. This chapter looks at looking, and at how new ways of
monitoring behavior are changing policing.

Smith runs a company known as Axon, which today is best known
for the body cameras it makes and sells to police forces. Until 2017,
the company was called Taser, after its main product and source of
revenue. The name change reflected the firm's shift in focus, away
from its chief product, which has become a generic word for a category of products (like Xerox or Kleenex), and toward its growing
camera business.

In 1993, Smith, then twenty-three years old and fresh out of business school, headed to Tucson, Arizona, to meet Jack Cover, a seventy-three-year-old inventor of nonlethal weapons. As a youth, Cover loved a book called *Tom Swift and His Electric Rifle*, about a boy who invents a gun that shoots bolts of electricity. Cover used that book title's acronym to name his prospective weapon, which was intended to incapacitate but not kill someone using electricity: TASER.

I met Smith when he was on a publicity tour for his book *The End of Killing*. Part memoir and part argument in favor of widespread deployment of nonlethal weaponry, and against guns, it is essentially an extended, thought-provoking, engagingly written advertisement for his firm's products.[1] If that sounds derisive, it isn't intended to. Smith is the founder and CEO of a public company. He has a fiduciary duty to his shareholders, and he should be trying to get people to buy his products.

After graduating from Harvard with a neuroscience degree, he built his company from a garage in Arizona into the leading provider of bodycams and electric weapons to American police forces, becoming Ernst & Young's entrepreneur of the year in 2002.

In *The End of Killing*, Smith credits Cover, a physicist, for having "a brilliant, inventive, fertile mind . . . overflowing with ideas and enthusiasm." But Cover, he says, "stumbled when it came to figuring out how to take an idea in his head and turn it into a product that people would pay for." Enter Smith, who figured out how to market and sell nonlethal weapons to police departments.

First he and Cover had to tweak the design. Cover's original version used gunpowder to launch electrified darts, and the federal government classified it as a Title II weapon, the same category as machine guns, sawed-off shotguns, and rocket launchers, all of which are illegal without special licenses. This was, of course, not an ideal designation for a weapon intended as a nonlethal alternative to a standard police sidearm.

The next iteration used compressed nitrogen rather than gunpowder. Sales picked up, both for law enforcement and personal use. Today, at least fifteen thousand police agencies around the world use

Tasers. In 2017, the firm rebranded itself as Axon to highlight the growing importance of its non-Taser business—specifically, its body-cams. Axon posted revenues in 2018 of $428 million, 84.5 percent of which came from bodycams, the remainder from Tasers.[2]

The new emphasis was a shrewd business decision—Axon is now America's leading provider of bodycams. Tasers make money for Axon once: when a police force buys them. But with bodycams, Axon makes money when police forces buy them, and then they make more for storage costs. Axon also offers Evidence.com, a data-management system that lets departments upload, organize, tag, share, and quickly retrieve audio and video recordings.

The head of information technology (IT) for a modestly sized East Coast county police force (around 1,200 sworn officers, not all of them regular bodycam users) told me that her agency generates around four terabytes of data per month. That's about four thousand full-length movies' worth of data. Like most agencies, they do not have the server space to accommodate that swiftly growing mass of information, so they store it in the cloud. That represents an ongoing cost to the agency. It also raises thorny questions about chain of cus-tody and the private hosting of sensitive public information.

But they are no thornier than the many other questions sur-rounding bodycams that agencies grapple with. What do they record? What *should* they record? How do they change the relationship be-tween police and the policed? Where is the footage stored and for how long? Who gets to see it? For what purpose? When should it be admissible in court, and how should jurors evaluate it? How should we respond to being filmed? How should the police respond when they find themselves on the other side of the camera? In short, how should we think about the cameras that look at us?

There is an apocryphal saying—often cited as a Russian proverb, but possibly invented by Julian Barnes—"He lies like an eyewitness." One of the greatest films ever made, *Rashomon*, from 1950, revolves around conflicting accounts of the same incident (in fact, a crime, according to some of the witnesses): four characters see the same kill-ing, but each interprets it differently. Today, bodycams and cellphone cameras record police encounters with citizens. They provide visual, reviewable evidence where previously there was just written and oral testimony. But just because they provide something for us to see does not mean they provide an objective view of an encounter, or that we are all seeing the same thing.

As with much else in this book, the questions that police bodycams—and civilian use of cellphone cameras to record encounters with police—raise are not primarily legal. They are instead questions of expectations, process, and information security. These cameras record public encounters in which the subjects have little or no reasonable expectation of privacy. In recent years, bodycams and dashcams (cameras mounted on windshields that record video) have become standard issue for many police forces.

A police bodycam is a small device, usually a little larger than a deck of playing cards, that an officer clips to his shirt front. An even smaller version can also be worn as a headset attached to sunglasses. They are designed for an entire shift, so their batteries can last up to twelve hours, and they can record an immense amount of high-definition video. They usually have a broad, raised button on the top so that officers can turn them on and off with minimal effort—or with none at all, because some departments sync bodycams and dashcams to sirens and flashers. As soon as an officer turns on the siren and the lights, both cameras start recording. They can also be synced to an officer's holster, to turn on automatically when officers draw their guns. At the station, they usually live in a dock that charges them and downloads their information.

Most cameras have a perpetual prerecording buffer, meaning they record constantly on a thirty-second to two-minute loop to let people see what took place just before the officer decided to turn on the camera. In the spring of 2018, I embedded in a West Coast police department that at the time mandated full shift recordings for all patrol officers. The officers I spoke with seemed resigned (or perhaps just used to) the cameras. But I spent an afternoon shift with one patrol officer who told me that because the cameras start recording as soon as the officer removes it from its dock, officers had to learn to pick up their cameras from the dock after, rather than before, their preshift bathroom stops.

The widespread police use of bodycams is largely a by-product of tragedy. At around noon on August 9, 2014, in Ferguson, Missouri, Officer Darren Wilson shot and killed eighteen-year-old Michael Brown. The events leading up to Brown's death remain murky. In their first exchange, Wilson asked Brown and another man not to walk in the middle of the street. Then, according to Wilson's grand jury testimony, he noticed that Brown was carrying cigarillos, and Wilson suspected he may have been involved in a recent convenience-store theft. (A Justice Department report alleges that "Brown stole several packages of cigarillos" from Ferguson Market and Liquor.)[3] Wilson parked his SUV at an angle, blocking Brown.

Wilson and some witnesses say that Brown reached in through the patrol-car window and punched the officer; other witnesses say that Wilson reached out through the window and grabbed Brown by the neck. Wilson reached for his gun, the two men struggled for it, and Wilson fired, hitting Brown in the hand at close range. Wilson then got out of his SUV and chased Brown on foot. He says Brown charged him as he was shooting; some witnesses said that Brown had his hands raised. Wilson says he feared for his life, because he believed that Brown was reaching under his shirt for a gun.

In fact, Brown was unarmed, and died as a result of being shot at least six times. Days of unrest followed Brown's death, stemming from frustration not just at the killing of an unarmed young man, but at years of fractious relations between Ferguson's majority-white police force and its majority-black citizenry. An investigation by the Justice Department found that Wilson's use of force was not "objectively unreasonable" under federal law. Another wave of protests broke out three months later, after a grand jury declined to indict Wilson, who has since left the Ferguson police force.

On that same day, Brown's family issued a statement asking for support for their "campaign to ensure that every police officer working the streets in this country wears a body camera." Had Wilson been wearing a camera on the morning of August 9, the grand jury—and eventually the public—would probably have known whether Wilson instigated the conflict by grabbing Brown by the neck, or Brown reached into the car and began punching him, and whether Brown was shot to death while charging or while trying to surrender.

The Justice Department heeded the family's call: in May 2015, it announced a pilot program that distributed around $20 million in grants to cover the cost of 21,000 bodycams for 73 law enforcement agencies (the grants paid for cameras, technical assistance, and programs to study the effects of bodycam use).[4] This is a small fraction of the total number of law enforcement agencies in America, but the number is growing, and that funding stream continued from the Obama to the Trump administration. From 2015 to 2018, the Justice Department disbursed more than $70 million in bodycam grant money, according to the *Washington Post,* and it maintains a clearinghouse of information on bodycam best practices through the Bureau of Justice Assistance.[5]

Those funds turned bodycams from an interesting experiment into standard-issue products for most big departments. In April 2018, the Police Executive Research Forum (PERF), an education and research group for law enforcement, surveyed a nationally representative sample of 893 police agencies (including a range of locations and sizes—most of them small, with 99 or fewer officers, as most agencies across America are). In the results, 35.2 percent said they were using bodycams; another 46.6 percent said they planned to use them in the future. Forces with more than 250 officers are slightly likelier than their smaller counterparts to use or plan to use bodycams.[6]

This Congress, as well as the two previous, have all seen bills introduced that would require federal law enforcement officers to wear bodycams.[7] None passed, but eventually, similar legislation probably will. Nearly 92 percent of agencies said the most important reason to use them is to promote transparency, accountability, and legitimacy. Most agencies gave bodycams either to all sworn officers or just to patrol (meaning, in essence, uniformed police in cars and on foot, as opposed to plainclothes detectives or undercover officers).

As of May 2016, according to a study from the Johns Hopkins Applied Physics Laboratory, agencies could choose from over 60 different types of bodycams.[8] The range is no doubt greater today. Axon remains the market leader; its products are used, according to a company spokesman, by more than 18,000 law enforcement agencies in 100 countries, including forces in 48 of America's biggest 79 cities.

Bodycams are the rare form of technology that garners support from police and their critics, though not without initial skepticism. Many police unions opposed them—or at least were wary of them— in part because they feared that supervisors could use them to levy punishments for petty and technical rule infractions on officers in disfavor. GovTech, a website focused on technology and the public sector, reported that the head of El Paso's Police Officers' Association said he didn't want his officers "recorded 24/7. . . . What happens if I'm driving and somebody jumps out of the car and you get into a scuffle instantly? Well hold on sir—let me turn my body camera on so it can show what you are doing to me."[9]

Others viewed—and still view—bodycams primarily as a way to surveil already over-surveilled communities. Albert Fox Cahn, who heads the Surveillance Technology Oversight Project at the Urban Justice Center in New York, wrote in the *New York Times* that body-cams "would allow the police to turn a walk down the block into a warrantless search of where people go and with whom they associate. An officer standing outside an abortion clinic or political protest, for example, could chill some of our most fundamental constitutional rights."[10] Others worry that because many departments let police view bodycam footage before writing their report on using force, it will be easier for them to fit their narrative to what the tape shows, rather than what they remember happening.

Police critics believe that the cameras will compel officers to behave better and use force more judiciously. Police who support bodycams believe they protect officers against false accusations of misconduct. A poll taken by the Cato Institute, a libertarian think tank, in 2016 showed that 89 percent of Americans support requiring police to wear bodycams—and that this support "extends across demographic and political groups."[11]

But bodycams—or, more broadly, recording citizen encounters with police—also highlight a central tension in liberal societies' views of law enforcement. We want justice to be impartial, but not rigid. We do not want people to get away with lawbreaking, but neither do we want every legal infraction punished harshly. I'll ask the same question again: Would you want every single instance of jaywalking, or driving a mile over the speed limit, to be maximally punished?

In May 2019, *Slate* published an article by an ex-cop named Katie Miller, who wrote that bodycams eliminate the informal interactions and discretion that help make policing more humane. She told the story of pulling over a woman who ran a stop sign in pre-bodycam days. She had groceries and an infant in the backseat, and it turned out she was driving with an expired license. By law, she should have been arrested. But that would have separated her from her child. Miller instead told her to call a friend to pick her up. "I couldn't have gotten away with that today," she wrote.

"If I discovered a homeless person urinating in public," Miller explained further, "the video forced me to fine him, arrest him or violate general orders by not recording the interaction. . . . [B]odycams may have made it easier to hold cops accountable for their actions, but they also have the effect of holding citizens strictly accountable for theirs." Miller also mentioned the tacit agreement that permits drinking alcohol from a paper bag. Public drinking is illegal, but arresting everyone outside drinking a beer on a hot day would be a tremendous waste of police resources. The paper bag, she said, "provided a workaround for police and citizens." Bodycams do the opposite: because the footage might be minutely reviewed, everything has to be done by the book. Bodycams did not create that tension between fair and unnecessarily rigid applications of the law, but they certainly appear to heighten it.[12]

Some cheer them because they provide evidence of misconduct. "Nobody hates a bad cop more than a good cop," Rick Smith, Axon's CEO, told me (though of course the head of a bodycam company would make the case for bodycams). He recalled a recent meeting with some big-city police chiefs who were frustrated by how difficult it was to get rid of poor officers. They were asking, "What am I supposed to do as a police leader, if I've identified someone who probably isn't a good fit for policing, and yet we can't get rid of him because of the employment protections for public employees?" The chiefs, Smith said, "really like the idea of accountability," and bodycam evidence helped them "prove the case" when they wanted to get someone off the force "to protect the image of the profession."

More prosaically, bodycam footage can help in training: departments can see where officers need to improve. They also show patterns of behavior across entire departments. As a former San Diego police chief noted in a Justice Department report, "When it comes to collecting data, the raw numbers don't always fully capture the true scope of a problem. . . . But by capturing an audio and video account of an encounter, cameras provide an objective record of whether racial profiling took place, what patterns of officer behavior are present, and how often the problem occurs."[13]

Bodycams also gather and store evidence. Crime scenes can be tense and chaotic. First responders have to secure the scene, keep onlookers at bay, and field questions from superior officers. Sometimes people on the scene will have witnessed something, but they don't want a crowd to see them telling police what they saw. A detective working the case can review the first responders' bodycams, identify people who were at the scene, and try to talk to them later in a calmer and less crowded environment.

So far, so uncontroversial. But what happens to the footage once it's uploaded to a central server? Do police get to edit it? If so, they can hide evidence of misconduct. Do officials get to decide what footage to release and when? If so, they can choose the footage that best serves their narrative. The more that people believe bodycams show an objective record of an event, the more tempting it becomes to do what officers in Baltimore allegedly did in 2017: stage, or "reenact," drug seizures for the cameras' benefit.[14]

How should police departments balance the privacy concerns of those captured on bodycam footage with the public's right to know, enshrined in sunshine and freedom-of-information laws? How well secured is the server where the footage is stored, and what happens in the event of a breach? These are the sorts of questions that well-crafted usage policies have to answer.

How long a department stores footage often depends on the crime, if any. The police department in Newark, New Jersey, for instance, stores nonevidentiary footage—meaning footage in which nobody was arrested—for 90 days. This footage is unconnected to a crime: it may be a traffic stop, for instance, in which the driver pays the ticket and does not complain. Other departments store such footage for as little as 30 days or as long as 210. Newark stores footage that shows an arrest for seven years. Footage from major crimes and ongoing investigations can get stored indefinitely.

That is where the real costs of these programs lie. Cameras are not terribly expensive. The Axon 3, for instance, which, as of this writing, is the company's latest bodycam, starts at $699. That is not nothing—particularly for a big-city force buying them by the thousand—but neither is it cripplingly expensive, even assuming a department has to upgrade them every few years.

PERF's survey found that many agencies spend $5,000 or less per year on bodycam programs. But that's because most police departments are small, or do not distribute bodycams to many officers. Yet even a modestly sized department with a robust program can generate enormous amounts of data that need to be stored, cataloged, archived, and easily retrievable.

A larger agency surveyed by PERF reported paying $1.4 million per year for equipment and $4 million for storage costs. Newark's police department, faced with an estimated annual cost of $1.3 million to store its footage in the cloud (that is, on a remote server operated by a private firm, like Axon), opted to store it in-house. Some departments save money by putting older videos into cold storage, effectively archiving them, which costs far less than having them readily available. PERF found that most agencies opted for in-house storage, with just 27.3 percent using the cloud, though that share may grow along with the amount of information that needs storage.

Firms that offer cloud-based storage promise safety and rigorous chain-of-custody documentation, which is essential when presenting evidence at trial to ensure that nobody has tampered with it. But breaches do happen (no doubt Equifax also promised its customers that their data was completely secure, right up until the data breach that exposed the personal information of 147 million people). With bodycam footage, breaches endanger not just sensitive personal information but also public safety and due process. More worryingly, as *Wired* reported in 2018, bodycams are easy to hack: malicious actors can download footage from a bodycam, edit it, and reupload it without leaving a trace.[15] That negates the promise of transparency that led to their widespread adoption.

Then there are the hours and extra personnel that bodycam programs require: for procurement, administration, analysis, and reviewing the footage. PERF's survey found that officers spent an average of 25.5 minutes per day reviewing and tagging bodycam footage. Agencies received an average of 9.1 Freedom of Information Act requests per month, each of which required an average of 9.8 hours of staff time to respond to (that's an average of all agencies of all sizes; presumably those figures are bigger for bigger departments). Still, most footage goes unexamined. Chris Fisher, executive director for strategy in the Seattle Police Department, told me that only around 5 percent of the "millions of hours" of video captured by his colleagues ever gets looked at. But 5 percent of millions is still at least 100,000.

No doubt machine learning and AI-driven analytics will reduce the amount of time that people need to spend reviewing bodycam footage. Axon has been working on AI-driven redaction, review, and reporting. Yet while AI might help officers spend less time on some of the more tedious tasks—including transcription and blurring the faces of bystanders in footage released to the public—the police encounters they record are often complex and unfold quickly. Automated video- and image-searching platforms may be a reasonable first step. But it is unthinkable that a department would release a machine-redacted video, without final human approval, in response to an open-records request; or that a prosecutor would use an officer's footage at trial without first scrutinizing both the footage itself and other footage featuring that officer to determine credibility and habits.

Bodycam policies vary widely from department to department. In itself, that is neither surprising nor wrong. Federal forces notwithstanding, American policing is locally governed—the federal government can fund and advise, and if departments are found to have a

pattern of violating people's civil rights, they can monitor and recommend reforms. But they can and should no more dictate bodycam
policies than they can mandate what uniforms or service weapons
locally employed officers use.

Still, some policies are better than others. As early as 2014, Chuck
Wexler, a Boston Police Department veteran who now heads the Police Executive Research Forum, wrote that "if police departments
deploy body-worn cameras without well-designed policies, practices,
and training of officers to back up the initiative, departments will in-
evitably find themselves caught in difficult public battles that will undermine public trust in the police rather than increasing community
support for the police."[16]

Even then, when just sixty-three of five hundred departments
surveyed used bodycams, a report that PERF wrote with the Justice
Department worried about whether departments had the right privacy guardrails in place. When should officers record? Who gets to
look at the footage? How available should recordings be to the public? A bodycam recording of a disputed shooting doesn't do much
good if the public can't see it. But police often respond to calls at
people's homes—should just anyone be able to see that intimate domestic footage?

Most departments do not film particularly sensitive conversations—with a child, for instance, or with a victim of sexual assault or
domestic violence. But, echoing Chief Ambrose's concerns, would recording every encounter risk making the sorts of casual conversations
essential to cementing good community-police relations awkward or
impossible? Should officers get people's permission before recording
any conversation?

Four years later, another PERF report found wide variance in
practices concerning when officers turn on their cameras, with 55.7
percent of agencies requiring officers to record any interaction with
a citizen involving "law-enforcement related activity" or any response
to a call for service, 19.3 percent requiring them to record all citizen
interactions, 9.8 percent leaving decisions to the officer's discretion,
and 6.4 percent with no policy at all.[17]

In November 2017, a coalition of civil rights groups led by the Leadership Conference on Civil Rights, along with Upturn, a technology-focused nonprofit with a strong interest in criminal justice reform, wrote a scorecard that rated the bodycam policies of America's seventy-five biggest departments.[18] There are some bright spots: most departments clearly delineate when officers have to record, and most have some safeguards in place to protect certain vulnerable people—people who believe themselves to be victims of sex crimes, for instance—from being recorded without their consent. But there were also plenty of gaps. Boston's police department, for example, had no publicly available usage policy, allowed broad officer discretion on when to start and stop recording, encouraged officers to watch footage before writing a report, set no limit on footage retention, and did not prohibit officers from editing or deleting footage.

And Boston is not an outlier. Most departments set no limits on footage retention, and few protect footage against tampering or deletion. Most allow the unfettered use of biometric technology, such as facial recognition, to identify people in the footage. Many do not make footage available to people filing misconduct complaints. The PERF survey found that although 79.2 percent of agencies had policies requiring them to release footage to the public, all but two of those agencies permitted exceptions. Seventeen percent of the agencies did not have to turn over footage at all.

Determining the ideal bodycam policy is difficult. In my view, it should lean toward disclosure, certainly in the case of credible misconduct reports, but some exceptions will always be essential. Figuring out what those exceptions should be, and who gets to declare them, is the tricky part.

These are not easy questions to resolve. But not having a readily available policy and making the footage difficult for the public to access contravene the principles of transparency and accountability that bodycams were intended to promote. Imagine an incident in which an officer shows up at a local jail at 4:00 a.m., having arrested a young man who has a bloody nose, a cut above his eye, and a sore shoulder. The officer says the young man was a belligerent drunk who attacked him outside a bar just after closing time; the young man insists he did no more than move too slowly for the officer's taste. He files a complaint. If the department lets the officer view bodycam footage before filing a report and testifying, but does not extend the same courtesy to the complainant, then the bodycam seems more like a police insurance policy than a program designed to promote transparency, accountability, and legitimacy.

There is ample research suggesting that people tend to behave differently when watched. That is one of the hopes underlying the widespread adoption of bodycams—that civilians will be more courteous, and police more likely to follow procedure. But a randomized, controlled trial of 2,224 police officers in Washington, DC, found that wearing bodycams had no statistically significant effects either on police use of force or on civilian complaints. Washington's police chief suggested to a journalist from National Public Radio that perhaps that was because his officers "were doing the right thing in the first place," and that bodycams had value beyond the study's parameters. He mentioned an incident in which footage showed that a fatal shooting by officers was justified because the person they shot was brandishing a knife.[19]

A similar trial of officers in Las Vegas, however, found that officers equipped with bodycams generated fewer complaints and use-of-force incidents than officers without them.[20] The officers with bodycams also arrested more people in Las Vegas than those without—although a study conducted two years later, in Mesa, Arizona, found the opposite: officers who wore bodycams were less likely to make arrests than those who did not.[21] The first finding matches the result of one of the earliest bodycam studies, conducted in Rialto, California, in 2012, before their general use; it found that use-of-force incidents dropped by 50 percent, and civilian complaints to almost zero.[22]

Perhaps the most interesting result came from a ten-site randomized trial conducted by criminologists in Israel, Britain, and the United States. It found that overall, bodycams had no effect on use-of-force rates (meaning, in this case, any use of physical restraint greater than handcuffing). But that overall finding masked variance:

in some places, police with bodycams used force more often, in other places less.

It turns out that when officers followed the experiment's protocol, recording every encounter starting from the time they arrived on the scene, use-of-force incidents dropped by 37 percent. When officers decided on their own when to turn on their cameras, use-of-force incidents increased by 71 percent (both rates were in comparison to the control group). This finding suggests two things. First, that turning on a bodycam mid-encounter may escalate already tense situations. And second, that having the right policies in place—mandating that officers record entire encounters—is essential to deriving positive effects from bodycams.[23]

Bodycams purport to show an event as it really happened—to relieve people of the need to consider conflicting testimony, decide who is the more credible of two witnesses who say different things, weigh alternate perspectives, and adjudicate between different viewpoints. But even though they may show things that oral or written testimony would omit, they can still distort the truth.

Bodycams provide just one more viewpoint. A camera mounted on an officer's chest can make people appear bigger or more threatening than they are, providing a more plausible justification for using force than may actually exist. Bodycams only show the actions of one person, so viewers see, for instance, a suspect getting increasingly agitated, but not whether an officer was reaching for his gun. Bodycam footage only shows what it shows. What is just outside the frame?

In an article for *Fordham Law Review*, Jeffrey Bellin, a professor at William and Mary Law School, and Shevarma Pemberton, a clerk for the Thirteenth Judicial Circuit of Virginia, posit "a thorny question that courts have yet to answer . . . whether police officer statements captured on a body camera . . . are admissible in court." The authors note that statements such as "Your breath smells of alcohol" or "He just threw something into the bushes" would generally be considered hearsay if offered at trial. But in recorded footage, they may qualify as admissible under a range of hearsay exceptions. This provides an incentive for police to narrate, and perhaps even embellish, events as they occur when they are being recorded.[24]

Yet in *Scott v. Harris*, decided in 2007, an eight-justice majority of the US Supreme Court endorsed the view that police camera footage provides an objective record of facts.[25] The case concerned Victor Harris, who led police in Coweta County, Georgia, on a high-speed chase. It ended when Deputy Timothy Scott deliberately bumped the back of Harris's car, causing Harris to lose control of the vehicle, which crashed. Harris's injuries left him a quadriplegic, and he sued, claiming that Scott had violated his Fourth Amendment rights by using excessive force. Scott, citing qualified immunity, asked for the case to be dismissed.

District and appellate courts denied Scott's request, allowing the case to proceed. When considering a request for summary judgment, courts must consider the facts in the light most favorable to the opposing party. So at this stage, they did not affirm that Harris's rights had definitively been violated, only that there was sufficient evidence, viewing the matter in a light favorable to Harris, to let the case proceed.

The Supreme Court reversed these rulings. Justice Antonin Scalia, who wrote the majority opinion, explained that ordinarily, summary judgment requests required "adopting (as the Court of Appeals did here) the plaintiff's version of the facts." But, Scalia said, there was "an added wrinkle in this case: existence in the record of a videotape." The footage showed Harris's car, as Scalia described it, "racing down narrow, two-lane roads in the dead of night at speeds that are shockingly fast."

The ruling mentions Harris swerving around other cars and running red lights. "Far from being the cautious and controlled driver the lower court depicts," Scalia wrote, "what we see on the video more closely resembles a Hollywood-style car chase of the most frightening sort, placing police officers and innocent bystanders alike at great risk of serious injury." He then chided the appellate court for accepting Harris's interpretation of the facts instead of viewing "the facts in the light depicted by the videotape."

But the Court's lone dissenter, John Paul Stevens, noted the lack of pedestrians and bystanders on the roads that Harris and his pursuers traveled. The police also ran red lights, and the cars in those inter-sections were stationary, as they should be when sirens are blaring. He posited that the cars on the shoulder had not been forced there to avoid injury from Harris, but because they heard and saw police in pursuit. Harris, he observed, consistently used his turn signals, and he did not come close to hitting anyone. Stevens wondered whether his colleagues might have taken a different view if they had learned to drive on two-lane roads, where overtaking in the opposite-traffic lane is common, rather than on "superhighways." To those objections the majority primly responded, "We are happy to allow the videotape to speak for itself."

But of course that is precisely what the video does not do. Witness the rulings by the two lower courts, made by judges who, as Justice Stevens pointed out, were probably far more familiar with driving on rural Georgia roads than was Justice Scalia, who was born and raised in Queens. The footage was grainy and in black and white, which made the headlights look like they were passing in the opposite lane, as though Scott were zooming past—and barely avoiding—oncom-ing traffic. But when the footage was viewed in color, the headlights seemed to be stationary—as though from cars that had already pulled onto the side of the road to avoid the chase.

Seven years later, another case, *Plumhoff v. Rickard*, also took dash-cam footage as an objective source rather than as just one view of a situation, and therefore subject to dispute like any other.[26] The bot-tom line is that this technology, which was supposed to help citizens hold officers accountable, may have the opposite effect: it may come to be viewed as not just one piece of evidence that can be contra-dicted by others, but a record of objective truth that can trump any opposing testimony.

That is not what video footage is or does: it is not the eye of God. It is a record of a single, fixed perspective. It can prove or disprove certain discrete and sometimes crucial facts. But no eyewitness—not even a camera—provides a single, complete, objective record of an event that brooks no disagreement.

Just as police can record their views of citizens, citizens can record right back, via their cellphones. While some officers may not like being on the other side of the camera, multiple federal courts have found that the First Amendment protects the public's right to film police officers in public. As early as 1994, the Eleventh Circuit Court of Appeals (the federal appellate court covering Alabama, Florida, and Georgia) recognized that citizens had a right to film public meetings.[27]

In 2000, the same court recognized that citizens—and not just journalists—had "a First Amendment right, subject to reasonable time, manner and place restrictions, to photograph or videotape police conduct." People cannot impede police activity in order to film, but the First Amendment protects their right to film. After all, the First Amendment right to possess, distribute, and watch audio and video recordings gets pretty hollow pretty quickly if the law bans their production.[28]

Several years later, another federal court brought that right into the cellphone camera age. In 2007, police in Boston arrested a man named Simon Glik, who was filming them making an arrest. They charged him with violating the state's wiretap statute, as well as with disturbing the peace and aiding in the escape of a prisoner. The last charge was quickly dismissed because the prisoner did not, in fact, escape. A court ruled in Glik's favor on the other two charges, holding that the state's wiretap law forbids secret recordings, while Glik was recording openly. Glik then filed a complaint against the Boston Police Department for violating his First Amendment rights (and his Fourth Amendment rights, though that claim concerns the Massachusetts wiretap act and is of limited broader utility).[29]

In 2011, the First Circuit Court of Appeals (which covers Maine, Massachusetts, New Hampshire, Rhode Island, and Puerto Rico) ruled in his favor, finding that the First Amendment's "aegis" extends beyond just the textual proscriptions against laws that restrict freedom of the press, and includes a positive right "to gather news 'from any source by means within the law'"—a right enjoyed by ordinary citizens as well as journalists. The court recognized that "police officers are expected to endure significant burdens caused by citizens' exercise of their First Amendment rights": citizens should be able to verbally oppose and challenge them—nonthreateningly, of course, and without interfering in their work—without the risk of punishment or arrest. Moreover, because police "are granted substantial discretion that may be misused to deprive individuals of their liberty," the public has a particularly strong interest in scrutinizing them (the court approvingly quoted an older judgment finding that "many governmental processes operate best under public scrutiny").

One month after a federal court in Boston ruled in Glik's favor, the ACLU of Illinois pressed a similar case in a federal court in Chicago. The ACLU had planned a "police accountability program," which would have encouraged people to record police officers performing their duties in public without the officers' consent.

The former Cook County state's attorney (Chicago's head prosecutor) argued that this would violate the state's eavesdropping law, which forbade audio recording of any conversation anywhere without the consent of all parties. Usually the penalty was minor, but if a police officer was recorded, the person convicted could have been subject to up to fifteen years' imprisonment. The ACLU asked the Seventh Circuit Court of Appeals (which covers Illinois, Indiana, and Wisconsin) for a preliminary injunction against enforcing the eavesdropping law.

The court sided with the ACLU, finding that the state's eavesdropping law was too broad. Protecting people's privacy rights by forbidding people to secretly record the private conversations of others was permissible, but that was not the same thing as forbidding them from openly recording the public activities of police. It held that such recordings fall within the First Amendment's protection of free expression, speech, and press rights, and that banning the recording of public events would be analogous to banning note-taking or photography in public.[30]

The court charmingly quoted Thomas Gordon, an early eighteenth-century Scot much beloved of the founding generation ("It is the Interest, and ought to be the Ambition, of all honest Magistrates, to have their Deeds openly examined, and publicly scann'd"), and Thomas Cooley, a nineteenth-century constitutional scholar and chief justice of the Michigan Supreme Court, who noted that the purpose of free speech and press rights was to "enable any citizen at any time to bring the government and any person in authority to the bar of public opinion by any just criticism upon their conduct in the exercise of the authority which the people have conferred upon them." Recording government officials in action is thus just as integral to the rights guaranteed by the First Amendment as writing or speaking about them, and deserves the same legal protection.

In 2017, appellate courts in the Third Circuit (which covers Delaware, New Jersey, Pennsylvania, and the Virgin Islands) and the Fifth Circuit (Louisiana, Mississippi, and Texas) joined the consensus, both finding that people had a First Amendment right to film the police engaged in their official duties in public.[31] The Fifth Circuit, which is often deferential to government power, ruled that "filming the police contributes to the public's ability to hold the police accountable," though a dissenting judge urged her colleagues not to propound any broad First Amendment right ahead of the Supreme Court, which had not then—and, as I write these words, still has not—ruled on the matter.

The Supreme Court had the chance in 2012, but denied certiorari to Anita Alvarez, then the Cook County state's attorney, who appealed the ruling against her. But the appellate courts that have found a public right to record police cover more than half of America's population. Their judges, who hold both broad and limited views on government power, have issued similar rulings, using nearly identical reasoning and language. No appellate court has ruled in the other direction. While it is of course not impossible that the Supreme Court could reverse them all—and the precedents on which they have based their decisions—neither is it likely. The police will have to get used to being on the other side of the lens.

◉

Videos of police encounters have long had a galvanic effect. At around 1:00 a.m. on March 3, 1991, the sound of sirens and helicopters woke George Holliday, then thirty-one years old and the owner of a small plumbing firm in California's San Fernando Valley. He had recently bought himself a Sony Handycam, a handheld video camera that recorded onto 8mm tape. He stepped out onto his balcony and began videotaping what he saw: white police officers brutally kicking and beating a young black man, whom America later learned was named Rodney King.

If it were not for Holliday's tape, four officers would probably not have been indicted for assault and excessive use of force. Without the tape, the officers' story—that King had resisted arrest and tried to attack them—would probably have been believed. But the tape did not show him resisting, and while he repeatedly tried to rise, it looked more like a desperate attempt to stagger away from a brutal beating than an effort to attack the cops. The officers were charged with using excessive force, but they were tried in the much whiter suburb of Simi Valley, rather than in Los Angeles County, and found not guilty. Their acquittal sparked five days of rioting in Los Angeles, resulting in over fifty deaths and around $1 billion in property damage.

Today, we all have a video camera in our pockets. Smartphone cameras are easier to use than a handheld camera that records onto a tape. They can also record for a longer time, produce clearer footage, and stream online in real time. That makes them especially useful for documenting spontaneous occurrences, as police encounters often are.

The ACLU has a host of apps that let users record and report encounters with the police. The group's live-streaming "Mobile Justice" app is available in eighteen states and Washington, DC. It lets the user record, report, and witness police interactions. The app automatically sends recordings to the user's local ACLU chapter, along with as much information about the encounter as the user wants to provide. It also lets users locate others recording police stops nearby, in case they want to act as witnesses.[32]

Brandon Anderson, a young black man from Oklahoma, is working on a similar product called Raheem AI, which will let anyone, anywhere report police misconduct.[33] On his website, Anderson notes that being killed by a police officer is the sixth leading cause of death for young African American men.

Raheem AI is an intensely personal project for him. His partner was killed by a police officer during a traffic stop in 2007. I met

Anderson at a vegan café near Madison Square Park in Manhattan late one spring morning in April 2019.

Anderson is also an army veteran and a graduate of Georgetown University, where he studied sociology. After his partner's death, he began thinking about police misconduct: how difficult it is to report, and how few consequences it brings. Procedures for reporting misconduct vary from agency to agency. Most require you to file a report in person, at a police station during business hours: a process both needlessly burdensome to working people and intimidating—so a lot of people just don't do it. Anderson said the officer who killed his partner had "a history of being violent in the community, but nobody reported him." That is not unusual: many people who believe they have been mistreated by the police never file complaints.

And even when complaints are filed, says Anderson, "information is locked away in police departments." The doctrine of qualified immunity, which shields government officials from lawsuits for violating people's civil liberties for actions performed in the course of their duties, unless they break a "clearly established" statutory or constitutional right, provides a broad shield. This doctrine is not in the Constitution; it was simply invented by the Supreme Court in 1967.[34] Police say it is necessary to protect them from frivolous lawsuits and excessive litigation, though of course they rarely bear the cost of lawsuits—their employers and insurance do—and qualified immunity is rarely applied early enough in the legal process to forestall a suit. In effect, the doctrine allows police to get away with egregious misconduct unless a court has previously addressed whatever specific form of misconduct they engaged in. For instance, in March 2019, the Ninth Circuit Court of Appeals held that police officers could not be sued for allegedly stealing $276,000 in cash and rare coins while executing a warrant.[35] Because "appellants did not have a clearly established Fourth or Fourteenth Amendment right to be free from the theft of property seized pursuant to a warrant," the ruling said, "the City Officers are entitled to qualified immunity."

Reread that sentence. Because no court had explicitly stated that police officers couldn't steal people's money while executing a warrant, the police officers couldn't be punished for (allegedly) stealing people's money while executing a warrant. I realize how strange that sentence sounds. On rereading, it grows no less strange or infuriating. As part of an investigation into illegal gambling in Fresno, California, a judge approved a warrant to seize money found on the defendants' property that police believed to be connected to illegal gambling. As in any such seizure, police are supposed to fill out an inventory sheet explaining what they took, and give it to the people from whom they took it. On that inventory sheet, police said they seized around $50,000; the defendants claimed that in fact they took $151,380 in cash and another $125,000 in rare coins—and kept the difference. The court held that it did not have to decide whether the police officers had violated the defendants' Fourth Amendment rights by stealing their cash and coins. It ruled instead that because no court had clearly established a constitutional right for people to not have their property stolen by police during the execution of a search warrant, the officers were entitled to qualified immunity.

I hope that even the most ardent defender of qualified immunity would struggle to plausibly argue that it was intended to protect alleged thieves—that a doctrine intended to protect public servants from frivolous lawsuits was also intended to provide them complete immunity from the consequences of allegedly blatant lawbreaking.

Raheem AI cannot reverse qualified immunity, but it can provide a public record of complaints about police behavior (or compliments—Anderson's product will allow positive reports, too). "We think reporting bad police should be as easy as ordering takeout," Anderson explained to me. His app will let anyone report an encounter, anonymously or with contact details, along with the officer's name and badge number. It will also make that information public, because, as he put it, "it should be easy to see how [officers] stack up against their peers around the country. That information should be accessible to police departments when hiring, to journalists writing stories about violent officers, and to community members who want to rally against a department or an officer."

Raheem AI's data will also be available to civilian oversight boards and to public defenders and prosecutors, so they know the record of a police officer called to testify during trial. "My theory," says Anderson, "is that police departments won't dispatch officers who they know can't testify in court. Which means we stop departments from dispatching violent officers to [make arrests], because they have no credibility." Insurance companies can use the data to determine police departments' liabilities, so "departments can either reduce the number of violent officers in their department, or increase the amount of money they pay to insurance companies."

Both of these apps—the ACLU's and Anderson's—answer an obvious question: Now what? Cellphone videos of police encounters abound on YouTube, but what happens to that information? The ACLU's app ensures that an organization charged with defending Americans' civil liberties sees it; Raheem AI should let the public see reports of officer misconduct, because sometimes the act of recording—or of recording and then posting it online—is not enough.

That is not always true. As I write, I can switch windows and watch a cellphone video shot in the past week of a police officer in Phoenix, Arizona. He threatens to "put a fucking cap right in [the] fucking head" of a young pregnant woman whose daughter reportedly took a doll from a dollar store; he punches and kicks her fiancé, the girl's father, before declining to arrest either of them. That particular video, which went viral in June 2019, was so egregious that it prompted apologies from Phoenix's mayor and police chief, as well as offers of legal aid from Jay-Z.

But cellphones have captured a number of police killings, including, among others, those of Walter Scott, a forklift operator and Coast Guard veteran who was unarmed and pulled over for a broken taillight, whom a police officer shot several times in the back as he ran; Philando Castile, a thirty-two-year-old who worked at a Montessori school, whom a police officer shot four times during a routine traffic stop (the officer seemed to believe that Castile was reaching for a gun); and Eric Garner, suspected of selling single cigarettes, whom a policeman choked to death on a street in Staten Island, in broad daylight, as Garner gasped, "I can't breathe," eleven times. All of those killed were black men. All of their deaths appear to have been avoidable. The videos show agitated or angry police officers escalating conflict rather than trying to defuse it.

Along with the death of Michael Brown in Ferguson, Missouri (which was not captured on video), these unjustified killings—and the visceral reaction to seeing them play out in real time—helped inspire the Black Lives Matter movement. They also inspired welcome and long-overdue agitations for police, prosecutorial, and broader criminal justice reform.

I'm writing this sentence on the morning of June 6, after days of protests in Minneapolis and across America over the killing of George Floyd, who died after a police officer pressed a knee into his neck for nearly nine minutes—almost three of them after police failed to find Floyd's pulse. The excruciating video of his death—its slow inexorability, as former officer Derek Chauvin stares nonchalantly into the camera as he slowly chokes Floyd to death—sparked those protests, which in turn sparked calls for changes to police policy.

This suggests a more important second-order effect of body-cams—one not captured by studies that try to assess whether they produce immediate changes to police behavior: they galvanize support for reform. That seems true *especially* when they produce no immediate behavioral changes. Chauvin knew he was on camera, and believed (wrongly, as it turned out) that he would face no consequences for his behavior—he had, after all, successfully faced down eighteen previous excessive-force complaints. He had no reason to believe this one would be different. But it was, and it probably would not have been had it not been caught on camera.

Many videos like these were captured by people who happened to be passing by and decided to start recording. But some people use their phones and presence more systematically. Copwatch is a loosely organized group of activists devoted to filming the police. The group, founded in Berkeley in 1990, was inspired by police-watching organizations that one of the founders first saw while she was working in South Africa. I first encountered one of their chapters in Atlanta in around 2011 or 2012. As with other criminal justice reform movements, it has grown in strength since the killing of Michael Brown in 2014.

Copwatchers probably take a more skeptical view of the police than the average citizen does. Some posted videos show them badgering police rather than simply observing them neutrally. A banner on a Copwatch website boasts of "exposing dirty pigs" and offers for download posters proclaiming, among other things, "Cops have more in common with criminals than with normal citizens," "Most police officers are uneducated and dangerously undertrained," and "High IQ applicants are rejected by the Police Academy." But remember that the movement is decentralized; just because one Copwatcher has juvenile and repellent views of the police does not mean that any other Copwatcher shares those views.

And a few repellent posters do not invalidate the group's core mission, which Jacob Crawford, a veteran Copwatcher featured in a short film about the movement shot by *Vice*, described as "the direct, nonviolent observation of the police." Copwatch, he said, aims to deter rather than capture police misconduct. That makes sense: people tend to behave differently when they know they're being filmed.

At a café near Howard University one warm spring afternoon, I met members of a Copwatch group that has been active in Washington, DC, since the summer of 2017. (They spoke to me on the condition that I quote and refer to them collectively as "Copwatch DC.") In one sense, Copwatch DC does what other Copwatch chapters do: they monitor the police. For the most part this passes uneventfully. Copwatch DC said some cops can get confrontational, but the "by the book" ones ignore them—they understand that citizens have the right to film the police as long as they do not interfere.

Copwatch DC said their activism is "not just about literal watching, but also about challenging what the police state has become. When the police start to interact with someone, they're trying to put a wedge between the neighborhood and whoever they're talking to." That wedge often forms physically—police surrounding a suspect, with their backs to the public—but it's also a psychological wedge: many people believe that the police would never stop an innocent person. So when most people walk past police officers questioning someone, they think to themselves, "What did that person do?," rather than, "Does that person need my help?"

Copwatch DC sees its job as not just preventing police misconduct, but, more importantly, as doing what it can to remove that wedge—to let the person being questioned by the police know that they see him as "a human being, and we know that cops can be lethal, and we're not going to leave you in this situation by yourself." In this sense, it may differ from other chapters, in that its goal is as much to be present for a person in distress as it is to simply document police activity. Copwatch DC does not try to be a neutral party; they are there for the suspect's benefit, without regard to what the suspect might have done or is accused of doing.

Copwatch DC's role only begins in watching; it does not end there. They use monitoring the police as a way to build solidarity with other surveilled people. My simple question about why they do what they do prompted this response: "Think about what it means to be accountable to the people around you. If this was your parent, if this was your kid, if this was your sibling [being stopped by the police], would you just walk away, or would you stop and say I'm accountable to these people? . . . My liberation is tied to your liberation, and your liberation is tied to my liberation. . . . When I fight for you, I'm fighting for me."

This is activism on a more personal and intimate scale. "A lot of times," said Copwatch DC, "activists can be really good at mobilizing a lot of people, but get super nervous about talking to one person on the street. . . . We can show off and say we have all these people but we're not building power. . . . This [meaning individual people bearing witness and offering help and support] challenges us to break that tendency. I think that's where a lot of the power is."

Brandon Anderson is similarly clear about his ultimate goals with Raheem AI: "I want to level the playing field," he said, meaning between police and those on the receiving end of police misconduct. He wants to eliminate institutional barriers to reporting and disseminating information on bad officers. "People of color should have more control over how they're policed," he told me. "That starts with communities getting the information that they desperately need. . . . Most crime is because of need. People need stuff.

We're increasing the budgets of police instead of increasing opportunities for communities to get what they need so that we don't need police. But police maintain order, so they're well funded. Our ideology of safety has been shifted to depend on police. That's very dangerous."

You may not agree with all of Anderson's formulation, but it is undeniably true that police today have a much larger societal remit than they once had—probably one larger than they can capably handle. They are often the first responders to mental-health crises, but they aren't psychologists or social workers. They provide security in schools, and they're often called when a mentally ill person is in distress. We've all seen those videos of police officers treating unarmed, recalcitrant students or disturbed people like criminal suspects instead of children or people who need medical help. That happens not because the individual officers are bad people, but because they've been put into situations for which they aren't trained. Not every public display of disobedience, and not every mentally ill person in distress, require a police response. In fact, most probably do not—and yet police have become our principal social response to public risk.

You may find this analysis—mine or Brandon Anderson's—offputting or disrespectful. You may think that and still think Raheem AI is a good idea. You may find Copwatch's rhetoric offputting, particularly if you are encountering Copwatch for the first time in these pages, and disagree with the derisive words someone affiliated with Copwatch has used to describe police. Some may read "power," as Copwatch DC uses the word, as referring to the power of a community united against the police. But I don't think that's quite a fair reading, and even if it is, remember that not all people and communities have the same view of law enforcement. As I said in the prologue, my interactions with the police have been overwhelmingly positive, and I'm a middle-aged white man raised and living in the suburbs. Some see police officers as protectors, friends, brothers, sons, fathers. Not everyone has that privilege.

Imagine going to a store with your four-year-old daughter and finding yourself held up at gunpoint and threatened with death because she happened to walk out of the store holding a doll. That is what happened to the African American mother in Phoenix in the viral video from June 2019. The four-year-old took a doll from a Dollar Store without her parents' knowledge. A police officer approached their car with his weapon drawn and repeatedly threatened to shoot them; another officer punched and kicked the girl's father even as he was obeying them. (The officer was ultimately fired.) Imagine a policeman holding a gun to your head, or threatening to shoot your pregnant wife or fiancée, because of a four-year-old's innocent mistake. Or imagine police killing the person you loved during a traffic stop, while you were in uniform serving your country. That's what happened to Brandon Anderson.

Studies might debate the extent of racial bias in police shootings, but it is a simple fact that being killed by police is a leading cause of death for young black men, but not young white men. And according to a 2019 study by Frank Edwards, Hedwig Lee, and Michael Esposito—respectively, sociologists at Rutgers and Washington University in St. Louis and a postdoctoral fellow at the University of Michigan—people of color (African Americans, Native Americans, and Latino men) face a higher lifetime risk of being killed by police than do white Americans.[36] Nonwhite people also constitute an overwhelming majority of those arrested on drug-related charges, despite roughly equal usage rates across racial groups. Nearly 80 percent of inmates in federal prisons for drug offenses, and 60 percent in state prisons, are either black or Latino, according to the Drug Policy Alliance.[37] Prosecutors are twice as likely to pursue a mandatory minimum sentence for black people as for white people facing the same charge. These patterns have consequences. And a functional relationship between police and policed requires honestly acknowledging those differing views of the police and the circumstances that caused them.

Perhaps bodycams and cellphone cameras can help in that endeavor, but only if they are used—and their footage judged—properly.

I've spoken with officers in multiple police departments who support bodycams, because in their view and experience they reduce the number of false complaints against officers and encourage citizens to behave better. People pointing their cellphone cameras the other way are betting that the same is true when officers are in front of the camera rather than behind it.

4

MISSION CREEP

"You can tell me who you are. But give me fifteen minutes with your phone and I'll tell you who you really are."

ON THE MORNING OF DECEMBER 2, 2015, SYED RIZWAN FAROOK, A twenty-eight-year-old inspector with the San Bernardino County Department of Public Health, dropped his six-month-old daughter off at his mother's house and went to work. His department had scheduled a full-day training session and holiday party, but he left after just a couple of hours. Around thirty minutes later, he returned with his wife, Tashfeen Malik. Both were heavily armed and wearing combat gear; in the minutes that followed, they fired more than one hundred rounds, killing fourteen people and wounding another twenty-two. Four hours later they joined the dead, both killed in a gun battle with police.

Shortly after the attack began, a post went up on Malik's Facebook page in which she pledged allegiance, on behalf of both herself and Farook, to Abu Bakr al-Baghdadi, then the head of the Islamic State in Iraq and Syria. Authorities wanted to know whether they had any help from abroad in planning the attack, but the couple had destroyed their personal computers; they thought they had done the same to their smartphones.

Police managed to recover Farook's iPhone 5C, but because he was dead, and they didn't know his passcode, they were stuck. (Technically, the phone belonged to his employer, but he had chosen the passcode.) Because of the iPhone's standard encryption system, after ten incorrect passcode guesses the phone's data would be inaccessible. In common parlance, someone might call the data "deleted," but that isn't quite right: after ten wrong guesses, the iPhone destroys its encryption keys, which allow the user access to the phone's data. So the data would still be on the phone, but it would be permanently encrypted, with no way to decrypt and read it.

The FBI asked Apple for help unlocking the phone. To its credit, Apple refused. Alone among the tech giants, Apple appears to actually care about its customers' privacy. So the FBI obtained a court order requiring Apple to help it obtain the data on Farook's phone by creating a custom version of its operating system with markedly weakened security features; the FBI could then load this operating system onto Farook's phone, rendering its data easily accessible.[1]

Apple again refused. Tim Cook, the firm's CEO, released a letter on the same day the order was issued, warning that the court order set a terrible precedent: "If the government can use the All Writs Act to make it easier to unlock your iPhone," he said, "it would have the power to reach into anyone's device to capture their data. The government could extend this breach of privacy and demand that Apple build surveillance software to intercept your messages, access your health records or financial data, track your location, or even access your phone's microphone or camera without your knowledge."[2]

Creating an encryption-bypassing back door (which is what the court-ordered version of its operating system would be) "would hurt only the well-meaning and law-abiding citizens who rely on companies like Apple to protect their data. Criminals and bad actors will still encrypt, using tools that are readily available to them." And while the government argued that these were extraordinary circumstances, and they only wanted to unlock this one phone, Apple suspected, as did many others, that compliance would become precedent: governments would be able to compel Apple to unlock any phone whose contents they wanted to see.

Nine days later, Apple filed a motion to vacate the order, calling it unprecedented and unconstitutional. Previous rulings had treated code as speech protected by the First Amendment. Apple argued that forcing it to create code violated their employees' First Amendment rights against compelled speech. A court hearing was set for March 22, 2016.

The future of legal, popular encryption hung in the balance. The hearing, however, never took place. One day before Apple and the Justice Department were due to duke it out in federal court, the government requested a delay. An "outside party," it said in a court filing, might be able to unlock the iPhone without Apple's help. And that is precisely what happened. The FBI found another way to break into the phone, via a third party, and a week later, the Justice Department dropped its suit.

Had Apple lost, people who wanted to make sure the data on their phones stayed private would probably have had to go out of their way to install custom software—and even that may not have worked. Cellphone operating systems may have had to come with government-accessible back doors. At the very least, the precedent allowing America's federal government to use the All Writs Act, an obscure statute written in 1789, to compel tech firms to grant them access to customer data would have been set. The standard that Apple had set—and, more importantly, the belief behind it, that average users' data should be just as secure on their phones as it would be in a safe at their homes—would have been effectively gutted.

◉

Encryption is the practice of encoding information so that only authorized people will be able to read and understand it; anyone else will find it incomprehensible. Decrypting it requires a key—not a physical key, but a cryptanalytic one, a code of some sort. Those codes can be cracked—during World War II, British cryptanalysts famously defeated the Enigma machine, which the Nazis used to encrypt their communication—but doing so requires time and ingenuity. Digital encryption, of course, is far stronger and more complex than what was used for the Enigma machine.

Encryption used to make people nervous: it was a tool for spies and hackers. A veteran European intelligence analyst I met in early 2018 joked that "encryption was dodgy when I joined. Now the modern economy runs on it."

Today, encryption is reassuring. Without it, you probably would never use your phone to check your bank account, buy things with credit cards, or store other sensitive personal information. Apple uses it as a selling point. WhatsApp, Telegram, Signal, and Facebook Messenger all use end-to-end encryption, meaning that messages can only be read by the sender and the recipient. They cannot be intercepted in transit. Nor can the firms themselves read them, because they do not have the decryption key: by design, only the sender and recipient do. If they did not offer end-to-end encryption, fewer people would use or trust their apps.

As more of our lives has moved onto our encrypted smartphones, the need for law enforcement agencies to see what is on them has also grown. This is not inherently objectionable: if police have probable cause to believe that the contents of someone's phone could help them solve a crime, or stop one from happening, then they should be able to get a warrant to examine those contents, just as they can search someone's home with a warrant.

But as Adam Ghetti, a cybersecurity entrepreneur, pointed out to me, "The law and the constructs that it was built on were written at a time when everything you had was near you and could be touched." That is no longer the case, he said. "The average human in a developed country has more data that they created in a faraway place than in a tactile place at home." Most countries have laws offering people's homes protection from intrusive searches. But laws governing devices are not nearly so clear. Cloud computing—putting private data on servers that do not belong to us, and are often in countries with different data privacy laws than those in which the data's creator resides—makes things even more complex.

This chapter tries to unravel some of that complexity. It examines how police can bypass encryption, and even without doing so, how they can use your phone's metadata—the nonconversational parts of your calls—to track your location. And it asks what safeguards are and should be in place to ensure that people's data is as secure, even if hosted in that faraway place, as it would be if it was locked in their home filing cabinets.

Let's go back to Apple's standoff with the FBI. Constitutional concerns notwithstanding, there were three immense dangers in what the FBI wanted Apple to do. The first is technical. Creating a custom operating system might be challenging the first time, but Apple would only need to solve that challenge once; after that, it would just need to tweak it slightly for any specific phone the government wanted to access. It's like any other technological breakthrough: creating the first iPhone was a years-long challenge; subsequent iPhones have effectively been variations on the first.

The second danger was, for lack of a better word, hygienic. Apple's weakened OS could have leaked, letting anyone break into any iPhone. An operating system that police could load onto a suspected terrorist's phone to see who else helped him plot his act of terrorism could just as easily be loaded onto your phone or mine by someone who wanted to drain our accounts using our banking apps or steal our identities.

The last and most alarming danger was precedential. If a magistrate can compel Apple to write code to get information about this particular crime, why could another court not compel Apple to do the same for other crimes? What would the threshold be—only acts of suspected terrorism? Are lives taken by religiously motivated murderers somehow more worthwhile than those taken by murderers with other motivations? Could a judge order decryption in a civil case, where only money is at stake? Slippery slope arguments are often the last refuge of scoundrels, but in this case the slope is not just slippery; it is frictionless and nearly vertical.

That risk is particularly acute in repressive countries, or those that lack an independent judiciary. One can imagine China, for instance, or Russia, Iran, or any of dozens of other countries, salivating over a way to crack phone encryption, and not just for criminals or terrorists, but for political dissidents, opposition politicians, student activists—anyone, really. They could demand that Apple provide them with the back-door OS, and either manipulate it to their demands or, better still, show their experts how to do it as often as they like. One can equally well imagine Apple refusing, and having its executives hauled before one of those countries' courts on some trumped-up charge of abetting criminality, and after a "trial," Apple being ordered to pay a great deal of money, or having its local employees jailed.

Apple seemed to see a hard refusal as the only way to hold the line against these sorts of disastrous consequences. It has continued to do so. A Saudi Air Force pilot murdered three people and wounded eight in a shooting at Naval Air Station Pensacola in December 2019, and police recovered the shooter's phone. In January 2020, Attorney General William Barr held a press conference where he called on Apple to unlock it. Law enforcement has long held up a parade of horribles—the proverbial terrorist ticking time bomb, human trafficking, organized crime, and so forth—as reasons why they need an encryption back door. Apple held the line, as it did five years earlier.

Had the San Bernardino case reached a conclusion, the position of either Apple or law enforcement might now be bolstered by court precedent. An inspector general's report into FBI testimony regarding Farook's phone notes that the head of the FBI's cryptographic unit "was definitely not happy" that the legal proceeding ended—intimating that some in law enforcement may have wanted a legal precedent as much or more than they wanted to unlock the phone.[3]

In explaining why the Justice Department dropped its suit, Eileen Decker, the US attorney trying the case, issued a statement saying simply that "with the assistance of a third party, we are now able to unlock that iPhone without compromising any information on the phone."[4] The FBI did not reveal who the third party was. But informed rumor pointed to an Israeli firm called Cellebrite.

I visited Cellebrite's offices in Petah Tikva, just east of Tel Aviv, in March 2018. The company's nerve center is a hushed, spotless, air-conditioned room—a library of sorts—but instead of books, cellphones line the shelves and fill the cabinets. If Cellebrite does not have every phone ever released anywhere on earth, they're pretty close. They have to be: to break into a phone, first you have to study it.

And what does someone's phone reveal, once police break into it? Everything. "You can tell me who you are," says Leeor Ben-Peretz, an executive at Cellebrite. "But give me fifteen minutes with your phone and I can tell you who you really are." Ben-Peretz's office windows have a lovely vista of the low-slung skyline of Petah Tikva and the burnished mountains beyond, but I was more interested in the view on a large monitor in front of him.

A young engineer entered his office and connected a smartphone to what looked like a desktop computer with several ports on the front. After a quick login and a few clicks, the computer identified the phone type. The user can then bypass the locked phone's passcode and continue to use one of several extraction methods. "Logical extraction" reveals immediately accessible data: stored text messages, emails, pictures, and instant messages. With more time, Cellebrite's machines can also perform a "physical extraction" revealing more information, including data that may have been deleted. The neatly organized, labeled data can then be viewed, saved, shared, filtered, and searched.

Police officers can also carry with them a tablet-sized Cellebrite device that does a basic phone search—a sort of digital triage that lets them decide quickly whether a fuller investigation and extraction is merited. "Crime scenes in the past were about fingerprints and footsteps," says Ben-Peretz. "Today it's digital: mobile devices, connected cars, and tablets. Our digital footprint: this is the strongest indicator for what really happened."

Cellebrite is cagey about revealing precisely how their technology works, as are the companies that have developed encryption for their devices: to reveal how this sort of technology works, on either side, is to give a sophisticated opponent a road map to defeat it. So what follows is not, and should not be read as, an explanation of how Cellebrite does what it does, but as a discussion—based on my talks with several sources well versed in cybersecurity—of how encryption on a device, generally speaking, works and can be defeated.

Sitting inside most encrypted smartphones is a coprocessor. One of its functions is to ensure that only the user-chosen password can decrypt the phone's content. One of the ways it does this is by increasing the amount of time required to input successive passcode guesses. So the first couple of times you type in a wrong password, for instance, it may require no extra time at all before the next guess; people mistype their codes all the time (they enter an old code, or their finger slips and they enter a wrong number). The coprocessor allows for that sort of error.

But after the third or fourth wrong guess, it may lock your account for an hour or two. After the fifth, it may increase the amount of time required before the next guess by ten, after another wrong attempt by one hundred, and so forth—making it functionally impossible, or at least extremely cost-ineffective, to brute-force guess the passcode (i.e., to try every conceivable combination of letters and numbers). Eventually, a well-encrypted phone will delete its data—or render it functionally inaccessible—by destroying the encryption keys.

According to an analysis from the Electronic Frontier Foundation (EFF), the custom OS that the FBI wanted Apple to write would have lacked the encryption keys' auto-delete function, the increasing-delay function, and the requirement that passcodes be typed into the phone. The FBI wanted to try every mathematically possible passcode quickly in a brute-force attack, and the custom code would have eliminated the system functions that usually make that impossible.

Still, it is unclear whether designing such software quickly would have even been feasible in the time-pressured context of a criminal investigation. As EFF's analysis notes, "This is a little bit like asking General Motors to build a new truck with a fifth wheel by next month. Of course they could theoretically do this with enough effort. They're in the business of building cars. But it would be expensive and time-consuming."[5]

Encryption-cracking devices appear to trick the phone's coprocessor into allowing an unlimited number of guesses, either by figuring out a way to lie to it about the number of times it has guessed (for instance, on the ninth guess the counter resets to zero instead of proceeding to ten), or by just bypassing the counter. On phones without coprocessors, they can simply clone the device's memory, load it onto another device, or upload it into the cloud, and then guess as many times as it takes (needless to say, encryption-crackers generate guesses quickly and in parallel rather than the way people do it: slowly and sequentially).

Once the device gets the passcode right, it uploads the phone's memory, organizing and labeling each type of file—for instance, photos, texts, emails, and so on. It can also upload operating system database files that the user never sees but that can reveal information about every time the user turned his or her phone on or off as well as other sensitive data.

Encryption-crackers do not damage the phones they break into; in fact, they generally leave no traces at all. If you or I were stopped at the border and had our phones briefly taken by police, we might surmise that they plugged it into an encryption-cracker, but we would probably not be able to tell by using the phone that anything had been done to it.

Phones vary in their vulnerability to hacking or cracking. Apple's disk-encryption system means that the iPhone's memory cannot be physically removed and examined; decrypting the data requires an owner-selected passcode. Not even Apple can defeat its own encryption without that code. Apple also controls both the hardware and the software on its phones, which means that patches to discovered flaws can be discovered and pushed through faster than with less vertically integrated phones.

Defeating encryption can be pricey: *Motherboard*, the *Vice* empire's tech-news outlet, reported in 2017 that a one-year Cellebrite subscription cost $250,000, though unlocking a single device would be far less expensive.[6] Grayshift, an American firm, makes an increasingly popular American encryption-cracker called GrayKey, which costs $15,000 for a basic model, or $30,000 for an advanced one. Cellebrite sells to lawyers and law enforcement agencies around the world, but alarmingly, secondhand Cellebrite products show up on eBay for less than $100.

A popular encryption-cracker must be easy to use, but that ease is an artifact of design, not function: what they do is difficult and complex, and it varies slightly with each type of phone. Encryption, like crime, is a game of cat-and-mouse: one side figures out and exploits a vulnerability; the other patches the hole and hardens its defenses; one finds a weakness in the patch or new model; and the cycle repeats.

In June 2018, Apple announced that the port on its phones that can be used either for charging or for downloading its contents to another device would henceforth lock one hour after the owner had last locked or used the phone. It can still be used for charging phones, but users must enter a password before using it for data transfers. This made it impossible for encryption-crackers to upload the phone's memory or coprocessor without first knowing the password (assuming, of course, that their unlocking attempts came more than an hour after the user locked the phone).

But this fix seems to have been short-lived: in early 2019, Cellebrite boasted that it could once again unlock any iPhone. Apple seemed to have figured out the flaw, because by 2020, America's top law enforcement official was once again trying to publicly pressure Apple into giving the FBI access to a phone.

Under what circumstances should police be permitted to use encryption-cracking tools? I'd like to propose two principles to guide this exploration. People on opposite sides of the debate over encryption-cracking behave as if they contradicted each other. They do not.

The police should not have the right to unlock any phone they like, anytime they like, for any reason they like. At the same time, criminals should not be able to use encryption to keep relevant information hidden from law enforcement. One can—one should (I do)—support giving police all the tools, guidance, and support they need to do their jobs quickly and within the confines of the law, while also favoring maximal protections for individual citizens against unwarranted searches by the government. I would no more want governments poking around our phones without probable cause than I would want them rifling through my filing cabinets.

Cellebrite's terms of service provide some comfort. To their credit, the terms say that before the company decrypts a phone, it requires the customer to provide them with "a valid and legally-issued search warrant, assistance order, subpoena, court order, owner consent form, or other authorization (including as authorized by applicable law) . . . that permits Cellebrite to perform such Services lawfully on the Device." Citizens of countries with independent, noncorrupt judiciaries will find those terms considerably more comforting than those in countries where judges do what they are told or paid to do. It is also just a contract between the user and Cellebrite. If the user of one of Cellebrite's products breaks into your phone with it, that contract doesn't protect you or give you any recourse against Cellebrite or the user. If Cellebrite decides not to enforce the contract, there's nothing you can do about it.

It also only applies to devices sent to one of Cellebrite's offices to decrypt. It says nothing (nor could it say anything, of course) about decryption done by law enforcement on a Cellebrite terminal or tablet that an agency purchased. Ultimately, the requirement to provide an official court order only provides as much of a safeguard to civil liberties as a country's judiciary does. In countries with strong rule of law, judicial warrants are safeguards; in others, they are rubber stamps.

In the United States, police usually have to have a warrant to use an encryption-cracker. In *Riley v. California*, decided in 2014, the Supreme Court ruled unanimously that police needed a warrant to search someone's cellphone, even after a lawful arrest.[7] Although they may physically search a person who was arrested—meaning they can pat him down and turn out his pockets—that right was intended to protect officers and preserve evidence; it does not apply to digital data.

This ruling makes intuitive sense. The police cannot pull you over for speeding and search your car; nor can they show up on your doorstep because of a noise complaint and ransack your house. So they should not be permitted to troll through your digital life just because they arrested you.

Chief Justice John Roberts's opinion in *Riley* was perhaps the Court's most thoughtful explication of the Fourth Amendment's reach in the digital age (though that says as much about how little the Court has said as about the substance of the ruling). The government argued that searching a cellphone was "materially indistinguishable" from searching someone's physical person. Roberts's ruling said that that's "like saying a ride on horseback is materially indistinguishable from a flight to the moon. Both are ways of getting from point A to point B, but little else justifies lumping them together. Modern cellphones, as a category, implicate privacy concerns far beyond those implicated by the search of a cigarette pack, a wallet, or a purse."

Smartphones do not just contain a lot of information. The information they contain reveals a tremendous amount in aggregate: emails AND personal photos AND your favorite books and articles AND instant messages AND banking information, and so forth. "The sum of an individual's private life can be reconstructed through a thousand photographs labeled with dates, locations, and descriptions," the Court explained. "The same cannot be said of a photograph or two of loved ones tucked into a wallet. . . . A decade ago police officers searching an arrestee might have occasionally stumbled across a highly personal item such as a diary. . . . But those discoveries were likely to be few and far between. Today, by contrast, it is no exaggeration to say that many of the more than 90% of American adults who own a cellphone keep on their person a digital record of nearly every aspect of their lives—from the mundane to the intimate." Letting police search that digital record is qualitatively different, in privacy implications, from letting them pat someone down after an arrest to look for weapons or secreted contraband.

The Court noted that some files that appear to be on a user's phone are in fact in the cloud. The government tried to distinguish between the two, arguing that officers' right to search a phone incident to arrest would not extend to cloud-based files. The Court swatted away that distinction, noting that for privacy interests, "it makes little difference" where a user's private data is stored.

The Court also rejected a number of attempted false equivalencies. The government argued that searching an arrestee's phone was like searching a car, but phones hold both more and more revealing information. The government suggested limiting a cellphone search to data relevant to the crime at hand, but police would not always be able to discern in advance and in practice where that information might be.

The government suggested that officers should always be able to search an arrestee's call log, just as previous case law let them search call logs at a phone company. But on a cellphone, lists of recently made calls are not just lists of who someone called when; they may also contain "identifying information . . . such as the label 'my house.'" Finally, the government suggested that officers be allowed to search phone data for any information they could have legally found in the predigital era. That analogy fails because phones contain much more information: "The fact that someone could have tucked a paper bank statement in a pocket does not justify a search of every bank statement from the last five years," the Court held.

Of course, this ruling does not mean that a phone can never be searched, or plugged into an encryption-cracker, only that doing so requires a warrant. And, as the Court noted, the exigent-circumstances exception remains in effect: police can search a phone without a warrant if they believe that not doing so would cause imminent harm or the destruction of evidence. The Court acknowledged that the ruling would "have an impact on the ability of law enforcement to combat crime," but concluded that "privacy comes at a cost."

A separate but related question concerns whether to limit warrants permitting cellphone searches, and if so, what those limitations should be. Search warrants for homes or offices, for instance, can be limited to looking for certain things in certain places, but warrants for phone searches often grant police blanket access. According to Jennifer Lynch, the EFF's surveillance litigation director, a few judges have begun to push back on such requests in view of the amount of sensitive information people keep on their phones. But those remain individual quibbles; warrants granted to search a phone entitle police to do just that, in toto.

And *Riley* does not apply at American borders, where law enforcement agents can search anyone entering the country, citizen or not, without a warrant or the need to show probable cause. The Supreme Court has repeatedly held that this exception extends up to one hundred miles inland, hence encompassing territory home to around two-thirds of all Americans. Police cannot search or detain anyone for just anything—they must have "reasonable suspicion" that someone has committed a crime or violated immigration law—but this rule still permits far more intrusive practices than the Fourth Amendment's warrant requirement usually allows.[8]

Riley will almost certainly not be the Supreme Court's last word on searching digital devices. But as first words go, it is an encouraging start.

Still, governments do not have to crack your phone's encryption keys to derive useful information from it, as Daniel Rigmaiden discovered. Rigmaiden is a fascinating person: penetratingly thoughtful and curious, softly and quickly spoken.[9] After graduating from high school he decided to more or less drop out of society. Itinerant in coastal California, he made and sold fake IDs. He then began filing fake tax returns in the names of dead people and pocketing the returns. That drew some unwelcome attention: in 2008, when he was just twenty-seven years old, the FBI arrested him on seventy-four counts, including fraud and identity theft.

Rigmaiden explained to me that during that period, he was "using a lot of methods to hide [his] location and identity." He moved from town to town, used fake names to rent places to live, and went online anonymously. The only link between his real-world identity and online capers was the aircard he used to connect to the Internet. But the card had no GPS tracker in it, and at first he couldn't understand how the police found him (he was arrested leaving his apartment). He had been vigilant about protecting his identity. He had assumed that, without a GPS tracker in the aircard, they would only be able to track him to a broad area, rather than a specific location.

From his prison cell, Rigmaiden deduced that the government must have some sort of technology able to detect a specific cellphone's signal with far greater accuracy than had ever been disclosed. He sketched out what he thought the device might do and sent it to his lawyers, who declined to present a defense centered around this claim. So he represented himself. Poring over thousands of pages of discovery documents that the government turned over to him, he found that his theory was correct: the government had a tool called a Stingray.

Stingray is a brand name, but it is often used metonymically for its entire class of devices—much like Taser. Stingrays are IMSI-catchers. IMSI stands for "international mobile subscriber identity," which is a fifteen-digit number that identifies every unique user of a mobile telecommunications network. An IMSI-catcher, as the name suggests, can determine a user's IMSI, thus facilitating tracking and interception. These devices are also called cell-site simulators, because they mimic a cellphone tower, tricking all the cellphones in a certain area into connecting to it rather than to a legitimate tower. For clarity's sake, in the following discussion, I will use the term "cell-site simulators" rather than IMSI-catcher or Stingray.

Few pieces of police technology are as hidden from public scrutiny as cell-site simulators. Agencies that use them are often required to sign nondisclosure agreements (NDAs). *Wired* reported that federal marshals raided the Sarasota Police Department to prevent it from turning over documents related to cell-site simulator use to the ACLU of Florida.[10] Prosecutors in some jurisdictions have reached settlements to avoid having to disclose details of cell-site simulator use in open court. A paper by Adam Bates, then an analyst with the Cato Institute, mentions an NDA signed by the sheriff's department in Erie County, New York, which allowed the FBI to compel it to drop a prosecution rather than disclose any details of cell-site simulator use.[11]

The ACLU of Delaware obtained an extraordinary NDA and cover letter from the Harris Corporation, which makes Stingrays, to a detective with the Delaware State Police, who signed it in 2010. The letter warns that "only officers with arrest authority are permitted to use them or have knowledge of how they work. . . . [They] should not be discussed or demonstrated in any public setting where the general public may overhear or see, such as an open courtroom or a 7-Eleven parking lot." The NDA forbids police from disseminating information relating to the Stingray and requires them to inform

Harris of any "court order or judicially mandated disclosure." It also purports to give Harris veto power over any disclosure to "governmental agencies"—meaning that a state police chief, say, could only discuss his force's use of Stingrays with his state's legislature or governor if Harris approved.[12] (Unsurprisingly, Harris declined my interview request.)

These devices are small and portable. They can be carried by hand and deployed in cars or even airplanes. And they are widespread. According to the ACLU, as of November 2018, state and/or local police departments in at least twenty-seven states had them, as did at least sixteen federal agencies. (Given the widespread use of NDAs, take the "at least" in that sentence very seriously.)

Because their use is shrouded in such secrecy, much of what we know about how cell-site simulators operate comes from Freedom of Information Act requests, public-document searches, diligent defense attorneys, and academic research.[13]

Before you can understand how these devices work, you need to understand how a phone operates within a network. When a cellphone is turned on, it identifies itself to its network's nearest tower every few seconds. In essence, your phone is saying to the tower, "I'm here; do you have anything for me?" If the network has something—a text, email, call—it sends it on to you. But whether it does or doesn't, the tower notes your location. I'm sure you've used your phone's GPS navigation; the GPS not only tells you how to get where you're going, but also, necessarily, lets your tower know where you are. Your Wi-Fi also constantly reveals your location, as you can see in your phone's settings. These features let your cellphone service provider locate you quite precisely, all the time. As a matter of course, service providers track and retain this location information, in some cases for years.

Cell-site simulators and IMSI-catchers mimic cellphone towers, tricking all the phones within a certain radius into connecting to them rather than to an actual tower. IMSI-catchers, as the Electronic Frontier Foundation explains, operate passively. Instead of transmitting signals, they grab "cellular transmissions out of the air, the same way an FM radio works. They then decode (and sometimes decrypt) those signals to find the IMSI of the mobile device and track it."

Cell-site simulators broadcast signals, and "this causes devices within range to disconnect from their service providers' legitimate cell sites and to instead establish a new connection with the cell-site simulator." As Cooper Quinton, an EFF technologist, explained to me, both processes take advantage of an asymmetry in mobile telecommunications: phones must authenticate themselves to towers, but towers do not have to authenticate themselves to phones. That allows a phony tower to intercept data from a real phone.[14]

Once they're connected, the simulator can see all the data transmitted to and from the phone. That includes the phone's IMSI number, which allows police to more easily track the user in the future. It also includes the phone's metadata, meaning it can see the numbers called and received as well as how long the calls lasted. Some can intercept calls and text messages. The EFF found marketing materials from a maker of cell-site simulators boasting that its devices could be configured to divert calls, divert and edit text messages, and impersonate another phone in calls and messages.

As with encryption-crackers, a user probably would not be able to tell that his or her phone was being tracked. At worst, the user might notice a brief service disruption, but only if the phone connected to the simulator while the user was using it or looking at it. A few simulator-detection apps exist, but nobody seems quite sure how accurate or reliable they are. A team of researchers at the University of Washington have built a broad-range network designed to deduce the presence of IMSI-catchers by detecting anomalies in cell-tower signals, but without actual simulators for verification, their detections cannot be verified.[15]

If these devices only collected information on specific phones belonging to specific people whom police had probable cause—or even reasonable suspicion (a lower standard, which is used, for example, for pat-downs)—to believe had committed a crime, that would be one thing. But cell-site simulators vacuum up data from every phone within range. In a densely populated area, that can amount to thousands of phones. It can include phones in sensitive locations, such as private homes, houses of worship, or doctors' and lawyers' offices.

Few, if any, technologies better illustrate the yawning legal gap between protections for physical and digital information. Imagine police searching for a suspected criminal in a neighborhood by forcing open the doors to every home and office and rifling through everyone's desks, bedside tables, and filing cabinets; thumbing through their photo albums, bank records, and love letters; and looking over their books, magazines, newspapers, and music.

Whether this violated the Fourth Amendment would not even be the question—of course it would. The better question would be whether it violated the common-law prohibition on general warrants, which permit police to search and apprehend someone believed to have committed a crime with virtually no limits. This noxious practice helped inspire the American Revolution.

Perhaps there really is no way to obtain critical information from a justly suspected criminal other than sifting it out from the data of thousands of innocent people. Perhaps, on balance, after careful consideration, most people are comfortable with this practice—and rely on the multiple state laws requiring that police delete all the data they gather from people who are not targets of their investigation. Police say they have no interest in amassing data from innocent people, and on the whole, I believe them. But that doesn't mean that data can't be gathered. And a broad view always has exceptions: just because most police officers don't want to peer into most people's private information does not mean that none will. And in a democracy, whether and how we want agents of the state to use this sort of information-gathering technology is a decision that ought to be made deliberately, collectively, and publicly, not shrouded behind NDAs.

If police only used cell-site simulators to catch dangerous criminals, that would also be one thing. But in October 2019, Univision reported that Immigration and Customs Enforcement had used them to locate and target undocumented immigrants—despite the acting director of ICE telling Senator Ron Wyden (D-OR) in 2017 that ICE did no such thing.[16] The ACLU sued ICE over its Stingray use after the agency took more than two years to "process" the ACLU's Freedom of Information Act requests.[17] And the EFF found documents showing that police departments had used them for less than worthy reasons: to find a husband who had snatched a phone from his wife during an argument, and to find someone who stole $56 worth of sandwiches and chicken wings.[18]

All of which illustrates another danger inherent to surveillance technology: mission creep. Cell-site simulators are expensive; to justify their cost, they must be used. Law enforcement agencies did not shell out hundreds of thousands of dollars for cell-site simulators to catch sandwich snatchers. Presumably, they bought them to stop genuine hazards to public safety. But there are always more minor than major criminals, and pricey tech does not justify its expense sitting on a shelf.

These devices began as tools for military and intelligence investigations. Through federal grants, they have trickled down to state and local police departments, and to far more mundane uses. This happened with weaponry and military equipment: they were moved from battlefield use to more routine use in police departments. Adam Bates from the Cato Foundation noted, "What the War on Drugs has done for police militarization, the War on Terror is now doing for police intelligence gathering, and the privacy of millions of Americans is at risk."[19] Battlefield combatants or terrorists overseas do not have constitutional rights. Americans, even those suspected of committing crimes, do. Cell-site simulators make it easier for police to catch criminals. So would repealing the Fourth Amendment.

This is not to say that they should never be used—only that their use should be subject to judicial scrutiny, just as a police search of a house or office would be. The Justice Department's guidelines on cell-site simulators, adopted in 2015, require their use to be approved by a supervisor, meaning that an individual agent cannot simply decide to deploy one at will. They also require that simulators "be configured as pen registers, and may not be used to collect the contents of any communication" (a pen register records all numbers dialed to and from a particular phone).

On one hand, Americans should be glad to see that the Justice Department forbids using cell-site simulators to eavesdrop on phone calls. On the other, the warning to configure them in a certain way strongly implies that they can be configured in another way—that at least some simulators can, if the user so chooses, intercept the content of voice calls.

More importantly, the guidelines state that federal law enforcement agents "must now obtain a search warrant supported by probable cause"—the same standard required before a search of a home or business—before using a cell-site simulator.[20] The guidelines require agents applying for a warrant to explain to the court that they have a device that will cause a phone to reveal its unique identifier, that the agents will use that identifier to locate the phone, and that all phones in the device's area of operation may experience a temporary service disruption; crucially, they must also tell the court how they will dispose of nontarget data and affirm that they will not make investigative use of any nontarget data. And they require that agents using simulators to target a known phone delete all data incidentally obtained from other phones "as soon as that device is located, and no less than once daily." If they are using a simulator to find a phone, they must delete data pulled from other phones within thirty days.

Still, these are only guidelines, not law. And they apply only to federal agents, not to any of the more numerous state and local departments that use cell-site simulators. Most worrying are the kinds of issues raised in a letter sent by Senators Chuck Grassley (R-IA) and Patrick Leahy (D-VT) to the former US attorney general, Eric Holder, and the former secretary of Homeland Security, Jeh Johnson, in December 2014. The senators were concerned about the FBI's Stingray usage policies—in particular, the broad exceptions to its policy of generally obtaining warrants before deploying them, such as the FBI's belief that it does not need a warrant in "cases in which the technology is used in public places or other locations at which the FBI deems there is no reasonable expectation of privacy."[21]

This lets the simulator's user, rather than a court, decide when an expectation of privacy is reasonable. It also overlooks a crucial distinction: people may have attenuated expectations of privacy for their actions in public, where they can be observed. But their expectation is not zero, particularly for their possessions, such as personal information on a phone. The police cannot stop you on the street to search your purse, briefcase, or wallet at will, just because you carry those things with you in public.

The Fourth Amendment, after all, affords people security in their "persons, houses, papers and effects." Until well into the twentieth century, that was understood only to protect people's homes from physical searches. But in *Katz v. United States*, decided in 1967, the Supreme Court held that attaching an eavesdropping device to a public phone booth violated the Fourth Amendment, which protects, as the Court explained, "people, not places." This case first introduced, but did not define, the concept of "reasonable" expectations of Fourth Amendment protections.

Two rulings in the late 1970s—*United States v. Miller*, decided in 1976, which dealt with bank records, and *Smith v. Maryland*, decided in 1979, concerning telephone records—together created what came to be known as the "third-party doctrine." This doctrine holds that when a person voluntarily discloses information to a third party, such as a bank or a phone company, that person surrenders his or her Fourth Amendment protection. In other words, police do not need a warrant to induce the phone company to provide a list of all the numbers a person called or was called from; nor do they need one to compel a bank to turn over a person's records.

In 2012, Sonia Sotomayor—the Supreme Court's most ardent Fourth Amendment champion—noted that in the digital era, the third-party doctrine was no longer tenable. We surrender a constant stream of information to our telecom providers routinely and involuntarily in the course of our daily lives. "I would not assume," she wrote in a concurrence to *United States v. Jones*, which held that attaching a GPS device to a vehicle constituted a search, "that all information voluntarily disclosed to some member of the public for a limited purpose is, for that reason alone, disentitled to Fourth Amendment protection."[22]

Still, technology moves faster than jurisprudence and policy (witness, for instance, the continued use of the phrase "pen register"—originally a device that used a fountain pen to write Morse code messages in dots and dashes on a strip of paper). In *Carpenter v. United*

States, decided in 2018, the Supreme Court ruled that police needed a warrant to obtain historical cell-site location information (CSLI) from a mobile telecommunications provider. Yet Chief Justice John Roberts, writing for the majority, warned, "Our decision today is a narrow one. We do not express a view on matters not before us [such as] real-time CSLI," which is what a cell-site simulator provides.[23]

Yet some believe the reasoning that supported the Court's decision in *Carpenter*—briefly, that people have a "reasonable expectation of privacy in the whole of their physical movements," and that the Fourth Amendment protects not just physical effects but also people's reasonable expectations of privacy—demands warrants for real-time surveillance. In 2019, the Massachusetts Supreme Judicial Court (the state's highest) held that when police caused a suspect's phone to reveal its location in real time, that constituted a search under the Massachusetts state constitution, and thus required a warrant or exigent circumstances. This issue may well wind up back before the US Supreme Court soon, and it is difficult to see how the justices could rule differently, given the views expressed in *Carpenter*. Yet, if most federal agents are following Justice Department guidelines (Homeland Security has similar ones, enacted at around the same time), that reduces the chances of a federal court case.

Some states, meanwhile, have passed their own laws requiring police to obtain warrants for any location information. The California Electronic Communications Privacy Act (CalECPA) is a paragon of citizen-focused privacy law. It requires a warrant, consent, or proof of exigent circumstances before police can obtain CSLI records from a service provider or access information stored on a person's "electronic device."

That is an encouraging development, as are the Justice Department's guidelines and the baseline that the Supreme Court set in *Carpenter*. To build on them, citizens should insist that similar laws—not just guidelines—govern their local police departments, and they should insist that personal data on a phone or tablet be treated in law identically to their personal papers in a filing cabinet.

5

THE END OF ANONYMITY

"The history of surveillance is the history of
powerful surveillance systems being abused."

ON DECEMBER 17, 2004, PRESIDENT GEORGE W. BUSH SIGNED THE
Intelligence Reform and Terrorism Prevention Act into law. It was a
sweeping set of reforms most notable for creating the director of national intelligence (DNI), a cabinet-level official who oversees America's intelligence community.

The bill also gave $20 million to the Transportation Security
Administration (TSA) "for research and development of advanced
biometric technology applications to aviation security, including mass identification technology." "Biometric" is one of those
words that sounds complex but refers to something quite simple:
unique physical or behavioral characteristics that can be used to
identify someone digitally. They include fingerprints, retinal scans,
voices, gaits, or—what we're interested in for the purposes of this
chapter—faces.

That act also laid the groundwork for a biometric entry and exit
system at airports, arguing that "completing a biometric entry and
exit data system as expeditiously as possible is an essential investment
in efforts to protect the United States by preventing the entry of terrorists." Of course, "as expeditiously as possible," when referring to

government work, should not be mistaken for actual speed. Customs officials began fingerprinting all foreign nationals between the ages of fourteen and seventy-nine upon arrival after the act passed, but not until December 2018 did America get its first biometric airport terminal, in Atlanta.

Since then, as I discussed in the prologue, passengers have been able to check in to their flights and go through the security line by having their pictures taken. The picture-taking replaces the traditional ID and ticket check; the picture is matched to the passenger's passport photo and to the biographical information that the airline and Customs and Border Protection (CBP) have on file.

Passengers can opt out—and, except for the experiment I describe below, I always do. Whether you want to do the same is up to you. But, as I mentioned earlier, opting out can be difficult. Facial-recognition screening is quick; the process is set up for it. Opting out slows everything down. Maybe you can feel, or imagine you can feel, the people behind you in line glaring and growing impatient. But to voluntarily use facial recognition in this way is to normalize it, and to signal to the airlines and government that you approve of it. Most importantly, bear in mind that the more you choose to use facial recognition, the more it will be used in ways and places that you do not choose. Your assent helps this technology spread.

CBP keeps American citizens' pictures for twelve hours—enough time to get them on the plane and into the air. They already have our passport photos and biographical data. They keep foreign nationals' pictures for seventy-five years, but they then fill the same function as Americans' passport pictures—on future visits, foreigners' faces are compared to the images that CBP already has on file.[1]

I flew out of Atlanta's biometric terminal to Quito, Ecuador, in early June 2019. Many people have no direct experience with facial recognition in their daily lives; I wanted to see how it works in practice. I had already checked in using my phone, but I was curious to see how good the facial-recognition cameras would be. In my passport picture, I am bearded and deeply tanned; at the time of my flight, I was clean shaven and, alas, much paler (that's what happens when your beat changes from roaming around Southeast Asia to a desk in Washington, DC).

At the same time, I had, and still have, tremendous misgivings about facial recognition. It worries me that around half of all Americans—the majority noncriminal, of course—have their pictures stored in police-accessible databases (the pictures are mainly passport and driver's license images; state laws vary in whether they allow police to access the latter). It also worries me that the technology has a reputation for bias against women and nonwhite faces. Although, in this case, facial recognition just replaces the existing practice of manually checking a passport picture, I worry about the acclimatizing effects. Airlines want to expand the practice to domestic flights, and I suspect that as people grow accustomed to checking in seamlessly with their faces, the technology will start showing up in more and more places—which means more and more databases will contain our faces. How well guarded are those databases? Who gets to see them?

Facial recognition presents a greater potential for abuse—for subjecting innocent people to permanent suspicionless surveillance and tracking—than any other technology in this book, even automatic license plate readers and cellphone tracking. After all, you can always take the bus or leave your phone at home. You can't shed your face so easily. And regulations governing its use are at best ad hoc, at worst nonexistent, and rarely include penalties for breaking them.

So after I dropped off my bags, I wasn't sure what I wanted to do: have my picture taken and go through the system for the sake of journalistic documentation, or opt out as a stand against an unreliable and potentially dangerous technology. In the end, I did not have to make a choice.

By the time I made it near the front of the line, the system was wonky. Both the punctiliously polite TSA agent and the well-dressed, middle-aged blonde woman in front of me were starting to lose their cool as she stood staring at a camera, repeatedly not having her picture taken. He ended up screening her, me, and who knows how many others behind me the old-fashioned way. He put the ticket's bar code on the scanner, compared my face to the one in my passport, and waved me through. If this were a novel, the whole exchange would have been a little too on the nose. Reality has no such narrative constraints.

Of course, just because one airport line's facial-recognition system failed to function does not mean that facial recognition is a failure. Just the opposite: it is improving constantly. Still, some might argue that my experience should allay people's fears. They might assert that the fevered imaginations of privacy activists have turned facial recognition into a perpetual-surveillance bogeyman, but in practice, facial recognition is clunky and only somewhat effective in a limited number of use cases. Police mainly use it to compare pictures taken under controlled circumstances to other pictures taken under controlled circumstances. So calm down, argue facial-recognition boosters; all it does is enhance and speed up what law enforcement already does.

This idea is complacent and wrong. Facial recognition may not be able to track us everywhere we go right now. But the technology is not quite in its infancy; it's in mid-adolescence, its big-paws-on-a-puppy stage. Amazon's Rekognition, for instance, is a plug-and-play system that uses machine learning to constantly improve. Facial recognition will only get better, cheaper, and—absent strong public outcry—more commonly used, risking the end of our ability to be anonymous in public.

Right now, and only right now, concern about its potential harms can be mobilized to outweigh its ability to actually do harm. This is not the time to laugh off its clunkiness. This is the time to consider carefully what facial recognition can do, what we want it to do, where we want it used, and, most importantly, where we do not want it used, and what we do not want it to do—and to take action and craft policy accordingly.

◉

At its core, the phrase "facial recognition," as ordinary people most often use and understand it, refers to a series of algorithms applied to a digital image designed to detect, recognize, and identify a human face. There are numerous specific, proprietary algorithms—at least one hundred available on the US market—that do each of these things. Parsing and evaluating the difference between them is beyond the scope of this book; instead, I'm going to try to give a very basic, general explanation of how this process tends to work.

Neurologists, programmers, and others who understand the more intricate scientific and technological aspects of facial recognition better than I do may be familiar with the description that follows. They may even find it simplistic. I don't apologize for that: I'm not a scientist, and this book is for the lay reader. But instead of skipping ahead or gnashing their teeth, I hope they keep reading; I hope they find the next section a helpful guide to explaining the technology's dangers to the general public.

The first step in facial recognition is face detection, and the first step toward both is training. Programmers show software numerous images of faces, telling the computer that these things are faces. The software can then deduce that in future images, these round-ish things with two roundish sunken spaces that might reflect light above a protrusion, with other protrusions on either side of the big roundish object, and a line or open space below the central protrusion, probably constitute a face (they are probably eyes, a nose, ears, a mouth).

With algorithms that use deep learning or neural networks, as the best ones now do, precisely how they reach this conclusion—or indeed, any conclusion—remains something of a mystery, even to the algorithms' creators. This is not entirely surprising: how human neural networks (also known as "brains") function at a granular, decision-making level is similarly mysterious. These algorithms are, in a sense, black boxes, and are judged by their output, not the routes they take to get there.

These sorts of opaque algorithms may be brilliant and efficient, but they also contravene the right to confront one's accuser, which is central to the concept and jurisprudence of due process. If that accuser is a complex neural network whose precise functioning cannot be explained—and which, unlike people, who use a complex neural network between their ears, cannot be confronted and questioned—then that right is violated.

Your phone's camera detects faces in real time. When you prepare to take a picture, boxes or circles probably appear around the faces in the image. When that happens, the camera's software is saying, in essence, that there is a high probability that this set of features—"features" here referring not directly to facial features, but to specific patterns: gradations of color relative to other gradations of color in the image, such as pools of white around a dark core (eyes), above a protrusion that catches or shadows light (nose), and so forth—constitute what it understands to be, based on previous experience, a human face.

Algorithms then determine whether the image of a face is occluded, say, or in profile. Such images are usually sufficient for detection as faces—a program can usually detect whether a face in profile, or in poor lighting, or turned downward, away from the camera, is indeed a face. But an image clear enough to be identified based on comparison to a picture in a database, usually taken under cooperative conditions (meaning when the subject is posed and looking directly at the cameras), requires rotating the image so that it is as close to a straight-ahead shot as possible, which most software can do quickly.

Next the algorithm will usually translate a color image of a face into grayscale. By getting rid of colors, the algorithms are left only with gradations of brightness. It will then search for unique points of reference on the image that collectively compose a unique face. Precisely which ones vary by algorithm, but they tend to include distances: between the eyes, from one side of the chin to the other, from the bridge to the tip of the nose, and so on—dozens of distance markers. The algorithm compares these unique features to those found on people's faces in its database and determines how likely it is that a match exists.

The introduction of "convolutional neural networks," as I will discuss later in this chapter, has improved facial recognition's accuracy well beyond the old method, which relied solely on comparing linear measurements between points on faces on file. Still, as far as I know, most facial-recognition systems have not yet reached the gold standard of "one to one in the wild," meaning a system that can reliably identify a person as they walk past a camera at their usual pace, occluded or poorly lit. But they will.

Nor will this recognition capacity stop at faces. In Israel I saw a system being trained to recognize gaits and bodies, so it can identify someone from behind or without a clear view of the face. Chinese systems recognize ages and genders; they are being trained to recognize emotions. And systems that use machine learning and neural networks, as the best do today, improve on their own; they can learn, just as we do.

Yet even the best facial-recognition systems determine probabilities, not certainties, and operators of these systems need to determine what level of probability they are comfortable with. Set the bar too high, and the system will produce a lot of false negatives: it will miss people who are in the database. Set it too low, and it will produce a lot of false positives: it will see likely matches where none exist. Or, in policing terms, set it too high, and the suspect will not be identified; set it too low, and innocent people will be bothered and possibly arrested.

This problem is not exclusive to facial recognition. Television shows like *CSI* paint biometrics and forensic science as practically infallible. These TV detectives talk of finding a fingerprint or other biometric "match," when in the real world such evidence is far less certain: it usually points to probable matches, at best, rather than toward certainty. And sometimes biometrics fail.

Consider, for instance, the aftermath of the Madrid train bombings in 2004. On March 11 of that year, terrorists detonated several bombs on commuter trains that killed around 200 people and injured another 1,400. Eight days later, the FBI identified a fingerprint on a recovered bag of detonators as Brandon Mayfield's. Mayfield was a lawyer in Oregon; investigators found no links between him and the attacks. Nonetheless, Mayfield was put under covert surveillance, and his home and office were searched. He was arrested on May 6 and detained as a material witness for two weeks—despite his lack of connection to the attacks, and, even more alarmingly, despite the Spanish National Police having told the FBI nearly a month earlier that the fingerprint did not in fact belong to Mayfield. Not until the

Spanish police publicly revealed that the fingerprint belonged to an Algerian national was Mayfield released. He ultimately won a public apology and $2 million from the federal government.[2]

Or consider also the well-earned discrediting of other quasi-biometric sources of data, such as bite-mark analysis. Often presented at trials as forensically accurate, in fact bite-mark analysis is wholly unscientific: it's just a person making an observed judgment. Bite marks shift and change when left on skin: they can be distorted by the skin's elasticity, or shift over time as the victim's skin swells, heals, or decays. Yet it has put people in prison, often incorrectly: bad bite-mark evidence has led to multiple exonerations.[3]

But where does facial recognition fall on the biometrics spectrum, which stretches from DNA analysis (fairly reliable, given an adequate sample and the proper interpretation) to bite-mark analysis (wholly subjective and without scientific backing)? How good is facial recognition at, well, recognizing the right faces?

Answering that question is difficult, not least because every algorithm is different. In that sense, asking whether facial recognition is accurate is a bit like asking whether cars are fast. Some are and some aren't. Some have higher top speeds than others. Some run smoothly at high speeds, and some rattle and shake on highways. A Lamborghini can reach higher speeds, and reach moderate speeds faster, than my trusty old Subaru. Some cars are generally faster than others, but almost all of them will get you where you want to go faster than if you walked, just as all facial-recognition algorithms are intended to recognize faces.

In testimony to the House Oversight Committee on March 22, 2017, Kimberly Del Greco, deputy director of the FBI's Criminal Justice Information Services Division, said that the system her agents used at that time "returns the correct candidate a minimum of 85 percent of the time within the top 50 candidates."[4] That's not very good.

It raises a question for trials: if a person is arrested based on a lead generated by a facial-recognition algorithm that ranked him the forty-fifth most likely match of fifty, how should a defense attorney use—and how should a judge and jury weigh—that information? Generally, police say that facial recognition is used to generate leads, not proof. Presumably, police and prosecutors will say that in this case, the lead that came from the forty-fifth person panned out, while the first forty-four did not, and it shouldn't matter where someone ranked as long as the police arrested the right person. But that contradicts testaments to the technology's effectiveness.

In July 2018, the ACLU of Northern California built a facial-recognition database using publicly available mugshots and Rekognition, Amazon's deep-learning facial-recognition software. Used by police departments and large corporations, it is part of Amazon Web Services' push into the surveillance market (Amazon also owns Ring). The ACLU, as mentioned in Chapter 1, ran every current member of Congress through the database, using Amazon's default settings. The database misidentified twenty-eight members of Congress as arrestees, including a disproportionate share (40 percent of wrong matches) of nonwhite representatives, including John Lewis, a hero of the civil rights movement who represented part of Atlanta from 1987 until his death in July 2020, and Luis Gutierrez, who represented parts of Chicago for twenty-six years.

Matt Wood, Amazon's vice president of AI, pushed back on the ACLU's experiment, claiming that it used Rekognition's "default confidence threshold" of 80 percent, not the 99 percent confidence level it recommends for law enforcement use. Moreover, Rekognition, he said, is "constantly improving." Twice he pointed out, in one brief post, that Rekognition has been used to fight human trafficking (though he never says precisely how).[5] But anything can be harmful in one case and helpful in others. Surface-to-air missiles have helped win wars; that doesn't mean that my neighbor needs one. They would be far less productive in solving minor lawn-care disputes.

The ACLU's is just one of many studies and experiments that have found racial and gender bias in facial-recognition algorithms. Sometimes those biases emerge without studies: in 2015, Google's consumer-facing facial-recognition app misidentified two African Americans as "gorillas."

In early 2018, Joy Buolamwini, a doctoral student at the Massachusetts Institute of Technology, and Timnit Gebru, an AI research scientist at Google, published a paper analyzing how well three leading facial-recognition algorithms—IBM's, Microsoft's, and Megvii's, which is more commonly known as Face ++—identified genders across races. They found that the error rates of all three were roughly 2.5 times as high when identifying women than men, and nearly twice as high for darker-skinned than for lighter-skinned faces. All performed at their worst when trying to identify the faces of darker-skinned women.[6]

Precisely why these algorithms perform worse at these tasks is not clear, but it may have something to do with the datasets on which they were trained. If these sets contain more men than women, and more white people than nonwhite people, then the algorithm may perform best with the most familiar characteristics.

This suggests that facial-recognition race and gender bias might be ameliorated by training algorithms using a more diverse set of faces (which only means the algorithms would perform equally badly for all genders and ethnicities). IBM, at least, seems to believe that theory may be true: in early 2019, it released a dataset of one million diverse faces, annotated in ten different ways to give facial-recognition algorithms a stronger starting point.[7] In response to Buolamwini's finding, Microsoft, according to the *New York Times*, said it was "investing in research to 'recognize, understand and remove bias.'"[8] (Microsoft, like Amazon and IBM, has called on the government to regulate facial recognition, although, with Congress as dysfunctional as it is, that more or less amounts to virtue signaling.)

In aggregate, the algorithms appear to be improving. The National Institute of Standards and Technology (NIST), a nonregulatory government standards agency in the Department of Commerce, has performed regular tests on commercially available facial-recognition algorithms. In 2018, it evaluated 127 algorithms from 39 different developers, finding that they were collectively 20 times more accurate than in 2014.[9]

The report attributes the improvement to the use of convolutional neural networks. Facial recognition, it says, "has undergone an industrial revolution, with algorithms increasingly tolerant of poor quality images"—in other words, as facial recognition improves, so does its ability to accurately identify people from imperfect photos.

The days of us having to stand still and stare directly into a camera in order to be recognized may soon seem as outdated as having to remain perfectly still for a daguerreotype.

But aggregate improvements can still mask microlevel differences. Just because facial recognition has grown more accurate does not mean that all algorithms perform equally well on all races and genders. An evaluation that NIST released in December 2019 found that, across 189 commercially available algorithms from 99 firms, systems fared notably worse at identifying African and East Asian people than they did at identifying Europeans. (That was not the case for algorithms developed in China, which displayed low false-positive rates for East Asians—suggesting that training networks on a broad array of faces could help ameliorate the racial false-identification gap.)[10]

Some systems will perform better than others. Still, without adequate benchmarks and policy guardrails, nothing compels police forces to choose a less biased algorithm if, for instance, it is more expensive than one that performs worse.

And even as facial-recognition algorithms grow more accurate across all demographics, they can still be used in a biased way—by being deployed, for instance, as some agencies currently deploy patrol forces: disproportionately in nonwhite neighborhoods. An algorithm that successfully identifies 99.8 percent of all the faces it sees, but is mostly used to identify black and brown people, becomes just another tool to perpetuate racial bias. As with any other technology that is used the wrong way, facial recognition risks calcifying, rather than ameliorating, society's biases. That statement raises a crucial question: What is the right way to use it?

◉

Perhaps the most targeted, limited way that police use facial recognition is to generate investigative leads. The sheriff's department in Washington County, Oregon, was the first law enforcement agency in America to use Rekognition, Amazon's facial-recognition tool. According to both its website and a presentation by Chris Adzima, a senior information analyst with the Washington County Sheriff's

Office, at a police-tech conference in May 2019, they do not use facial recognition to surveil people going about their daily business.

The department wrote a usage policy specifically vowing that their employees would "not employ this technology without a lawful justification that is based upon a criminal nexus," that it would "not employ this technology to conduct mass surveillance," and that facial recognition could "not be used to conduct surveillance of persons or groups based solely on their religious, political or other constitutionally protected activities." The policy also states that "facial recognition search results are potential leads that require follow-up investigation," and that those results alone do not constitute probable cause.[11]

If a criminal suspect is caught on camera while engaged in what appears to be criminal activity, an officer, with approval from a commanding officer, compares that image to a database of county mugshot photos dating back to 2001. The picture that starts the investigation might be through any of a variety of means: through surveillance footage, for instance; or because someone took a picture of an assailant with a cellphone camera; or because a suspect consented to have his picture taken by a police officer, or has been arrested and had a mugshot taken, but refuses to provide identification. Only trained officers are allowed to run the searches.

The usage policy contains penalties for violating it—sort of ("discipline as appropriate"). All requests to run searches are subject to audit, and photographs that do not turn up a match are kept for a year and then deleted from the server. As facial-recognition usage policies go, this is about as good as it gets, but it's really not all that good. The penalties are vague, and however benevolent the aims and limited the uses, the county is still building a database that could be used for broader and less benevolent purposes later on.

At the same conference where I saw Adzima's presentation, I met Daniel Steeves, the chief information officer for the Ottawa Police Service. He is everything you would expect a senior Canadian police officer to be: mild, bearded, reasonable, and wry. His department piloted a program similar to Washington County's: twenty-five officers in a robbery investigation unit received training and were then allowed to run images of people captured by surveillance cameras during what appeared to be criminal activity—Steeves mentioned stealing from liquor stores and gas stations—through a mugshot database.

"Without facial recognition," Steeves explained, "you'd have an officer sending out a broadcast email saying, 'Does anyone recognize this guy?' You'd have two thousand people looking at an image that maybe three people should have seen." He points out the privacy concerns surrounding that common practice and noted that a manual search of their mugshot database, which comprises fifty thousand images, could take weeks. The facial-recognition program returned possible matches in seconds.

"That acceleration of identifying a suspect created a different problem," though, he added. "Now they have to assign an officer to apprehend the suspect or deal with the issue. With such quick identification, they found that they didn't have enough officers on their team to deal with that pace—to go out and apprehend the suspect. We found we're identifying so quickly we don't have enough officers to deal with the dispatch." He also said that facial recognition let them quickly identify a number of serial offenders, getting them off the streets before they committed more crimes.

In a *New York Times* op-ed published on June 9, 2019, James O'Neill, commissioner of the New York Police Department, detailed how his department used facial recognition, and it was in much the same way as the Washington sheriffs and the Ottawa police. They treat possible matches as a lead, "comparable to tips to our Crime Stoppers hotline—no matter how compelling, they must be verified to provide probable cause for an arrest." Similarly, a guide for NYPD patrol officers released the following March said "the facial recognition process does not by itself establish probable cause to arrest or obtain a search warrant, but it may generate investigative leads through a combination of automated biometric comparisons and human analysis." In 2018, said O'Neill, detectives asked officers from the Facial Identification Section to run 7,024 searches, which led to 1,851 possible matches and 998 arrests.[12]

O'Neill claims that facial-recognition software has also "cleared suspects," though he provides no examples, only a bit of hopeful logic: facial recognition will make convicting innocent people less likely because—according to the Innocence Project, which seeks to exonerate the wrongly convicted—71 percent of documented false convictions stem from "mistaken witness identifications."

First of all, facial recognition's current accuracy rate, especially for nonwhite people, suggests that it will not function quite so perfectly. Second, O'Neill's portrayal of the technology is contradictory: on one hand, facial recognition is just a lead that must be pursued, no different from someone calling in a tip; but it is also powerful and accurate enough to rule suspects out. This formulation implicitly demands that police be skeptical of supporting evidence, but accepting of evidence that contradicts their conclusions, which isn't really how human nature works.

When detectives obtain a useful image in the course of an investigation, they provide it to trained officers from that section, who run it through a database of mugshots—"not," Commissioner O'Neill explained in his op-ed, "photos from the Department of Motor Vehicles, Facebook, traffic cameras or the myriad streams of closed-circuit TV video from around the city." The NYPD does not compare suspects' photographs to police sketches, as other departments do. O'Neill believes it would be "an injustice to the people we serve if we policed our 21st-century city without 21st-century technology."

That's a fair point. But the NYPD's rules are just that: self-imposed rules. What are the penalties for deviating from them? He does not say, and the NYPD appears to have no formal usage policy. Nor does O'Neill say what happens to photographs that generate no matches, who gets access to data generated by the system, or how accurate the system is overall: how many false matches it generated, whether any innocent people were questioned or arrested as a result of those matches, and what precisely he means by "match." If a "match" is, say, someone whom the system identifies with 95 percent or greater certainty, that's one thing; if it simply throws out a dozen people who might be the suspect, with a certainty of only 30 or 40 percent, and one of those leads pans out, is that better or faster than the old-fashioned method of investigation? That question is especially hard to answer, because nondigital methods of recognizing faces—i.e., leafing through police department mugshot books—do not have known error rates.

As Clare Garvie, a facial-recognition expert with the Georgetown Law Center on Privacy and Technology, pointed out in her report "Garbage In, Garbage Out: Facial Recognition on Flawed Data," precisely what other evidence officers need to corroborate a match or make an arrest is unclear.[13]

Garvie described a case in which detectives in New York put a suspect in a lineup "solely on the basis of a facial-recognition search." That suspect was then arrested based on witness identification that would not have happened had he not first been put in the lineup. In Washington, DC, an officer with the Metropolitan Police Department showed a witness a "possible match" photo from MPD's database, and then obtained an arrest warrant based on the facial-recognition match, witness confirmation, and a vague social media post about a possible birth date, containing only the day and month, as the only evidence.

Strictly speaking, these arrests were not made solely on the basis of the facial-recognition match. But it was pretty close to that. What makes this doubly worrying is the quality of images used. Some agencies permit facial-recognition searches to be run on artists' sketches, or on faces from partial photographs filled in using 3D modeling software, despite justified doubts about their ability to generate reliable results.

Still, some guidelines are better than none. In early July 2019, the *Washington Post* reported that federal agents were using facial recognition to trawl databases of state driver's license photos.[14] Those databases comprise hundreds of millions of pictures of people who have never been convicted of any crime. As the article noted, "Police have long had access to fingerprints, DNA and other 'biometric data' taken from criminal suspects. But the DMV records contain the photos of a vast majority of a state's residents, most of whom have never been charged with a crime."

Agents of the state searched these databases without the license-holders' knowledge or consent. Agents with ICE, the FBI, and other agencies executed hundreds of thousands of searches over the past several years. These searches did not require warrants, the consent of elected officials, or any other sort of official policy sanction; they were often executed, according to the *Post*, "with nothing more formal than an email from a federal agent to a local contact." Such searches do not just help ICE agents find the undocumented; in states that grant driver's licenses to undocumented immigrants (Maryland, for example, has issued nearly three hundred thousand since 2013), they lead agents right to their door. And a later article clarified that ICE no longer needed a friendly state contact. They have independent access to driver's license databases in some states, including Maryland's—a solidly liberal state that presumably never would have approved of giving ICE access.[15]

Indeed, among the most chilling aspects of this story is that nobody seems to know who granted ICE that access, or when or why—though it seems clear that voters and elected officials had nothing to do with it. The *Washington Post* quoted an ICE spokesperson saying the agency does not "routinely" use the database for civil immigration enforcement, but that should comfort nobody—it is in fact an admission that they have and do use it for precisely that purpose. ICE's conduct elicited that rarest of all things in Washington: bipartisan agreement. Both Jim Jordan (R-OH), a stalwart ally of Donald Trump, and the late Elijah Cummings (D-MD), who, as chairman of the House Oversight Committee, led one of the panels involved in investigating the president during impeachment proceedings, blasted ICE for its conduct.

Some twenty-one states, plus Washington, DC, have agreements allowing federal agencies to access their databases of driver's license photos. Those agreements stipulate that searches must pertain to a criminal investigation, but that is a low bar: it does not say that they can only search for criminal suspects, or with judicial approval, or after obtaining a warrant, only that they have to come up with a minimally plausible connection to a criminal investigation. Entering the country illegally is a criminal offense, which means as long as ICE is trawling for undocumented people, they clear the bar. According to the *Post*, agents searched not just for suspected criminals, but also for "possible witnesses, victims, bodies, innocent bystanders and other people not charged with crimes." No policy allows such activity, but neither does any prevent it.

To really understand how invasive this practice is, think back to when you got your driver's license. Did you assume that by obtaining a license to drive, you were automatically surrendering your face, birth date, address, size, ocular health information, and willingness to be an organ donor to the prying eyes of any federal agent who happened to have a buddy at a state DMV? I certainly didn't. I assume you didn't. It's one thing for a state to retain digital and physical copies of convicted criminals' biometric and personally identifying information. It's quite another to do the same for people who have never been convicted. It represents a monstrous expansion of state authority and control. It is the sort of thing that makes people less willing to trust their governments.

Moreover, at least four states whose databases ICE agents trawled (Utah, Vermont, Washington, and Maryland) offer driver's licenses to undocumented immigrants, reasoning (correctly, in my view) that if undocumented people are going to drive anyway—as many do, because they have to work—then for the safety of everyone else on the road, they might as well take driver's education classes and obtain auto insurance. To then allow ICE agents to access their personal information is careless and indifferent, at best, if not blatantly duplicitous.

But these sorts of searches are not unusual. According to Clare Garvie, of Georgetown Law, at least one-quarter of America's roughly twelve thousand police agencies have access to a facial-recognition system. At least forty-four states allow facial-recognition searches to be run on their driver's license photo databases, and more than thirty let law enforcement directly run or request searches without a warrant.

Add to this the FBI's database, which contains twenty-five million local and federal mugshots, along with all the local databases to which federal agents have access, and the faces of around half of all Americans are searchable in this way. It's part of a vast biometric trove overwhelmingly made up of people who haven't committed any crime, which now can be searched at will by the state's agents without a warrant.

This is not the only way police use facial recognition. In another report, "The Perpetual Line-Up," Garvie and her colleagues identified four of the most common police uses: "stop and identify," when police come across someone who cannot or does not want to identify himself, snap a picture of the person with a tablet or smartphone, and then run it through and possibly add it to a database; "arrest and identify," when a person is arrested and her picture is then entered in a police database, which may be accessible to federal agents who can run their own searches; "investigate and identify," when police have surveillance footage of a suspect committing what appears to be criminal activity, and they run the suspect's face through whatever databases they can access; and "real-time video surveillance," discussed below.[16]

In China, cameras equipped with real-time facial-recognition technology litter much of the country. In December 2017, a BBC reporter, John Sudworth, wanted to test this network's effectiveness.[17] At that time there were 170 million state-owned closed-circuit television (CCTV) cameras active around China, with plans to roll out another 400 million by the end of 2020, amounting to around one camera for every two people.

Sudworth captured his whole experiment on video. First, we see him submitting his picture to police in Guiyang, the capital of Guizhou in southwestern China. Guiyang's facial-recognition network has pictures and data on nearly every one of its roughly 4.3 million residents. A tech executive there boasts on the video that the cameras he sells power a network that can match any face with identifying information, including registered cars, friends, and relatives, and trace the person's movements back one week.

After giving the police his photograph, Sudworth turns up in the city center—he had not told the police precisely where he would start—and just starts wandering. The goal is to see whether the police can find him, and if so, how long it takes. For context: more people live in Guiyang than in any American city except New York. In square miles, Guiyang is around four times the size of Chicago or Madrid. Seven minutes after a car drops him off, cameras catch him entering the bus station, and six policemen—who seem unaware that it's supposed to be an experiment—surround him. Sudworth is friendly and disarming, but the police are unmoved. "Maybe these guys aren't in on the joke," he says on camera. They form a phalanx and walk him out of the station.

The most chilling thing about this experiment is that Chinese police said roughly the same thing American police do. "For ordinary people, we will only extract their data when they need our help," one policewoman told the BBC. Otherwise, she said, in a nifty little contradiction, "we won't gather their data. . . . [I]t only remains in our big database. We only use it when needed." To Chinese state agents, "when needed" means whenever a higher-up tells them it's needed. It could be to catch a thief or sexual assailant. But it could just as easily be to track parishioners walking home from an unauthorized church, or to keep tabs on people who have expressed political views that the authorities dislike.

Cameras equipped with real-time facial recognition exist in the West, too. Garvie found that, as of mid-2019, police forces in Detroit and Chicago have them.[18] In March 2020, OneZero, an online journal about tech and science run by a platform called Medium, reported that Wolfcom, a company that has sold bodycams to at least 1,500 law enforcement agencies around America, was beta-testing real-time facial recognition.[19]

Detroit's usage policy allows facial recognition to be run on "any interface that performs live video, including cameras, drone footage, and body-worn cameras"—which seems, at least to me, to mean any camera the police can get their hands on. Police in Detroit can run facial-recognition searches on their smartphones.[20] Detroit's police chief later said they wouldn't run real-time facial recognition, and they would only use the technology "when officers have reasonable suspicion that a crime has occurred."[21] A subsequent directive limited its use to violent crimes and home invasions, and limited image searches to still photographs. But the capacity exists, and it's just waiting to be turned on.

The array of available cameras in Detroit includes hundreds of city-owned ones at schools, churches, hotels, public housing complexes, reproductive health clinics, and addiction treatment centers. Do we really want the government knowing how often people in its mugshot database go to church, or how often someone with an old conviction takes his kids to school? Do you want the government to track when people visit facilities that provide abortions? Are you really anonymous if you have to pass by a camera equipped with real-time facial recognition on your way to your Alcoholics Anonymous (or Gamblers Anonymous, or Narcotics Anonymous) meetings at your local church?

Detroit's usage policy says the department vows not to "violate [the] First, Fourth and Fourteenth Amendments." But the very existence of facial-recognition-equipped cameras at sensitive locations—such as churches and clinics that provide abortions—risks at least chilling First Amendment–protected activity. And the Fourth Amendment prohibits the government from running general, warrantless searches. Of course, one could argue that Fourth Amendment protections attach to people and their possessions, not to photographs and information that they have already submitted to a government agency (i.e., mugshots or driver's license photos).

But, as noted above, I would wager that people submit their information to state DMVs with the belief that it will be used for limited identification purposes by the specific entity to which it was submitted, not suspecting that it might become part of an immense database searchable at will by multiple agencies from multiple levels of government. Though mugshots are less voluntary, their subjects still have constitutional rights.

How—and even whether—those rights and privacy expectations will be protected, in America and elsewhere, is not yet clear: there is too little jurisprudence. In 2015, three residents of Illinois filed a class-action suit against Facebook, claiming that the company had violated the Illinois Biometric Information Privacy Act by storing biometric identifiers—in this case, their faces—and subjecting them to facial-recognition technology without their express written consent and without a retention schedule. (The Illinois law requires companies that collect biometric information to obtain a subject's express permission, to notify people that their biometric data is being stored and how it is being stored, and to let them know why and for how long. Absent a court order, it cannot be stored indefinitely.) Facebook tried to get the case dismissed, arguing that the three plaintiffs had failed to prove any concrete harm resulting from Facebook's actions; the plaintiffs argued that Facebook's violation of their privacy rights was itself a substantive harm.[22]

The court agreed with the plaintiffs. Facebook appealed to the Supreme Court, which declined to hear the case. Facebook then settled with the plaintiffs for $550 million. Illinois's Biometric Information Privacy Act is among the more stringent such state laws. But Facebook's settlement shows that such laws need not be national to be effective. In much the same way that California's emission standards provide a floor for carmakers across America, perhaps stringent, thoughtful state privacy laws can do the same for tech firms.

Conversely, the High Court of Justice for England and Wales dismissed a case brought by a Welsh civil liberties campaigner who contended that use of real-time facial recognition by the police violated his civil rights. He sued over the collection and real-time processing of images gathered through CCTV cameras, arguing that the practice violated his human rights as well as Britain's data protection laws. The court disagreed, holding that a "clear and sufficient legal framework" governed the technology's use and that the police were using the technology in a fair, legal, and nonarbitrary manner. This ruling suggests that police use of facial recognition in England and Wales faces no substantive challenge, and that people who live in those countries will need to accommodate themselves to being constantly tracked and monitored in public.[23]

The US Supreme Court's ruling in *Carpenter v. United States*, decided in June 2018, gives Americans slightly more protection.[24] Seven years earlier, the FBI had arrested Timothy Carpenter based on evidence it obtained by tracking his cellphone. One of his partners in crime gave the police Carpenter's phone number, and the police obtained a magistrate's order—not a judicial warrant—that let them track Carpenter's location and call history.

The Supreme Court held that the government's warrantless acquisition of a suspect's cellphone records, which revealed his location and movements over a long period of time, violated his Fourth

Amendment rights. A narrow 5–4 majority held that the Fourth Amendment protects not merely a person and that person's possessions, but also that person's expectations of privacy. That is a heartening decision, one that could form the basis of a new understanding of privacy rights and expectations in the digital age.

Though it has not yet been applied to real-time facial recognition, it could. Real-time facial recognition contravenes our expectation that the state will not constantly track (and possibly record and store) our public movements, especially when we have not been suspected of a crime. But the sooner someone forces courts to answer whether *Carpenter* applies to real-time facial recognition, the better: police are not standing still. Officials in both Chicago and Detroit insist that they do not engage in real-time facial-recognition surveillance, but the capacity exists, and public opposition may be the only thing holding police back from using it more widely.

The ACLU of Northern California obtained documents showing that police in Orlando, Florida, had bought—and, at least for a time, used—real-time facial-recognition services from Amazon.[25] Amazon has said it will suspend the accounts of any customers found to be violating its terms of service. That vow is welcome as far as it goes, but it is ultimately hollow. There are no laws regarding how police can use real-time facial recognition, including disclosure. The only reason we know about the systems in Detroit, Chicago, and Orlando is that Clare Garvie and the ACLU attorneys took the time to file Freedom of Information Act requests, and then publicized the results.

To its credit, Amazon has endorsed what it believes to be an appropriate set of guidelines for police use of facial recognition. It should "always be used in accordance with the law, including laws that protect civil rights," wrote Michael Punke, the company's vice president of global public policy, in a blog post.[26] Actual humans should review any results before police decide to interview or detain a suspect, and police should only accept identifications for which the algorithm is at least 99 percent confident. Moreover, police should be transparent in their use of facial recognition, and citizens should know when, where, and how the technology is being used. These are all eminently sensible ideas, but in a free society, citizens' civil liberties should not depend on companies deciding to develop sensible policies, and police departments deciding they would like to follow them. Legislatures, composed of people elected by and accountable to the public, should debate and pass clear regulations, with swift and enforceable penalties for failing to adhere to them.

Axon, the leading provider of bodycams to police, decided in June 2019 against equipping its cameras with facial recognition. Its AI Ethics Board, an external advisory committee composed of academics, activists, and police officers, felt that the technology "should not be deployed until [it] performs with far greater accuracy and performs equally well across races, ethnicities, genders, and other identity groups."

The board also declined to answer the question of "whether face recognition on body-worn cameras can ever be ethically justifiable." Moreover, it said, "no jurisdiction should adopt face recognition technology without going through open, transparent, democratic processes, with adequate opportunity for genuinely representative public analysis, input, and objection." Again, this is a sensible and principled stance; and again, the civil liberties of citizens in a free society deserve better protection.[27]

Congress has begun, at last, to agree—or at least to start preparing to agree. In 2019 and 2020, the House Oversight Committee held multiple hearings on facial recognition, and members of both parties seem inclined to regulate the technology. The devil, as ever, is in the details, and Congress will probably not manage to pass substantive legislation before 2021: the presidential election of 2020, the priorities imposed by the Covid-19 pandemic, and the institution's endemic dysfunction make reaching agreement sadly unlikely. But I would encourage anyone who wants to see sensible federal regulation passed— meaning real restrictions on how long personally identifiable biometric data can be stored, strict limits on who can access facial-recognition databases and why, and real penalties for violating these regulations— to call their congressional representatives early and often.

Some places—such as San Francisco and Somerville, Massachusetts—have decided that the most reasonable approach to facial-recognition technology is not to regulate it, but to prohibit city agencies from using it at all. I wholeheartedly support these bans, though I don't think they're the only way we should combat facial recognition. For one thing, they are unlikely to pass everywhere: most places aren't as liberal as San Francisco and the Boston area, which both have highly educated, tech-savvy populations.

Matt Cagle, a technology and civil liberties attorney with the ACLU of Northern California who helped spearhead the San Francisco ban, argues that facial recognition is dangerous regardless of its accuracy. Inaccurate facial recognition risks ensnaring the innocent. But accurate facial recognition, when used without viable regulation in real time, risks chilling political expression and association. Some people would be less likely to attend a public protest or political rally—or perhaps to attend services at a mosque, or accompany a friend to an abortion clinic—if the police tracked and recorded them. It should unsettle you, in other words, that Rekognition misidentified a disproportionate number of nonwhite lawmakers. But the breadth and accuracy of Clearview, the facial-recognition app I discussed in the prologue, should also unsettle you.

And even if facial recognition starts out tightly regulated, Cagle contends, it is "vulnerable to mission creep." He noted that the Wiretap Act has been amended several times to broaden the range of crimes for which the government can intercept communication. As for those who argue in favor of facial recognition in a limited set of circumstances, like the ones approved by the Washington County Sheriff's Office in Oregon, that still requires building a database, which can easily be used for real-time mass surveillance. "The history of surveillance," Cagle told me, "is the history of powerful surveillance systems being abused, and the stakes are just higher with facial recognition."

Perhaps this view strikes you as alarmist. American police do not generally use real-time facial recognition. The technology is improving. Just because Chinese police can find one person in a city of 4.3 million in less time than it takes to drink a cup of coffee does not mean that European or American police will—we don't do that sort of thing.

But the technology permitting it exists, and abuses often begin as things "we just don't do"—until we do. For instance, there existed a general understanding that federal agents could not just demand identification from people without probable cause or a warrant. But then ICE agents started boarding Greyhound buses and demanding proof of travelers' citizenship (technically, they cannot do this without "reasonable suspicion" that someone has broken immigration laws; in practice, it happens). People learned that Border Protection officers have expanded powers within one hundred miles of a border, where two-thirds of Americans live; and they then learned that their "understanding" was really just an expectation.

Without clear regulation, the use of facial recognition could spread in a similar fashion. Those mugshot databases that police currently use just to identify legitimately suspected criminals today could easily fuel real-time facial recognition as soon as police decide they want it. ICE agents could show up at bus and train stations with facial-recognition-equipped tablets looking for undocumented people—and then other federal agents and eventually local police could just as easily do the same, because why should immigration violations receive higher priority than other crimes?

If this is not the world we want, then we need to organize and speak up now. There is no technological solution to these abuses. Those facial-recognition-defeating sunglasses are cool, but not scalable: they may protect you while you're wearing them, but only when you're wearing them, and only you—not people you love, or your fellow citizens. There is no rewind button to uninvent things. There is only democracy. We can shape the world we want, rather than just acquiescing to ever-increasing levels of surveillance and decreasing levels of privacy.

Kade Crockford, who directs the Technology for Liberty Program at the ACLU of Massachusetts, called the Somerville and San Francisco facial-recognition bans "a wrench [thrown] into the gears of technological determinism." She pushes back against "this story that if it's invented it will be deployed, and you'd better get out of the way," and says, "It's up to us to decide whether we think it's appropriate for governments to use this technology." This seems exactly right to me. Perhaps more people believe that facial recognition will keep us safe than believe it will imperil us. But whatever we decide, the important thing is that *we* decide, and do not passively allow our civil liberties to be whittled away more than they already have been in the name of public safety.

6

EYES IN THE SKY

"Where law enforcement leaders see a wonderful new tool
for controlling crime and increasing public safety, a portion
of the public sees the potential for a massive invasion of privacy."

SOMETIME IN 2009, ONE MAN KILLED ANOTHER IN AN ALLEY IN CIUDAD
Juárez, just across the Rio Grande from El Paso, Texas. It was a personal tragedy for the dead man and his family, but sadly, murder is
not unusual in Juárez. That year, the city was among the most violent
on earth. The Juárez and Sinaloa cartels battled for control of the
city, a crucial drug transshipment hub, and in 2009 the resulting murder rate was around 130 per 100,000 people.[1] By comparison, America's murder rate was 5.5 per 100,000, and its most violent city that
year was Detroit, with a murder rate of 49.2 per 200,000.[2] What set
this killing apart is that Ross McNutt, now the owner and chief technical officer at Persistent Surveillance Systems, discussed in Chapter
1, happened to catch it on video.

   McNutt is an air force veteran and an aeronautical engineer with
a PhD from the Massachusetts Institute of Technology. In 2004, when
he was with the Air Force Center for Rapid Product Development,
and US troops in Iraq were regularly being killed by improvised explosive devices (IEDs), he designed a system to catch the bombers. By
mounting a camera to the underside of a drone, he found he could

"watch an entire city the size of Fallujah. We could watch a bomb go off, follow the people who set it, and then go back in time to see where they came from."[3]

When he retired from the air force in 2007, he designed a new generation of that system and founded Persistent Surveillance. He later told a Baltimore City Council meeting that he regrets that name, because "it gives people the heebie-jeebies, and it doesn't accurately describe what we do." The first part of that clause may be true. But in fact his company is able to put an entire area of a city under persistent surveillance by flying drones with video cameras on them in a loop over an entire neighborhood and beaming images back for analysis. Sometimes these images help cities direct traffic flows. Sometimes they catch murders in progress. The name may have a slightly sinister connotation, but it is not inaccurate.

In the Juárez shooting that he captured on film, the only physical evidence recovered by police was a stray bullet casing. No witnesses came forward. But the images McNutt recorded told a fuller story. By rewinding the video from the time of the shooting, his system tracked four cars converging on the alley: one car carrying the shooter, a getaway car that waited half a block away, and two protection cars sealing off the street leading to the alley. The shooter got out of his car, took down his victim, then ran to the getaway car and sped off.

Almost immediately, people ran out of adjacent buildings to (ineffectually) chase the shooter—indicative, McNutt contended, that they were probably armed and had "some role in protection." McNutt's cameras tracked the getaway car to a house, where someone—perhaps the shooter—got out of the passenger side door and entered. By overlaying his cameras' maps onto Google Earth, his system could provide a clear view of the house as well as a street name and address that could be sent to an officer's smartphone.

In other words, what looked from the ground like an impossible whodunit or random killing looked from the air like a planned, professional hit. The people who chased the shooter probably had at least some idea of who killed their colleague and why. What's more, McNutt's firm could track the getaway car and see when and where the shooter got out, as well as everywhere all four cars went in the hours after—and, just as important, where they were before—the shooting. It also tracked the activity near the victim after the shooting, leading to the deduction that the murder appeared to have disrupted a major drug transaction. During the few months that Juárez could afford Persistent Surveillance's services, McNutt says, his technology led to multiple arrests and convictions.

McNutt's product stems from noble intentions: in his words, to "solve otherwise unsolvable crimes." Sadly, in many American cities, that doesn't mean crimes so carefully planned and brilliantly committed that they baffle the massive resources of the police and the best detectives on staff. It often just means one person shooting another in a vacant lot or deserted alley in the company of people who would never talk to the police.

An investigation from *BuzzFeed* and *The Trace*, a nonprofit news organization that covers gun violence, found that in the summer of 2017, more than 1,100 shootings in Baltimore, going back two years, remained unsolved. The city's understaffed, cash-strapped police department solved fewer than 25 percent of fatal and nonfatal shootings in the city. In 2016, Chicago cleared just 26 percent of its murders and made arrests in just 12 percent of gun assaults. The figures for nonfatal shootings were similarly bleak in Los Angeles (17 percent), San Francisco (15 percent), and Boston (10 percent).[4]

It is easy to see both the promise and the peril of Persistent Surveillance's technology. It gives police a new perspective, literally, on their city. It also gives them a time machine: when they get reports of a crime, they can both follow the perpetrators as they escape and rewind the footage to see where they came from. What police department would turn down that kind of tool? What politician would want to keep the best possible technology from the department they oversee? Everybody wants safer streets with fewer criminals on them.

On the other hand, the potential for abuse of the technology is vast. One can easily imagine an unscrupulous, vindictive politician using it to dig up dirt on his political opponents. Or a jealous police officer using it to keep tabs on ex-girlfriends. Or hackers manipulating the drones, or finding back doors into the server on which the footage is stored, and using it for all sorts of nefarious ends.

McNutt's technology may have performed well in Iraq. But military tactics, technology, and strategy are not always appropriate for policing. The missions are different: soldiers fight on foreign soil, against an enemy without constitutional rights; police protect the lives and rights of their fellow citizens at home. Whatever its benefits, Persistent Surveillance's technology seems to me fundamentally incompatible with the values of an open, liberal society—particularly at a time of low and declining crime rates. It subjects hundreds of thousands of people who are not suspected of committing any crime to, as the name suggests, persistent, archivable surveillance. Even those whom the system catches committing a crime were initially surveilled before they became suspects.

McNutt notes—and, having seen his system in action, I can attest that this is accurate—that his system covers a wide space in low resolution: about one pixel per person. The people captured on video in Juárez looked like dots; they had fewer distinctly human features than characters in old Atari video games. As McNutt explains, "At that level, I can't tell anything about you. The only thing I can tell is movement. The only way I can tell you're not a bush is you tend to run along the sidewalk. The only way I can tell you're not a dog is you jump into a car. I can't tell if you're black, white, green, red. I can't tell if you're a man or woman. Can't tell if you're dressed. And we don't care. All I can do is watch that dot run away from a reported crime." But, of course, if you can follow that dot back to a house that you can identify precisely on Google Earth, then the resolution becomes much less important.

This exemplifies one way in which the new, tech-based surveillance differs from the old in-person kind. A drone may not be able to see your face or read your expressions, just as a cellphone tracker may not be able to overhear your conversations. But both can, in effect, induce you from amassed data. If a drone can see a dot leaving your house, getting into a car in your driveway, and driving to where you work after stopping to drop off two little dots at a school where your children are enrolled, then a reasonable observer would assume that it is you, even if it's not possible to confirm it with fingerprints or a face.

Just fifteen years ago, drones were mostly in the hands of the military. America's armed forces began flying them as far back as World War II, when radio-controlled planes were used for target practice. But as of March 2020, according to the Center for the Study of the Drone at Bard College, at least 1,578 state and local police, fire, and emergency service agencies own drones, with police accounting for 70 percent of those agencies. Public safety agencies in every state own at least two drones (Rhode Island and Vermont own just two each), with the highest concentrations in California, Texas, and Illinois.[5]

More than twice as many government agencies own drones than own manned aircraft (though public safety helicopters are often shared among multiple nearby agencies). That makes sense: drones are cheap. They cost around 1/100th the cost of a high-end helicopter—or, as one officer told me, for half the cost of a standard police car, you can have 80 percent of the capabilities of a manned aircraft that costs $1 million. A drone's fuel costs are one-tenth those of a helicopter, and it costs nothing to store, while a helicopter can cost up to $500 per month.

Drones fit in the back of a police cruiser. Some premarket models can even fit in a pocket. Officers can fly them using a laptop and a remote control; and they send a live, high-definition camera feed to as many officers as an agency deems necessary. The most popular drones for public safety purposes are the DJI Phantom, a light quadcopter with a high-definition camera (no longer in production), and the Inspire series drones, which are also quadcopters, made by the same firm. Both are also popular with filmmakers, because they take great video. (Multi-rotor drones are classified by the number of rotors propelling them: a tricopter has three, a quadcopter has four, and so on.)

Most countries have established legal frameworks for drone flight. In the United States, Part 107 of the Federal Aviation Regulations forbids drones from, among other things, flying at night, or beyond the operator's visual sight line, or in controlled airspace (which generally means near airports), or more than four hundred feet above the ground, or above the nearest structure less than four hundred feet away. These regulations stem from public safety concerns rather than privacy; they are intended to prevent accidents.[6]

But public safety agencies can apply for waivers from these requirements, and many do—for search and rescue or crowd control, for instance, a waiver from the ban against flying over people and at night is all but essential. Public safety drones also have to weigh less than fifty-five pounds, including all attachments; drones this size more closely resemble hobbyists' craft than massive military versions.

Those rules do not assuage everyone's concerns, however. Ross McNutt may scrupulously avoid recording identifiable images, but that is his practice, not the law. Police could easily equip drones with high-definition cameras and automatic license plate readers.

They may not even need a judge's approval to do so. In *Florida v. Riley*, decided in 1989, the Supreme Court held that police don't need a warrant to subject someone's property to aerial surveillance.[7] A policeman had flown over Michael Riley's Florida property in a helicopter and had seen what he believed to be cannabis growing in a greenhouse. Based on that information, police had obtained a search warrant and found the cannabis. Riley argued that the initial aerial search violated his privacy expectations and therefore required a warrant.

A majority of five justices disagreed with Riley, but could not agree among themselves on why. Four focused on the fact that the police helicopter had followed Federal Aviation Administration (FAA) regulations and so could observe only what a member of the public could have observed. The fifth justice, who did not join the opinion but concurred in the result, instead argued that the test was not whether the helicopter was operating within FAA regulations, which concern safety, but rather whether the public regularly operates aircraft at the relevant distance from the ground. If so (and the justice concluded that was the case here), the property owner could not reasonably expect privacy, because the public would often observe him as well. Even the four-justice plurality admitted the potential relevance of this point: "There is nothing in the record or before us to suggest that helicopters flying at 400 feet are sufficiently rare in this country to lend substance to respondent's claim that he reasonably anticipated that his greenhouse would not be subject to observation from that altitude."

In an earlier case, *California v. Ciraolo*, decided in 1986, the Court reached a similar conclusion based on a similar rationale, finding that even erecting a ten-foot fence around one's yard did not establish "a subjective expectation of privacy from all observations of his backyard," and that it was unreasonable for the property owner to claim that a police overflight breached his Fourth Amendment rights when a telephone-line repairman could have seen the same thing.[8]

Still, people have some rights to regulate airspace above their property. In *United States v. Causby*, decided in 1946, Justice William O. Douglas wrote that landowners "must have exclusive control of the immediate reaches of the enveloping atmosphere." That case was brought by a chicken farmer whose birds were literally frightened to death by military aircraft flying at low altitudes. He sued the government for taking his property without compensation, and the court held that they had to pay him.[9] Property owners cannot ban jets from flying thirty-five thousand feet above their backyards, but regular, low-flying aircraft are different, at least if they cause "a direct and immediate interference with the use and enjoyment of the land." It is also unclear how such arguments would apply to drone-based observation, given that members of the public are not generally permitted to fly them above private property but may often do so.

Still, the questions raised by police use of drones are not, for now at least, primarily about legal issues. Police do not need a warrant to follow or film someone in public. If you spend any time at all in major cities, airports, or public transport systems, or even restaurants, gas stations, and convenience stores, you have almost certainly been filmed thousands of times, perfectly legally.

The questions, at root, are questions of expectation: What are citizens of a free country willing to tolerate in the name of public safety? Should we expect to be tracked and filmed whenever we leave our homes? In the investigation that led to *Florida v. Riley*, police flew a helicopter over someone's home; that required time, staffing, and command approval based on a tip the department deemed reasonable.

Drones, conversely, can be flown perpetually at low cost. Just as our privacy laws need updating for a world in which cellphone metadata—which has traditionally not required a warrant to obtain—can tell police more about us than the contents of our cellphone calls, they also need updating for a world in which warrantless aerial surveillance can tell police not just whether we have illicit plants growing on our property, but where we are going at all times.

◎

Police use drones for more than just covert surveillance. As Al Frazier, an aviation professor, retired Glendale (California) police officer, and deputy with the Grand Forks (North Dakota) sheriff's department, explained at the 2019 International Association of Police Chiefs Technology Conference, "The liberal media . . . wanted to paint a picture that we're going to be looking in people's windows, looking for pot plants," but "very few agencies are using [drones] for covert surveillance. Most are using them for overt purposes."[10]

Any reporter who covers police—whether for a "liberal media" outlet or my own center-right newspaper—gets used to hearing comments like this. They don't just come from the right, either: a law professor with whom I speak regularly told me that public awareness about police surveillance spikes after "sensationalist" stories—and concern rises with it. Most journalists do not set out to write sensationalist books and articles, however; certainly I do not.

Nor do I write about the risks of surveillance technology because I want to portray police in a bad light. Police officers do a difficult, dangerous, necessary job. The overwhelming majority of law enforcement officers have a genuine concern for public safety along with a genuine desire to protect people. I write about the risks of surveillance technology because those risks are real. They need to be considered and balanced against whatever benefits the technology offers. I write about those risks because our civil liberties deserve protection—and yes, that means protection from agents of the state, including police officers. It would be easier for police if nobody ever questioned their actions, and they could do as they wished. But most people do not want to live in such a world. Besides, standing up for civil liberties also means standing up for the civil liberties of police officers when they aren't in uniform.

Perhaps chief among those overt purposes that Frazier mentioned is search and rescue. Drones take less time to dispatch than manned aircraft and can stay aloft longer—for well over a day, given the right battery and storage capacity. Their size lets them reach places that helicopters can't go. Drones are more or less weatherproof. They can fly over fires, in severe cold, and into extreme danger (such as locations with unexploded ordnance or high levels of radiation) without risking agency personnel, who can monitor the feed from a safe location. They can survey damage from natural disasters, such as floods and volcanoes, while those disasters are still occurring.

And drones are modular: agencies can outfit them with conventional cameras, devices to monitor radiation or gas leaks, GPS trackers, license plate readers, or anything else, really, that a drone can carry. Equipped with a FLIR camera—an acronym for Forward Looking Infrared—drones are good at finding people lost in the woods. FLIRs are thermographic cameras that can detect infrared radiation, typically from a heat source.

If a hiker gets lost in, say, a remote part of a national park, a drone flying a few hundred feet off the ground may prove more effective at finding him than dozens of searchers at ground level. On a cold night, a person will stand out from her surroundings on a FLIR camera feed, though she will grow gradually less distinct as her clothes grow cooler. (Some people believe that FLIR cameras can see through buildings; they cannot, though they can be used to inspect buildings, because they can see where heat is leaking out of a structure because of, say, detached plaster or other facade coatings.)

Drones can also be used for overt surveillance, such as investigating unfolding crimes. A drone outside an apartment window can keep tabs on a shooter holed up in an apartment, for instance, to better inform a rescue team being sent up a staircase. Drones can also help track a fleeing suspect. They can be sent into toxic environments, such as a house where meth was recently cooked, with less risk to officer safety than a live search.

They can also be used to monitor traffic, map disasters, and re-construct accident and crime scenes. After an accident or crime, agencies can send a drone to fly over the scene and then use the images to create an accurate, navigable, storable map. In general, quadcopters (or hexacopters, octocopters, or other types of hovering drones) work best for mapping, accident reconstruction, and other uses that require a drone to remain in place for longer periods of time, while fixed-wing drones, which can fly for longer distances but cannot hover, are preferable for search-and-rescue operations.

Drones can be used for crowd monitoring, though here we start to get into areas of concern. Few people would object to police fly-ing a drone over a parade or concert to keep an eye on a potentially rowdy situation, and to ensure that police on the ground were de-ployed wisely. But many would rightly object to a drone flying over a public protest.

In practice, however, those two activities look similar. In both cases, a small, possibly undetectable aircraft circles above a large gathering of people. In both cases, the stated concern of the agency deploying the drone would presumably be public safety. Both uses implicate protected activity: the First Amendment, of course, protects the right to free speech, which the protesters are clearly exercising. But it also protects the right to peaceably assemble, which the concert-goers are also exercising. Some might argue that flying drones over both gatherings does not directly imperil people's right to speak or assemble. They are wrong: someone might be less likely to attend, say, a demonstration supporting reproductive rights if her boss opposed legal abortion and she knew there was a risk she would be filmed.

That does not make those uses inherently illegitimate any more than putting actual police on the ground would. But police stationed along a protest or parade route are visible: you can see the people seeing you. You can see what they are doing, whether they are writing down names, how they interact with you. Drones, as with other emer-gent forms of surveillance technology, can be hidden and perpet-ual. They remove the human connection that exists between police officers and the policed. They are the literal eye in the sky, silently watching and recording. Police officers are comprehensible: you can look them in the eye and talk to them. Drones are pitiless and beyond question.

That may be why, as I discussed this book with friends and family members and other people who have just a passing familiarity with these issues, drones came up more than any other single piece of surveillance technology. That is not because drones or the issues they raise are technologically complex; they are, after all, just flying cameras. But they instantiate perfectly the change that makes so many people uneasy—from being surveilled by people to being surveilled by machines. And their military heritage exemplifies another worrying trend: the militarization of policing. As a report from the Justice Department's Community Oriented Policing Service notes, "Where law enforcement leaders see a wonderful new tool for controlling crime and increasing public safety, a portion of the public sees the potential for a massive invasion of privacy."[11]

In 2016, the National Telecommunications and Information Administration (part of the Department of Commerce) released a set of best-practice recommendations on drones and privacy. They are geared toward hobbyists, and they are about as helpful and interesting as you'd expect a set of best practices collected by an obscure part of the government bureaucracy to be. Among the recommendations is this one: "If you think someone has a reasonable expectation of privacy, don't violate that privacy . . . unless you've got a very good reason." In addition to begging the question, this advises the public to violate people's privacy in a way that the government usually cannot without a warrant. And also these: "If you can, tell other people you'll be taking pictures and video of them before you do," and, "If anyone raises privacy, security or safety concerns with you, try and listen."[12]

Many of us would like the government to do more than just politely listen to our privacy concerns. I don't object to the police ever using drones. No one should: They can find people lost in the wild easily. They can provide a bird's-eye view of a volatile public gathering. They can fly up to a fourth-floor window and monitor someone holed up with a gun and some hostages. But they can also monitor all of us, all the time, without our ever knowing we're being filmed.

At least eighteen states require police to obtain a warrant before using drones for surveillance or to conduct a search, though all have exigent circumstances exceptions.[13] But drone jurisprudence has been scattershot. As a report from the drone study center at Bard notes, "There appears to be little consistency in how, and by whom, infractions involving drones are prosecuted." A few state and local courts have convicted people for flying drones over other people's property, but all were acting as private citizens, not law enforcement, at the time. (And who can say how many jurisdictions did not charge or convict people for the same activity?) The FAA has forbidden drones from flying over prisons, though that has not stopped people from trying: smuggling is a lucrative business.[14]

Some argue that drones receive a disproportionate amount of concern. They are, after all, just cameras with wings (or rotors). A report from the Brookings Institution cautions against paying more attention to what drones are than to what they do, noting that "this technology centric approach creates perverse results, allowing the use of extremely sophisticated pervasive surveillance technologies from manned aircraft, while disallowing benign uses of drones for mundane tasks like accident and crime scene documentation, or monitoring of industrial pollution and other environmental harms."[15]

Brookings worries that requiring police to obtain a warrant before flying a drone would limit their use for benign purposes, such as public events, where they might beneficially augment on-the-ground surveillance. Rather than focusing on drones themselves, Brookings sensibly recommends pushing for policies that (1) limit persistent surveillance and data retention; (2) protect privacy rights, by letting private citizens exclude aircraft from the space up to 350 feet above their property; and (3) mandate transparency, by requiring police to regularly publish details of how they have engaged in both manned and unmanned surveillance. This is a sensible approach not just for drones, but for technology and policy more broadly: focus on regulations and impact rather than the technology itself.

The last factor Brookings mentions—transparency—is the most important, and not just for post facto reporting, either. In December 2018, the New York Police Department announced that it had bought fourteen drones. It explained what they would be used for—search and rescue, hazmat operations, crime-scene documentation, hostage situations, monitoring of traffic and pedestrians at large events, and for emergencies with the approval of the police chief. More importantly, the NYPD vowed that drones would not be used for warrantless surveillance, traffic control, routine patrol, or immobilizing suspects; would not be equipped with facial recognition; and would not be weaponized.

Those last vows are welcome, as far as they go. But they should go further. Drones may not have cameras equipped with facial-recognition capabilities, but the NYPD could still run its footage through a facial-recognition database. Monitoring large events leaves the door open for using drones to surveil political protests, and in any case, "large events" are undefined. The NYPD's policy lets the chief approve drone uses for "public safety and emergency situations," but does not define what those are, either. The NYPD keeps most drone footage for thirty days, but lengthens that retention period if it is needed for a "legal process"—which again goes undefined. The best one can say about this policy, and the NYPD's approach to drones, is that it disclosed the drone program's existence and purpose before the craft were launched.

Baltimore's police did not do that before engaging Ross McNutt's Persistent Surveillance for a ninety-day trial program. When the *Washington Post* broke the story, the pilot program quickly ended.[16] But in December 2019, Baltimore's police commissioner, Michael Harrison, announced its revival. A six-month pilot program began on May 1, 2020, first with just a single plane, but with plans to add more over the summer.[17] The ACLU sued (unsuccessfully) to stop the program.[18] Laura and John Arnold, two Texas-based philanthropists who have funded an array of criminal justice reforms, will pay for the program, which reportedly costs $2.2 million per year. Police will not have access to live video feeds; instead, Harrison explained at a news conference, the footage will be used for "evidence packages" for already reported incidents. Baltimore's mayor, Bernard Young, has expressed support for the pilot program, after which an independent team of civilian auditors will assess its efficacy. These safeguards may sound reassuring until you remember that a city's police department is putting entire swathes of a large city, including thousands of people not suspected of any crime, under perpetual surveillance.

McNutt had lobbied the city since his program was shut down, arguing that Persistent Surveillance not only helps fight crime but also improves police accountability. He took pains to explain to me that his firm shared data with public defenders as well as the police. His firm held over fifty community meetings in Baltimore, he said, and it was a hard sell. "Right now," he told me, "we face a huge fear based on lies."

That is not quite true. Some people may indeed be misinformed about what his drones can see and record, and they may repeat that misinformation. But for the most part the public's fear seems based on legitimate concerns: of being watched, tracked, and recorded by a police department that did in fact watch, track, and record swathes of the city without telling anyone. That the resolution is too low to discern individual people, that they're only concerned with the sorts of serious crimes that frighten everyone, that McNutt's drones may be able to solve murders that would otherwise go unsolved—all of these count in his favor. But without public trust, it may not matter.

7

WIDENING THE NET

"The public doesn't look at people with ankle monitors and say, 'There's an innocent person.' They say, 'What did that person do?'"

WHEN JOHN WAS BAILED OUT OF JAIL IN LOUISIANA AND FITTED WITH AN ankle monitor to await trial, he thought it would be easy. "I was thinking all I had to do was not do the wrong thing and be inside for the right amount of time," he told me. A bondsman paid his bail, and he was sent home with an ankle monitor and two hefty debts: $250 per month to repay the bondsman, and $180 per month to the parish (the name for counties in Louisiana) for the monitor.

But then the pain started. The monitor got hot, especially when he was charging it—which he had to do twice per day, each time for around two hours. People who wear monitors can't remove them, of course, so charging them essentially requires that they plug themselves into the wall. The monitor left burn marks on his skin, and he worried that it would interact badly with the bullet wounds in his leg.

John (not his real name) lives in a parish in Louisiana that uses electronic monitoring (EM) as a way to keep tabs on people before trial. EM use is on the rise: a study by the Pew Charitable Trusts found that from 2000 to 2015, the number of people on some form of EM rose from 53,000 to more than 125,000. The number is almost certainly higher now. Pew's figure only includes people accused or convicted of criminal offenses; it does not include the large and growing number of undocumented immigrants awaiting trial under EM.

Around 471,000 people each day are jailed awaiting trial, making up most of the total jail population. (In America's carceral system, "jail" is where defendants await trial, or where people serve short sentences for minor crimes; "prison" is where people serve longer sentences for more serious crimes. This figure is just for jails.)[1] Pretrial detention costs American taxpayers $14 billion per year. According to the Pretrial Justice Institute, an advocacy group, 95 percent of the growth in America's jailed population from 2000 to 2014 came from people who had not been found guilty of any crime.[2]

As in the rest of America's criminal justice system, racial bias helps determine who awaits trial behind bars and who gets released. Some studies have found that African American and Latino defendants face higher bail amounts than whites, are likelier to be detained for similar crimes, and are less likely to be released without bail. Despite laws that are supposed to restrict pretrial detention to people who are either dangerous or a flight risk, the overwhelming majority of pretrial detainees are in jail simply because they cannot afford their bail.

This obvious injustice (the United States and the Philippines are the only two countries that still routinely use cash bail) has prompted states and cities to begin eliminating it. Despite evidence showing that reminders, such as texts and phone calls, get most people to show up for their trials, many judges—especially elected judges—are reluctant to simply release most arrestees on their own recognizance. EM lets the state monitor detainees and costs far less than jail; in fact, most places that use EM charge detainees for their own monitoring.

EM advocates argue that being monitored out of jail is better than being in jail. People with monitors can work, maintain the family relationships critical to reducing their chances of reoffending, and participate more fully in their own defense. But "better than jail" is a low bar to clear. EM often comes with conditions that set detainees up to fail.

EM has tremendous promise—but not so much as a way of subjecting people who are still innocent in the eyes of the law to state control. Rather, its promise comes from its use as an alternative to incarceration after conviction. In this chapter, I'll explain that distinction, and I'll do so by examining the aftermath of two fights that took place years and an ocean apart.

◈

We'll start with the later fight, which took place in Indianapolis in May 2019. Kathleen, a genial, red-haired fifty-two-year-old woman, told me about it on a quiet September morning in downtown Indianapolis. I met her at the offices of Project Lia, a nonprofit that trains formerly incarcerated women to make accessories and home furnishings from discarded materials. Kathleen had made several chic aprons from discarded fabric.

A few months earlier, when she was on probation for an earlier charge, she got into a heated argument with her roommate, who called the police. Kathleen was arrested for intimidation and disorderly conduct and taken to jail. There, she languished for three weeks, because she neither had $500 for her cash bond nor knew anyone who did. Eventually, her public defender contacted the Bail Project—a national nonprofit that, as of September 2019, had bailed nearly seven thousand people out of jail. The organization paid for Kathleen's release.

As a condition of her release, however, she had to go straight from jail to a municipal building to get fitted with an ankle monitor. She was charged a $50 "activation fee" and then $13 per day, which is one dollar less than the highest rate charged by Marion County, where she was jailed, for EM. That works out to nearly $400 per month; include the activation fee, and it's just $50 less than the bail she could not pay.

Tyler Bouma, Marion County's head of corrections, told me in an email that "there are several mechanisms in place to lower these fees, the court can set a lower fee, the court can find the client [which is a deeply weird and euphemistic way to characterize someone whom his county has imprisoned] indigent, our case managers can work with the client using a financial application to determine a need for a lower fee, or even indulgence." Kathleen found the application burdensome and confusing; Bail Project staff told me that was not unusual.

Kathleen said that detainees must pay the activation fee within forty-eight hours of the monitor being turned on or they get "violated"—meaning sent back to jail to await trial. She balked at the cost; her attorney said she would be arrested and in violation if she didn't come up with the money. But, as Kathleen noted, "just because you say I have to pay $50 doesn't mean I have $50."

The monitors have a GPS locator; some also have an alcohol-monitoring sensor. Like most monitors, hers used geotagging to make sure she was where she was supposed to be—namely, at her apartment, unless she got permission to be somewhere else. (Authorities can set the device's parameters as needed. They can restrict users to or from a certain area.) If Kathleen crossed the street to talk to a neighbor, an alarm would sound. "They'd call and ask what's happening," she told me, "and if you don't have a good answer, they'll violate you."

That seems reasonable enough, if annoying to the wearer: ankle monitors are supposed to keep track of the wearer's location. But a lawyer I contacted told me about a client on EM who found that an escape alarm sounded whenever he went to the laundry room in his apartment complex. Some who live in trailers found that the metal walls blocked the transmitter's signal, which also triggered an escape alarm.

A detainee who gets permission to leave home for two hours for a job interview must hope their interviewer keeps to schedule and the bus for the return home doesn't get caught in traffic. Then there are errands to run, child care to manage, and various minor emergencies—imagine having to completely plan outings in advance, asking permission days ahead of time for the most basic deviation from your usual habits. Triggering an alert requires wearers to plead their cases to the police, whose disbelief can send them back to jail.

Alarms also sound when the monitor runs out of batteries. Tyler Bouma said Marion County's monitors "hold a charge for greater than twelve hours if properly charged twice daily for one hour each time." But things happen. Perhaps the monitors don't always work as advertised. Perhaps, every so often, someone forgets to charge it:

many people on EM have unstable housing arrangements, which can make regular, predictable charging difficult.

Kathleen said her monitor sounded an alarm on her way back from a job interview. She had ten minutes of battery life left, but was still forty-five minutes from home. She had to get off her bus and go into the various businesses she passed, asking if she could plug herself into the wall for an hour.

John said the monitor cost him two jobs: one because his curfew wouldn't work with the hours he was offered, another because the alarm on his malfunctioning monitor sounded every two hours, which his manager found "unprofessional." That had costs beyond just a loss of income. "When you get fired, it's different from you quitting," John told me. "I can't go back to these jobs. My reputation is bad because of the monitor. . . . I was going through people to get those jobs. Because of my jacket, I can't get put on certain jobs. People I knew were speaking up for me. When the monitor backfired on me it made them look bad."

John was on EM for around four months, Kathleen for a month before her attorney convinced a judge to remove it, because she couldn't pay and the conditions impeded her from finding a job. I don't know whether John's lawyer made similar petitions; they were in different jurisdictions, charged with different crimes, and facing different judgments. But it still seems worth pointing out that John is African American, whereas Kathleen is white.

Collateral consequences linger for both of them. For John, it's his reputation. For Kathleen, even though her charges were dismissed after her ex-roommate failed to show up to court, she still owes Marion County hundreds of dollars for her monitoring.

The fees are onerous, but they represent just part of the problem with EM. James Kilgore, who spent six and a half years in prison before becoming a researcher and activist in Illinois, gently chided me when I called him to discuss EM's costs. "I'm concerned that a lot of journalists are flocking to stories where people are being charged outrageous fees," he said. "What readers take away from that is if we just got rid of the fees it would be okay. The real problem is it's a denial of people's freedom; it's a surveillance device; and it's doing a lot of things that mess up their lives in addition to the fees." Kilgore referred to EM as "e-carceration," and he's leading a campaign to restrict—or at least think more carefully about—its use.[3]

Through onerous conditions, EM can wipe out two major advantages of awaiting trial at home rather than jail. First, one of the reasons why jailed defendants have higher conviction rates than those accused of similar crimes who await trial at home is that the latter can actively participate in their own defense. They can meet with their lawyers more easily, find helpful witnesses, and so on. Restrictive EM conditions, such as having to request permission days in advance for a meeting with a lawyer or a potentially helpful witness, make that difficult.

Another reason why defendants jailed before trial have significantly higher conviction rates is that they plead guilty—particularly when accused of less serious crimes—just to move on with their lives. To someone who has never been caught up in the criminal justice system, this may seem incomprehensible: if you didn't do anything, then fight the charges, and the truth will (literally) set you free.

But imagine if you were jailed awaiting trial on a drug possession charge. You don't have money for bail; neither does anyone else you know. The drugs weren't yours—they were your friend's, but found in your car.

At your first and only pretrial meeting with your dedicated but overworked public defender, she presents you with a choice: Plead guilty, and the prosecution will agree to time served, with one year on probation. Or go to trial in ten months, in which case the state will seek a maximum sentence of fifteen years. You probably won't be sentenced to the maximum, but you could easily get five years, maybe eight. In other words, plead guilty, go home, and accept being convicted for a crime you didn't commit, or spend another ten months in jail and face an uncertain outcome at trial. This sort of thing isn't limited to drug crimes, or to cases in which the defendant is innocent. The "trial penalty," as it's known—the tendency to receive a stiffer sentence if you insist on taking your case to trial—can induce a lot of people to go along with the plea bargaining on offer.

EM is less coercive than prison. But it's still pretty coercive. If you are a poor defendant who owes (or whose family owes, on your account) $1,000 to a bail bondsman, and you face six months of daily $13 charges, adding up to well over $2,000, you may take a guilty plea to save the expense—and the stigma. People on pretrial EM have not been convicted of anything, remember—they are innocent in the law's eyes. And yet, says David Gaspar, the Bail Project's operations manager, "the public doesn't look at people with ankle monitors and say, 'There's an innocent person.' They say, 'What did that person do?'"

Instead of viewing EM as an alternative to jail, it may make more sense to view it as jail in an alternative location. Whether in jail or on EM, people who have not been convicted of any crime are subjected to perpetual surveillance and carceral control. They can have privileges revoked—be sent to solitary if they're in jail, or sent to jail if on EM—on a guard's or officer's say-so, with little chance for appeal.

James Kilgore has created a list of ten principles to make EM use more humane. Collectively, they call for fewer restrictions on movement, using GPS-tagging as a last resort rather than a default option, not charging wearers for their own surveillance, not implanting recording devices in monitors, and not using EM to widen the state's surveillance net. His recommendations are eminently sensible, though they are an indictment of the American criminal justice system. The system and the general public view EM—that is, subjecting people who are supposed to be presumed innocent to perpetual surveillance, in a way that holds their freedom in the balance, and charging them for the privilege—as a humane and progressive advance.

Clearly, EM is not the progressive advance that people so often deem it to be. But that doesn't mean it should be cast aside entirely—and here we come to our second fight. This one took place a couple of years back, just outside Stockholm, in Sweden. Carl went to a pub near his home with his two daughters, who were both in their early twenties.

Here's how he explained to me what happened: "We went to a local pub [near] where I lived with my two daughters, and they started arguing with some other girls and boys. I was thinking I must separate these guys now. Then I was dragged down to the ground and it all happened so quick. My side of the story is that I defended my two girls, and the other girls reported me for assaulting them. That's the crime I'm doing time for now. I feel misjudged in this. But this is how our government sees it."

Carl was sentenced to six months' imprisonment for assault. But under Swedish law, anyone sentenced to prison for six months or less can apply to serve their time at home, using EM. Applicants must have a job, stable housing, and no drug or alcohol problems. Carl's application was successful. At the time, he was forty-five years old, owned a painting firm that employed twenty-three people, and lived with his wife and daughters just outside Stockholm. He had never been convicted of another offense. All of these factors presumably counted in his favor. "It would have been a disaster if they had put me in jail—financially, economically—and I don't know how my marriage would have been," said Carl.

When I talked with him, he had just finished about a month and a half on EM. "This works pretty good for me," he said. "I can go to work. I have a schedule from our government that says between 6 a.m. and 5 p.m., that's my work hours. So I must go about 5:45 every morning. If I go to my office, I have a travel time of forty-five minutes. If I go somewhere else—to a meeting, or to visit my painter who isn't at work—I will send an SMS [to let police know] where I go. And every time I change places or directions, I just send a text or SMS. They know where I am, and they have a car that scans, so they can scan if I really am at that address where I'm texting them. It's free. The only thing is I must remember to text them."

Carl says the monitor isn't too burdensome. On Sundays during the first month, he had two free hours. In the second it went up to three, then four after that. I spoke with Carl when I visited Stockholm in early March 2018. "Sweden, in the winter," he said, "is cold, it's dark, we don't do that much in the evenings. It would have been harder if I had this device in the summer." In addition, "in winter you wear long pants. You can't see this device. People don't notice. . . . People don't know unless I tell them."

Alcohol is forbidden to people sentenced to EM in Sweden, so at random times, probation officers come to Carl's house to make him blow into a Breathalyzer. "They can come whenever they want— 3 a.m., 10 in the evening, 6 a.m.," said Carl. They can also take blood and urine samples to test for drugs. A positive test for any banned substance sends the offender to serve the rest of his time in prison. Most of the 10 percent of people who failed to complete their sentences on EM and were returned to prison failed because of alcohol use.

The advantages of EM to people like Carl are clear. They can work and serve their sentence at home; conviction need not mean joblessness and strained or sundered family relationships. But there are broader societal advantages, too. People who work pay taxes, contributing to the state's general economic welfare, which imprisoned people cannot do. According to Helena Lundberg, a criminologist with Sweden's justice ministry, imprisoning someone costs Sweden just over $300 per person per day, as opposed to just $45 with EM.

In addition to using EM as a replacement for imprisonment, the Swedish system lets long-term prisoners (which in Sweden, believe it or not, means anyone who has spent more than six years behind bars) use EM to serve the last six months of their sentences. This program helps them reacclimate to living at home. Violent criminals are ineligible for replacement EM, but no such restriction exists for "back-end" EM.

Like replacement EM, back-end EM requires prisoners to apply and get approved. One probation officer explained, "The system knows them. We have documentation—they've been home on leave, they have good behavior. Of course, they can be murderers and rapists. But they're easier to work with [than, say, a tough young knucklehead arrested for the first time]. They understand schedules. They wake up and go to work. They have a goal: I want to go home with my family and go to work."

A different use of EM also helps keep Swedish prison costs down: it replaces some guards at low-security prisons. Prisoners are geotagged; if a prisoner crosses the prison's boundary, an alarm sounds.

I'm not sure exactly how much time I spent open-mouthed while talking to Swedish probation officers, ministers, and criminologists, but it was a nontrivial amount. Both probation officers I spent time with were trained social workers. The prosecutors were sober and deliberative. Prisoners and people on EM get job training, life-skills classes, and more—Swedish prisoners can study psychology, law, and economics. They get cognitive behavioral therapy. The system was different from anything I had previously studied—focused, to its everlasting credit, almost entirely on rehabilitation rather than retribution.

Even before Sweden introduced EM in 1994, its criminal justice system was biased toward letting people serve noncustodial sentences whenever possible. Jan Bungerfeldt, a legal adviser for the Swedish National Board for Institutional Care, explained in a 2013 article that the whole concept stems from a belief that "prison is at best unproductive and in some cases counter-productive in terms of reducing re-offending, and then creates a problem of resocialization back into the community." Just 17 percent of Swedes sentenced to EM reoffend within a year of completing their sentence, compared to over half of those who do six months or less in prison.[4]

Yet the most interesting study related to EM comes not from Sweden, but from Argentina. This study tried to determine whether EM or imprisonment was better at cutting recidivism rates. This is where you will probably scratch your head (as I did) and say, "EM, of course"—assuming there must be a sheaf of studies from multiple states showing just that.[5]

But there's a problem: since EM usually goes to nonviolent prisoners serving brief sentences—in Sweden, much of the rest of Europe, and the United States—these studies don't really compare like with like. Perhaps prisoners eligible for EM were already on the glide path toward nonrecidivism, and would have done fine even if they'd been sent to prison, criminogenic as it is, to serve their brief sentences.

The study from Argentina addressed that problem by examining a group of offenders, violent and nonviolent alike, who received EM more or less at random. (They were assigned randomly to judges with strong ideological differences; some almost never used EM, while others used it freely.) The study found "a large, negative causal effect on criminal recidivism of treating individuals with electronic monitoring relative to prison." In other words, those on EM were less likely to return to prison after they had completed their sentences than those who had served their time behind bars. To be precise, the ones on EM—regardless of the crime committed, their education levels, or their ages or employment status—had a recidivism rate 11 to 16 percent lower than those who were sent to prison. Moreover, in Argentina those on EM received none of the counseling or intense supervision that the Swedes on EM receive. All of this suggests that the best way to keep people from repeatedly committing crimes and returning to prison is never to send them to prison in the first place.

Given how different Sweden's system is from America's, in particular—but really, from much of the non-Scandinavian world—it is tempting to dismiss its use of EM as commendable, but not replicable. And as long as a justice system remains focused on punishment rather than rehabilitation, that dismissal would not be entirely wrong.

But there are still lessons that other systems can take from Sweden. First, as someone with the Swedish probation service told me, "if you want to change someone, just putting a monitor on won't do it. It's how you work with them. [Someone on EM] is given trust, responsibility, and confidence that he can come through it." They also get training and coursework—not just to help them cope better with the outside world, but to remind them that they have minds worth using. In other words, Sweden does not warehouse prisoners; they do not lock them up and throw away the key. Eventually, almost everyone in jail—even in the United States—will get out, and become someone's neighbor. The Swedish system trains prisoners to be the best possible neighbor.

Ankle monitors differ from other forms of tech discussed in this book. The monitors gather information, but as far as I know they do not store it indefinitely. Ankle monitors with recording devices that can be turned on at the state's will should make everyone nervous, but they do not threaten the general populace in quite the same way as facial recognition or automatic license plate readers.

EM still represents a way in which technology expands the carceral state—and therefore, another opportunity for us to think about what we want from our criminal justice system. Putting people on EM costs the state less than sending them to jail, and, superficially at least, it seems to comport with the widely accepted societal goal of incarcerating fewer people.

Jailing people before their trials as a matter of course is unjust, but it's also bad policy. Many believe that it's the only way to get people to show up for trial. But there is evidence to the contrary. The Bronx Freedom Fund paid bail for around two thousand low-income New Yorkers charged with misdemeanors who could not afford bail between 2007 and 2017. During that time, 96 percent of the people they bailed out showed up for all their court dates, and in 55 percent of the cases the charges were dismissed. Robin Steinberg and David Feige, the Freedom Fund's founders, said the best way to get people to show up for court is also the best way to get anyone else to show up for a necessary appointment: frequent reminders—phone calls and text messages.[6] A study by the University of Chicago Crime Lab reached a similar conclusion—text messages dramatically reduce failures to appear.[7]

But surveilling people who have been accused of a crime all the time, with the risk of jail hanging over their heads for slight rule infractions, is not much better than jail. Some people, of course, are hardened criminals, and ought to be locked up to keep the public safe. But most people aren't. People who run bail funds will tell you that the most effective way to get someone to show up for trial is simply to remind them—call them, text them, bang on their door in the morning. EM may cost less than prison, but texts and phone calls cost even less, and do not subject innocent people to constant surveillance.

8

THE BLACK BOX OF JUSTICE

"In a racially stratified world, any method of prediction will project the inequalities of the past into the future."

SCENE ONE: A MUNICIPAL COURTROOM IN TRENTON, NEW JERSEY, ON A dreary morning in November 2017. A rake-thin, bearded man, shackled and wearing an orange jumpsuit, sits quietly, in that almost hibernational, jail-patient way, as his lawyer reels off numbers to the judge. "He was listed as a three, Your Honor. He's a two on the raw score. On danger to the community, he scores a five."

This was a pretrial hearing in the infancy of a bold experiment: Eleven months earlier, on January 1, New Jersey became the first state to almost completely eliminate cash bail. Instead of relying on hunches, judicial discretion, or a fixed schedule matching bail amounts to indicted crimes, judges now use an algorithm to determine bail. It uses nine factors to assess the risk of suspects absconding or harming another person if they're released before trial.

Most people in New Jersey's jails were there not because they were dangerous, but because they were poor. An analysis of New Jersey's jail population, done by the Drug Policy Alliance in 2013, found that 1,547 people, around 12 percent of the total jail population, were being held because they could not afford bail of $2,500 or less. Around 800 of them were there because they could not come up with $500.[1]

Rich people don't have that problem: Harvey Weinstein paid his $1 million bail with a check. To New Jersey legislators, algorithms based on suspects' personal history seemed like a better way to determine who posed enough of a flight or public safety risk to be locked up before trial and who didn't.

◉

SCENE TWO: A conference room, eight stories above downtown Los Angeles, February 2018. An intense, eagle-featured man with a perfectly shaved head stares intently at a laptop in front of him on the table. It's Sean Malinowski, then chief of detectives for the Los Angeles Police Department. A large screen at the front of the room mirrors the laptop's display, showing a map of the LAPD's Foothill Division, the easternmost of the seven areas that make up the Valley Bureau, just north of North Hollywood and Glendale. Before becoming chief of detectives downtown, Malinowski served two command positions in the district; he knows the area well.

Colored dots representing different types of reported crimes freckle the map. Red squares sit adjacent to some of the dots, each representing a 150-by-150-meter area. These are the areas that PredPol, the crime-prediction software used by the LAPD and numerous other law enforcement agencies around the world, has flagged as being at greater risk of crime.

Areas forecast to be higher crime risks get assigned extra "dosage"—meaning patrol officers are told to spend more time there, walking or in their cars. Malinowski says that if he were still in charge of policing in the Foothill Division, he would ask his officers to drive through those areas whenever they could, "so we're there randomly—it throws the criminals off." Command can track how much time officers spend in their assigned quadrants because their cars have GPS trackers on them. People like to compare these sorts of algorithms to *Minority Report*, a 2002 Steven Spielberg film in which police arrest people for crimes that they are forecast to commit. But PredPol is not Samantha Morton in a bathtub sending police out to arrest specific people who are going to commit specific crimes. PredPol focuses on geography, not individuals, and the idea is not to nab people red-handed, but to deter crime through increased police presence.

Predictive-policing programs use algorithms to forecast where future crimes are likely to occur. New Jersey's nine-factor risk-scoring program uses algorithms to predict which defendants will abscond or hurt people. There is nothing inherently wrong with using algorithms, which are, after all, just sets of steps designed to answer a question or perform a task (a recipe, for instance, is a sort of algorithm). Nor is there anything wrong with police being proactive rather than just reactive. People make decisions based on hunches all the time; algorithms, in a sense, are just hunches in evening dress.

Backers of using algorithms in law enforcement say their programs can remove, or at least help reduce, confirmation, ethnic, and racial biases, as well as simple human error, and deliver more consistent, bias-free results. That is a worthy goal. Bias infects America's criminal justice system. African Americans are nearly four times as likely as white people to be arrested on marijuana-related offenses, for instance, even though whites and African Americans use marijuana at relatively equal rates.[2] African American drivers are likelier than whites to be stopped and searched by police.[3]

A study conducted in Miami and Philadelphia by economists David Arnold and Will Dobbie and law professor Crystal Yang found evidence of bias against black defendants from both black and white judges: black defendants were routinely assigned higher bail and were likelier to be detained pending their trials.[4] The drive to eliminate such biases is not just commendable; it is essential if the system is to credibly deliver justice. But simply swapping mechanized judgment for human judgment is not enough.

The story of predictive policing begins in the 1990s with a process developed by the New York Police Department. Today New York is one of the safest big cities in America. In 2018, 289 people were murdered in the five boroughs. The city's murder rate—3.31 per 100,000 people—was the lowest measured in fifty years.[5]

In 1990, it was a different city: 2,245 people were murdered, a rate of around 31 per 100,000 (the city's population increased markedly in the intervening twenty-eight years).[6] Here's what the *New York Times* said about its hometown at the end of 1990: "The streets already resemble a New Calcutta, bristling with beggars. . . . Crime, the fear of it as much as the fact, adds overtones of a New Beirut. . . . And now the tide of wealth and taxes that helped the city make these streets bearable has ebbed. . . . Safe streets are fundamental; going out on them is the simplest expression of the social contract; a city that cannot maintain its side of that contract will choke."[7] To stop the choking, the city knew it had to get crime under control, but the police didn't have the right information.[8]

In 1993, New York elected its first Republican mayor in almost thirty years—an ambitious former federal prosecutor named Rudy Giuliani. It may seem hard to believe now, but back then Rudy seemed to have at least a modicum of political nous. He ran a law-and-order campaign, and soon after taking office appointed Bill Bratton, formerly Boston's police commissioner, then head of New York City's Transit Police, to head the NYPD.

Bratton soon ran into a problem: he found that his new department had no focus on preventing crime. At the time, that was not unusual. Police did not have crystal balls. They saw their job as responding to crimes, and to do that, the crimes had to have happened already. They were judged by how quickly they responded, how many arrests they made, and how many crimes they solved.

Police did not have access to real-time crime data. And, as Lou Anemone, then the NYPD's highest-ranking uniformed officer, explained in a 2013 report, "The dispatchers at headquarters, who were the lowest-ranking people in the department, controlled field operations, so we were just running around answering 911 calls. There was no free time for officers to focus on crime prevention."

So the department began using computers to crunch statistics. For the first time, crime data became available in near-real time. The department also began calling regular meetings, where commanding officers grilled captains and lieutenants, asking what they were doing to combat crime in their precincts. The department named this practice—the agglomeration and mapping of real-time crime data, as well as the legendarily terrifying meetings—Compstat. Its progenitor, Jack Maple, said it stood for "computer statistics or comparative statistics—no one can really be sure which."

Maple's invention rested on four main principles: accurate and timely intelligence, rapid deployment, effective tactics, and relentless follow-up and assessment. It sounds simple, even obvious: of course police should try to prevent as well as respond to crime; and of course, to do this effectively, they will need as much data as possible. Neither of those ideas were obvious at the time.

At around the time that Compstat was put in place, crime began falling. I do not intend to analyze, litigate, or even hypothesize about the precise causal relationships of Compstat to falling crime. With apologies to Dorothy Parker, eternity isn't two people and a ham; it's two criminologists arguing over the causes of the late twentieth-century crime drop. Perhaps the key was altered police practices. Perhaps it was changing demographics. Perhaps it was regulations that got the lead out of household paints and gasoline. Perhaps it was some combination of environmental, political, and demographic factors. Determining the correct answer is, mercifully, beyond the scope of both this book and my time on this planet.

Still, the fact is that Compstat transformed American policing (in much the same way as, and not long before, data-driven approaches transformed baseball). Other departments adopted it. New York has maintained and tweaked it. Today, a major-metro police department that considers only response and not prevention, and that purports to fight crime without data and accountability, is all but unthinkable. Predictive algorithms seem to be the natural outgrowth of the Compstat-driven approach: perfectly suited to departments concerned about preventing crime, not just responding to it.

How such algorithms make their predictions is not clear. Some firms say that publicly revealing the precise factors and weights that determine their predictions will let criminals game the system, but that hardly passes the smell test: a guy isn't going to decide to snatch wallets on Thirty-Fourth Street today because he knows his local police department uses XYZ Safety Program, and their algorithm currently forecasts high crime—and hence recommends increased police presence—on Thirty-Eighth Street.

The algorithms are proprietary, and keeping them secret is a matter of commercial advantage. There is nothing inherently wrong with that—Coca-Cola keeps its formula secret too. And, as I said earlier, there is nothing inherently wrong with using algorithms. But, as Phillip Atiba Goff of the New York University's Center for Policing Equity said to me, "Algorithms only do what we tell them to do." So what are we telling them to do?

Jeff Brantingham, an anthropologist at the University of California, Los Angeles, who cofounded PredPol, told me he wanted to understand "crime patterns, hot spots, and how they're going to change on a shift-by-shift or even moment-to-moment basis." The common understanding of the geography of street crime—that it happens more often in this neighborhood than that one—may have some truth in the long run, but has limited utility for police shift commanders, who need to decide where to tell their patrol officers to spend the next eight hours. Neighborhoods are big places; telling police to just go to one is not helpful.

So PredPol focuses on smaller areas—those 150-by-150-meter blocks of territory. And to determine its predictions, it uses three data points: crime type, crime location, and crime date and time. They use, as Brantingham told me, "no arrest data, no information about suspects or victims, or even what does the street look like, or neighborhood demographics. . . . Just a focus on where and when crime is likely to occur. . . . We are effectively assigning probabilities to locations on the landscape over a period of time." PredPol does not predict all crimes; instead, it forecasts only "Part 1 Crimes": murder, aggravated assault, burglary, robbery, theft, and car theft.

PredPol is not the only predictive-policing program. Others use "risk-terrain modeling," which includes information on geographical and environmental features linked to increased risks of crime—ATMs in areas with poor lighting, for instance, or clusters of liquor stores and gas stations near high concentrations of vacant properties. Other models include time of day and weather patterns (murders happen less frequently in cold weather).

All of these programs have to be "trained" on historical police data before they can forecast future crimes. For instance, using the examples above, programs treat poorly lit ATMs as a risk factor for future crimes because so many past crimes have occurred near them. But the type of historical data used to train them matters immensely.

Training algorithms on public-nuisance crimes—such as vagrancy, loitering, or public intoxication—increases the risk of racial bias. Why? Because these crimes generally depend on police presence. People call the police when their homes are broken into; they rarely call the police when they see someone drinking from an open container of alcohol, or standing on a street corner. Those crimes often depend on a police officer being present to observe them, and then deciding to enforce the relevant laws. Police presence tends to be heaviest in poor, heavily minority communities. (Jill Leovy's masterful book *Ghettoside: A True Story of Murder in America* is especially perceptive on the simultaneous over- and underpolicing of poor, nonwhite neighborhoods: citizens often feel that police crack down too heavily on nuisance crimes, but care too little about major crimes.)

Predictive-policing models that want to avoid introducing racial bias will also not train their algorithms on drug crimes, for similar reasons. In 2016, more than three-fourths of drug-related arrests were for simple possession—a crime heavily dependent on police interaction. According to the Drug Policy Alliance, a coalition that advocates for sensible drug laws, prosecutors are twice as likely to seek a mandatory-minimum sentence for a black defendant as for a white one charged with the same crime.[9] I could go on for a few hundred more pages, but you get the idea: America enforces its drug laws in a racist manner, and an algorithm trained on racism will perpetuate it.

Police forces use algorithms for things other than patrol allocation, too. Chicago's police department used one to create a Strategic Subject List (SSL), also called a Heat List, consisting of people deemed likely to be involved in a shooting incident, either as victim or perpetrator. This differs from the predictive-policing programs discussed above in one crucial way: it focuses on individuals rather than geography.

Much about the list is shrouded in secrecy. The precise algorithm is not publicly available, and it was repeatedly tweaked after it was first introduced in a pilot program in 2013. In 2017, after losing a long legal fight with the *Chicago Sun-Times*, the police department released a trove of arrest data and one version of the list online.[10] It used eight attributes to score people with criminal records from 0 (low risk) to 500 (extremely high risk). Scores were recalculated regularly—at one point (and perhaps still) daily.

Those attributes included the number of times being shot or being the victim of battery or aggravated assault; the number of times arrested on gun charges for violent offenses, narcotics, or gang affiliation; age when most recently arrested; and "trend in recent criminal activity." The algorithm does not use individuals' race or sex. It also does not use geography (i.e., the suspect's address), which in America often acts as a proxy for race.

Both Jeff Asher, a crime-data analyst writing in the *New York Times*, and Upturn, a research and advocacy group, tried to reverse-engineer the algorithm and emerged with similar results.[11] They determined that age was a crucial determinant of a person's SSL score, which is unsurprising—multiple studies have shown that people tend to age out of violent crime.

Shortly before these studies were published, a spokesman for the Chicago Police Department said, "Individuals really only come on our radar with scores of 250 and above."[12] But, according to Upturn, as of August 1, 2016, there were 280,000 people on the list with scores over 250—far more than a police department with 13,500 officers can reasonably keep on its radar. More alarmingly, Upturn found that over 127,524 people on the list had never been shot or arrested. How they wound up on the list is unclear.

Police have said the list is simply a tool, and that it doesn't drive enforcement decisions, but police have regularly touted the arrests of people on the SSL. The algorithm's opacity makes it unclear how someone gets on the SSL; more worryingly, it is also unclear how or whether someone ever gets off the list. And the SSL uses arrests, not convictions, which means some people may find themselves on the list for crimes they did not commit.

An analysis by reporters Yana Kunichoff and Patrick Sier published in *Chicago* magazine found that just 3.5 percent of the people on the SSL in the dataset released by the CPD (which covered four years of arrests, from July 31, 2012, to August 1, 2016) had previously been involved in a shooting, either as victim or perpetrator.[13] The factors most commonly shared by those on the list were gang affiliation and a narcotics arrest sometime in the previous four years.

Advocates say it is far too easy for police to put someone into a gang-affiliation database, and that getting into that database, which is 95 percent black or Latino, reflects policing patterns—their heavy presence in the mostly black and Latino South and West Sides of the city—more than the danger posed by those who end up on it. The above analysis also found that most black men in Chicago between the ages of twenty and twenty-nine had an SSL score, compared with just 23 percent of Hispanic men and 6 percent of white men.

Perhaps mindful of these sorts of criticisms, the city quietly mothballed the SSL in late 2019—and, according to the *Chicago Tribune*, finally stopped using it in early 2020.[14]

As with predictive-policing algorithms, the impulse to create this list is understandable. Repeated studies have shown that a small number of people are responsible for a disproportionate share of violence. If police could figure out who they were before they committed crimes or became victims, especially with gun crimes, they could keep more people alive and out of prison.

This approach—of trying to identify potential malefactors before they end up convicted and imprisoned—has a nonalgorithmic antecedent in a policing strategy known as Drug Market Intervention (DMI). DMI was created by David Kennedy, a criminologist at John Jay College in New York. Its strategy starts with police surveilling open-air drug markets and building cases against drug dealers. But instead of arresting them, police call them to a meeting with their families, social-service providers, and community leaders, where they present them with a choice: stop now, and we will help you; continue dealing, and we will prosecute you.[15]

Chicago offered something similar to people on the SSL. People with high scores got a visit from the police—despite having committed no crime—along with social-service providers and community leaders. But, as Kunichoff and Sier found, only a small number of people on the list attended these "call-ins," while hundreds were arrested. The more important difference between the two approaches is that DMI is based on physical, shoe-leather surveillance of specific subjects: the people whom the police call in can see actual photographic evidence of their drug-dealing. Algorithms offer no such reassurance.

But did the SSL work? To answer that question, we first have to determine what we mean by "work." If we mean did it reduce the number of people who died by gunshot, then in Chicago's case the answer appears to be "probably not," or at least it did not appear to be a determinative factor.

A Rand Corporation study of the first version of the SSL found that individuals on the list were no more likely to be shot or murdered than the people in a comparison group. They were, however, more likely to be arrested for a shooting. Chicago's police department told the authors of the Rand study that "the list was used as an intelligence-gathering source," and the authors posited that "when there was a shooting, the police looked at the members of the SSL as possible suspects. This suggests that the impact of the SSL was on clearing shootings, but not on gun violence in general."[16]

There is nothing wrong with the police building a tool that helps them quickly clear shootings—but that is not quite the same thing as a tool that improves public safety, or effectively reduces the level of gun violence. In 2013, when the SSL was introduced, Chicago recorded 415 homicides. In 2018, it recorded 539. In between, the numbers were 407, 468, 762, and 650.

The evidence for bail algorithms and geospatial predictive policing is similarly equivocal. A study by Hany Farid, a computer science professor, and Julia Dressel, who was then a student at Dartmouth, tested an algorithm known by the acronym COMPAS (Correctional Offender Management Profiling for Alternative Sanctions), which courts use to predict the likelihood a defendant will reoffend.[17] It draws from 137 features of the defendant's life and criminal history to predict whether he or she will commit another crime within two years.

The study's authors selected 1,000 defendants at random from a pool of 7,214 people who had been arrested in Broward County, Florida, in 2013 and 2014 and assessed by COMPAS. They divided the subjects into 20 groups of 50 each. Participants were randomly assigned to assess each defendant in a group of 50, and each group was seen by 20 people.

Participants read the criminal histories of each defendant along with their current charges, age, and sex, but not race. They were then asked to predict whether a defendant had been rearrested within two years of his or her initial arraignment. They guessed correctly 62.1 percent of the time. When the guesses of everyone in a group of 20 were pooled, the figure rose to 67 percent—slightly higher than COMPAS's rate of 65.2 percent.

The authors then repeated the experiment with another 400 volunteers, but this time they added the subject's race to the list of disclosed factors. It made little difference; the "crowd-based accuracy" rate was 66.5 percent. But an analysis by ProPublica, an investigative journalism nonprofit, of a larger group of defendants arrested in the same county, during the same time period, who were also assessed by COMPAS's algorithm, found that the algorithm was almost twice as likely to falsely identify black defendants than white ones as high risk, and similarly likely to misidentify white defendants as low risk.[18]

Brisha Borden, for instance, was an eighteen-year-old who picked up someone's unlocked bicycle, tried to ride it before realizing it was too small, and dropped it as soon as someone shouted that the bike belonged to her child. Still, a neighbor who saw the incident called the police; Borden was arrested for petty theft and burglary of an $80 bike that she did not in fact steal. COMPAS's risk scale rated her 8 out of 10—a high risk of reoffending. By contrast, Vernon Prater—a forty-one-year-old white man who stole $86.35 worth of tools from a Home Depot store, and had previously been convicted of armed robbery and attempted armed robbery, for which he had served five years in prison—got a 3 on the COMPAS scale. Two years after their arrests, Borden had been charged with no other crimes, whereas Prater had ended up serving an eight-year prison term for breaking into a warehouse to steal thousands of dollars' worth of electronic goods.

(Northpointe, the company that makes COMPAS, objected to ProPublica's work, sent a letter to the ProPublica writers saying, "Northpointe does not agree that the results of your analysis, or the claims being made based upon that analysis, are correct or that they accurately reflect the outcomes from the application of the model." Keen-eyed readers will note the utter lack of substantive objection— or indeed of substance, full stop—in that anodyne statement.)

The work done by Dressel and Farid raises two crucial questions about algorithms that predict recidivism. The first is one of value. COMPAS's algorithm takes in 137 factors, including subjects' answers to questions such as, "How many of your friends/acquaintances are taking drugs illegally?," "How often did you get into fights at school?," and whether defendants agree with statements such as, "A hungry person has a right to steal." Precisely how it weights those factors is a trade secret.

Dressel and Farid's algorithms performed just as well as COMPAS's knowing only seven things, all pulled from people's criminal records. They then slimmed that down even further and found that combining just two factors—age and number of previous convictions—produced results just as accurate as COMPAS's. A study conducted by five researchers led by Cynthia Rudin, a computer science professor at Duke University, reached a similar conclusion: taking into account just three factors—age, number of prior convictions, and sex—yielded results as accurate as COMPAS's.[19]

That is fundamentally unsurprising: if you are young and inclined toward crime, you will probably commit more crimes than someone older and less inclined toward crime. But it does call into question the fundamental promise of algorithmic risk assessments: that they will perform better than humans, getting more accurate results. And so the question that procurement officers and other criminal justice officials should ask themselves is this: If an algorithm predicts recidivism slightly less accurately than a random group of 20 people, and its accuracy could be matched using just two easily obtainable factors, should states and counties really spend taxpayer money on it?

A second question concerns fairness, and what kind of legal system people want judging them and their peers. In 2013, a judge in

Wisconsin, relying in part on COMPAS's risk assessment, sentenced a defendant, named Erik Loomis, to six years in prison, and gave another five supervised release. Loomis sued, arguing that relying on COMPAS—an algorithm that made a judgment using a secret methodology—had violated his due-process rights. A trial court and the Wisconsin Supreme Court both ruled against him. But the latter held that algorithmically determined risk assessments alone cannot determine a sentence, and that judges who use them must be warned that, among other things, they are opaque, not individualized, and may be unfair to nonwhite defendants.[20]

All of those factors contravene a liberal society's sense of justice. Among the most fundamental rights in the Anglo-American court system is the right to confront one's accuser. Opaque risk-assessment algorithms do not entirely vitiate that right—they assess risk; they do not, on their own, accuse or pass judgment. But as a decision that cannot be questioned, they come closer than many would like. They also may impede appellate review. A judge has to provide reasons for a decision, whereas a black-box algorithm does not—an appellate court may know what factors the algorithm considered, but not how they interacted or were weighted. And to what end? Again, it seems to perform no better than a group of people effectively chosen at random. And the accuracy of both people and algorithms tops out at around 66 percent, which is not great: that score, on a school test, would earn the test-taker a D. Is this really what we want from our justice system?

Studies of predictive-policing algorithms raise similar concerns. The fundamental problem, as William Isaac, an artificial-intelligence research scientist, explained to me, is that "reported crime is not a census of all crime. When you forecast where crime will happen based on reported crime, you're introducing institutional biases." The police are not everywhere in equal numbers. Their presence tends to be heaviest in poor, majority-minority neighborhoods.

Higher crime and arrest rates in those neighborhoods reflect force-allocation decisions—which themselves reflect societal expectations and preferences. And when you train an algorithm on data derived from those decisions, you replicate them in the algorithm.

That creates, as Isaac spelled out in a study he conducted with Kristian Lum, a statistician with the Human Rights Data Analysis Group, "a feedback loop where the model becomes increasingly confident that the locations most likely to experience further criminal activity are exactly the locations they had previously believed to be high in crime: selection bias meets confirmation bias." (Selection bias results from using an unrepresentative data sample—in this case, overpoliced neighborhoods; confirmation bias is the human cognitive tendency to look favorably on data that confirms what we already think, and disfavorably on data that challenges or disproves it.)[21]

A team from New York University, Rashida Richardson, Jason Schultz, and Kate Crawford—respectively, the director of policy research at the university's AI Now Institute, which examines the social impact of artificial intelligence in policymaking; a clinical law professor who directs the law school's Technology and Policy Clinic; and a research professor who cofounded the AI Now Institute—examined the data that feeds predictive-policing programs in a paper titled "Dirty Data, Bad Predictions: How Civil Rights Violations Impact Police Data, Predictive Policing Systems and Justice."[22]

This paper centers on a simple question: What sort of data is being fed to predictive-policing systems? To answer it, the authors examined thirteen jurisdictions that were using at the time of publication or had previously used predictive-policing systems, and had also been found to have engaged in "corrupt, racially biased or otherwise illegal police practices." They examined publicly available data on these jurisdictions' use of predictive-policing algorithms alongside evidence from adjudications and federal investigations to determine whether these algorithms were using "data that is derived from or influenced by corrupt, biased and unlawful practices, including data that has been intentionally manipulated or 'juked,' as well as data that is distorted by individual and societal biases," and data derived from deliberately false arrests. In other words, they wanted to know whether predictive policing, as it is actually used in thirteen cities, relies on data tainted with precisely the biases that it is advertised to correct.

In nine jurisdictions, they found that it had—that the algorithms used by these departments ingested data "generated during periods when the department was found to have engaged in forms of corrupt police practices." Chicago, for instance, created its Strategic Suspect List as it was engaging, according to the ACLU of Illinois, in illegal stop-and-frisk activity that disproportionately targeted African Americans. (The ACLU's report led to a settlement agreement mandating independent oversight of police practices and data collection as well as reform of the CPD's stop-and-frisk practices.)

Does this evidence prove beyond a reasonable doubt that specific arrests made at specific times in particular cities were wrong, and stemmed from racist practice? No. But it suggests that bias-infected data at least partly undergirds these cities' predictive-policing programs. As Sandra Mayson, a law professor at the University of Georgia, noted in her paper "Bias In, Bias Out," "In a racially stratified world, any method of prediction will project the inequalities of the past into the future."[23]

If this discussion of feedback loops and biased data and patterns of practice sounds vague, well, that is partly because, as discussed earlier in this chapter, we do not know precisely what goes into each algorithm, how those factors are weighted, or what the decision-making tree looks like. Just as determining exactly why Facebook or Twitter showed you this story and not that one is all but impossible, isolating precisely which factors in a predictive-policing algorithm produced which result is also difficult.

I met Rashida Richardson to discuss her work in a rapidly emptying office suite in Lower Manhattan (New York University's Center for Data Science was in the process of moving). Before joining the AI Now Institute, she was legislative counsel at the New York Civil Liberties Union. Richardson explained to me that she believes her "Dirty Data" paper represents "the tip of the iceberg when it comes to mapping algorithmic use through the criminal justice system." She said, "There are also collateral consequences. What about housing data that uses criminal justice inputs? [Some jurisdictions bar people with criminal records from public housing.] Gang databases?

Crime and police data used in pretrial assessments? It's this compounded harm that we don't even understand because of the lack of transparency around these systems, and around what data is being used and why."

Some places have begun trying to remedy that. In January 2018, the New York City Council passed a law mandating "the creation of a task force that provides recommendations on how information on agency automated decision systems may be shared with the public and how agencies may address instances where people are harmed by agency automated decision systems."

Bill de Blasio, New York's mayor, created that task force four months later. Unfortunately, it was unfunded—usually a signal that the politicians who created a committee do not take it all that seriously—and it spent much of its first year trying to satisfactorily define "automated decision systems." (Richardson's group, the AI Now Institute, has compiled a nonexhaustive list of dozens, including not just criminal justice algorithms, but also those used to assess which students are at risk of violence, which landlords are likely to harass tenants, how to allocate funding to fire departments, and many more.)

Following New York's lead, Vermont created an Artificial Intelligence Task Force to recommend how the state should use and regulate AI. And in the US Congress, Senators Ron Wyden (D-OR) and Cory Booker (D-NJ) and Congresswoman Yvette Clarke (D-NY) introduced the Algorithmic Accountability Act in April 2019. This bill, which of course went nowhere in the dysfunctional morass of the 116th Congress, would require companies to conduct impact assessments on their automated decision-making for bias, privacy, and security and to correct any flaws they find.

I have made this discussion as up-to-date as possible, but obviously I cannot know what will have happened with these task forces or pieces of legislation by the time the book is in readers' hands. I would be willing to bet money or pride that the Algorithmic Accountability Act will not become law, and that the task forces in New York and Vermont will fizzle, going the way of so many well-meaning, unsexy reform efforts—by releasing a thoughtful, high-minded report written in bureaucratic English riddled with hedges and throat-clearings and "to be sures," to be read only by people already primed to agree with its conclusions (or by reporters like me).

At the same time, the impetus that led to the creation of those task forces has not vanished. More people than ever before understand that justice by algorithm imperils our civil liberties. It deprives us of the right to confront our accusers, calcifies the racial bias that has distorted our justice system for far too long, and focuses the state's eye on people who have committed no crime. The days of law enforcement agencies rolling out predictive-policing programs in secret appear numbered.

Concerned citizens may not be able to eliminate the use of algorithms in the criminal justice system (nor is it clear that elimination, as opposed to careful monitoring, should be the goal), but they can at least compel governments to think about the data that goes into them and how they are used. For instance, perhaps they should be scrubbed of any data gleaned during a period when a department was found, by an independent agency, to have engaged in racist policing.

An equally good place to start would be to rethink what place-based predictive-policing algorithms actually reveal. The answer seems obvious: they show places where crime has occurred, repeatedly and in detectable patterns. But a map of crime is also a map of need. If cities can use that map to decide where to send police, they can also use it to decide where to target social services, such as job training and mental health care. As William Isaac, the research scientist I spoke with, noted, "Police departments have a limited set of tools, but they are responsible for dealing with broad, complex social phenomena. . . . What do you do when you have this information? Can you use it to help communities, rather than just surveilling and arresting people in those communities?"

9

THE CHINA PROBLEM

"We can now have a perfect architecture of control.
What democratic practices do we need to not become China?"

MY PREVIOUS CHAPTERS EACH CENTERED ON A DISCRETE PIECE OF TECH-
nology. Now I ask a broader question: What happens when a state
with weak institutions or scant regard for civil liberties combines
multiple forms of surveillance technology and turns them on its own
citizens? How bad can things get? To answer that question, I will examine Ecuador's emergency response network, which doubles as a
national surveillance system, and China's tech-enabled repression of
its Uyghur Muslim minority.

Before diving in, a word of caution: If you live in a developed
country with independent courts, security forces that generally respect citizens' civil rights, and well-established norms of political
redress, you may read this chapter with a sense of relieved remove.
Our institutions are resilient, you might think to yourself. Our courts
are independent. Our police are well trained. And our political arena
is well defined: Our politicians may not like each other, but they fight
for votes in well-run elections. They do not unleash the power of the
state on their opponents. Nor do they harass journalists or activists or
pose a threat to civil society.

But in many places, they have. They could do so anywhere. And if the geopolitical events of the past few years have taught us anything, it is not to take too much comfort from precedent.

Catherine Crump's question, which I introduced at the very beginning of the book, is still one I cannot get out of my mind: "We can now have a perfect architecture of control," said the law professor and codirector of the Berkeley Center for Law and Technology. Surveillance is effortless, cheap, and can be perpetual; as facial recognition and video analytics improve, we will be able to see, track, and keep tabs on everyone, everywhere. We cannot forestall the surveillance state through technology; we can only do so politically and democratically. So the crucial question, in Crump's words, is "What democratic practices do we need to not become China?" Ask yourself that as you read this chapter: What do we need to do to keep what I am about to describe from happening here?

◉

Quito, Ecuador's capital, sprawls up the side of verdant mountains and nestles itself into a long, narrow valley. With few streets more than two lanes in either direction and a profusion of parks and plazas, it feels more like a sprawling village than a major city. It has a charmingly scruffy soulfulness. A German Ecuadorian colleague of mine, who has been a resident of the city for eleven years but spent childhood summers in Quito well before then, complains that it used to be far more charming, before the government began replacing Quito's colorful old Spanish mansions with multistory blocks designed to accommodate its growth.

That may be true. But Quito has also avoided the miserable tangle of highways and flyovers that mar so many rapidly growing cities of the developing world. Quito's historic center is miraculously preserved, especially considering that it sits beneath volcanoes and above fault lines. UNESCO has recognized it as a World Heritage site for its unique blend of Spanish, Italian, French, Moorish, and indigenous architecture. Much of the district is car-free. Except for the towering Gothic and Baroque churches, the buildings are colorful and low, the streets cobblestone or brick.

The security cameras mounted on lampposts at intersections, however, are thoroughly modern. Filled with strolling Quiteños and tourists during the day, the area turns rough at night. At dusk, as the public spaces start to empty, the Baroque shadows of the buildings that loom over the tortuous streets take on a minatory cast.

Ecuador's crime rate has dropped significantly over the past decade. According to the United Nations Office on Drugs and Crime, in 2008 around 18 per 100,000 people were murdered within the country's borders.[1] It was not the most murderous country in South America that year—Venezuela's homicide rate was 51.4 per 100,000—and it was just one-fifth the rate that El Salvador would reach eight years later.[2] But in 2008, by comparison, America's homicide rate was 5.4.[3]

Ecuador's murder rate has since fallen markedly, but fear of crime remains viscerally present for many Ecuadorians. An American woman married to an Ecuadorian told me that her in-laws have strict rules about where they drive, park, and visit. A colleague told me that when he goes out at night, he takes taxis between bars and restaurants, even if they're just a few hundred meters apart. The former government opened numerous small police outposts throughout the city. These squat white buildings look resolutely uninviting, but my colleague said the police inside them tend to be responsive: officers convene WhatsApp groups with local residents, who use them to report crimes.

A card in my hotel room warned guests not to walk anywhere after 6:00 p.m. On my first night in the city, I asked the concierge how seriously to take that warning: the hotel didn't have a restaurant, and the nearest one open on a Sunday night, other than the Burger King across one street and McDonald's across another, was only three blocks away. He winced a bit, then looked me up and down. He told me I should be fine—as long as I walked quickly and "with purpose" (I did, and I was).

Purportedly in response to such fears, Ecuador's government unveiled ECU911, a national emergency response network, in 2012 (as I will discuss below, many ascribed less pure motives to ECU911's creation). It replaced an older system in which people had to dial separate numbers for police, fire, or ambulance. Now they simply dial 911, and an operator routes their call. If the caller is near an ECU911 camera, the operator can see where they are calling from.

Financed by a loan from China, ECU911 links 4,500 security cameras across Ecuador to twenty-seven centralized response centers. According to one government-watcher I met in Quito, it was the first Chinese loan that Ecuador used for something other than infrastructure, mining, or power plants.

The amount of Chinese investment flowing into Ecuador has alarmed many. Many of the complaints I heard sounded familiar. From 2014 through 2017, I covered Southeast Asia for *The Economist*. Anti-Chinese sentiment in that part of the world is rife. I got used to people resentfully talking about China throwing its weight around. China offered governments of smaller, poorer countries sizable loans that, unlike those that came from Europe or America, had no strings attached intended to encourage liberalization. Governments did not have to improve their human rights records or hold free and fair elections. The money did not really have to be accounted for; if some of it found its way into the pockets of the politically powerful and well connected, well, that was just how things worked.

Many in Ecuador were resentful: not only did the government indebt itself to China, but Chinese workers built the projects, including ECU911, for which Ecuadorian taxpayers would ultimately foot the bill. (This common practice lets China put excess labor, as well as capital, to work, providing the country a release valve for the pressure that thousands of underemployed young men in China might otherwise exert on government and society.)

According to the China–Latin America Finance Database, since 2005 Chinese government lenders—via the China Development Bank and the Export-Import Bank of China—have disbursed roughly $141.3 billion in loans across Latin America and the Caribbean. Ecuador is the region's second-biggest loan recipient by number and the third-biggest by value (Venezuela tops both rankings by far).[4]

A report from Freedom House, an American think tank, published in 2018 found that China had built Internet and mobile telecommunications infrastructure in thirty-eight countries and had sold surveillance equipment in at least eighteen. Some of these sales had alarming terms. For instance, CloudWalk, a Chinese firm, is building a national facial-recognition database for Zimbabwe, and Zimbabwe's government agreed to send citizens' biometric data—without their consent, of course—back to CloudWalk to help its AI learn to distinguish among dark-skinned faces.[5]

From 2007 to 2017, Ecuador's president was Rafael Correa, a left-populist gadfly whose politics were similar to those of Hugo Chavez in Venezuela and Evo Morales in Bolivia. He sought to downplay ties with the United States, leading him to turn toward China.

That made geopolitical sense: China was waiting with open arms—and wallets. But as Correa's popularity declined, suspicion of China and its interests grew. One source who knew the former government well told me that Ecuador could not so much as add a camera to the network without Chinese permission and licensing. The Chinese, said my source, even built the lampposts on which the cameras hang.

More than one reasonably well-informed Ecuadorian told me that the Chinese could access ECU911 cameras. Mario Pazmino, a former military intelligence official who has since become a staunch critic of Ecuador's government, told me that ECU911 represents "an attempt by China to use Latin America to expand Chinese social, military, and economic interests. It was a subtle infiltration of Chinese companies to gain market access, not just here but elsewhere in the region."

One afternoon, outside a loud but friendly demonstration of bus drivers agitating for better pay, I met a Venezuelan who had fled to Ecuador. He put it in slightly more mercantile terms. ECU911, he said, was "a franchise" of the surveillance system that China had already installed in his home country. Others in the region—potential customers—were watching. ECU911 had its perks: it could improve emergency response times, thus providing a plausible popular justification, but it could also be used for sub rosa surveillance as needed—and not just by local governments, either.

"I'm concerned," said Pazmino, "that data collected by ECU911 could be transmitted to China to gain an understanding of the habits and practices of Ecuadorian consumers for market-research purposes."

The data could also be used to monitor unrest. Pazmino mentioned a Chinese copper mine in eastern Ecuador that had met with sizable local opposition. "ECU911 is vital for that company and for Chinese interests," he said, "so they can monitor very specifically what is happening at that site, so they can defend their interests."

This struck me just at the paranoid edge of plausibility—but then again, Freedom House's report noted that, in January 2018, the African Union learned that its computer systems "had been sending confidential data back to Shanghai every day for five years." The backstory was similar to Ecuador's: "China had spent $200 million constructing the AU's new headquarters in Addis Ababa, including the computer network." In 2017, China's State Council announced that it wanted China to become the world's leading artificial-intelligence power by 2030. China also has a long and ignominious record of intellectual property theft and industrial espionage. It would perhaps be more surprising if it were not harvesting information.[6]

◉

ECU911's headquarters—which is also the response center for Quito, Orellano, and Napo Provinces—sits at the crown of Itchimbia Park on a hill overlooking much of the city. Despite the light landscaping and the spray of rainbow-colored tiles across one corner, the building remains an imposing, opaque, gray metal cube. For several days, my colleague and I had been trying to arrange a meeting with ECU911's director, to no avail.

So, early one afternoon, when we had a couple of hours between meetings, we just tromped up the hill, presented ourselves, and asked for a tour. After a few minutes cooling our heels in the nondescript lobby, to our surprise, three people from ECU911's public relations staff showed up and brought us inside.

Just behind the lobby was a cavernous entrance hall ringed with glass cases, each of which contained emblems belonging to an agency linked to ECU911: city police, transit police, fire brigade, paramedics, the Health Ministry, the Red Cross, and the military.

We learned that some taxis also have linked security cameras in them, as well as panic buttons that connect to local police: one in the front, one in the back, and another inside the trunk, in case a rider gets kidnapped and stuffed back there (it's on the interior roof of the trunk, the flack reassured me, in case you're on your back).

The last glass case contained ECU911's robot-mascot, Ecutron, whom they trot out for school visits. He has half-moon blue eyes, a giant head, barrel chest, and bandy legs. He looks like EVE (the robot love interest from the Pixar film *WALL-E*—and, why yes, I do have children; thank you for asking) after years on steroids.

After one of our guides flipped a card at a reader to unlock a restricted door, we came to a glass-fronted room. Etched on the glass in gold type, in Spanish and Chinese, was the name "Research and Development Laboratory for the Integrated Security System Between China and Ecuador." Behind the window there were nine desks, each of which had three computer monitors visible; when we visited, six desks were occupied. One of our guides explained that the people in that room "constantly review procedures to improve response times."

Despite the writing on the window, the guide said, ECU911 no longer had any contact with the Chinese. The Chinese built it, but the contract with them expired. Ecuador did not need their permission to add cameras, he explained. They did not have to buy equipment from China, and China did not have access to the network. But of course, if China did have access, it is doubtful that anyone on ECU911's press staff would know about it—and if they did, it is even more doubtful that they would tell a foreign journalist.

People around the world are concerned not just about what surveillance technology sees, but about what it stores, and who has access to that data. Maybe China can access ECU911's camera feeds, and maybe it can't. Similarly, I doubt Shotspotter's microphones can pick up street-level conversations, but I can understand why many people think they can. Maybe ICE can access your local police department's license plate database, and maybe it can't. But an ICE officer who happens to be friendly with one of your local sergeants can still call and wheedle that contact into running a few searches. The opacity of surveillance tech cuts both ways: because ordinary citizens find it hard to know when they are being watched, they also find departments' and companies' denials hard to swallow.

ECU911's main room is immense. It accommodates one hundred employees per eight-hour shift. They sit in long rows, each in front of a pair of monitors. The people in this room field calls, of which there are roughly two thousand per day, around 70 percent of which ask for police. Receiving a call starts a digital file, which follows the call to whatever agency responds.

At the front of the room is a movie-theater-sized screen divided into numerous smaller scenes. I counted fourteen, along with a few screens of analytics. Our guide said they were all showing accidents or crimes currently being monitored. I noticed a car crash, but the other scenes all looked unremarkable.

In a tidy little coincidence, as one of the guides was explaining how ECU911 had improved response times to natural disasters, a small earthquake shook the building. As far as I could tell, nobody was hurt; people barely even looked up from their monitors. It was my third, and while it did not toss me from my bed as one did in Indonesia, it was, like the other two, a humbling experience.

Down the hall is a second room only slightly smaller and less populated than the first. One of the guides explained that it was the "video vigilance" room. People here do not respond; they watch, calling up selected cameras to their feed from crime hotspots, intersections with a lot of accidents, or entrances to parks and other strategic sites, just to see if anything is amiss.

The guides then showed off what the linked cameras could do. On the screen at the front of the room—like the previous one, an immense one showing multiple scenes—an intersection in Quito's historic center came up: daytime crowds just milling around, much like those I had walked through a couple of days earlier, though the time stamp showed that this particular scene had occurred around eight months earlier.

At the center, a man crossed the street as he looked at his phone. On the side of the street that he had just left, and to his side, just behind him, were two other men in bright orange shirts and caps. From the camera's high vantage point, the men in orange were clearly stalking the third. They drew closer, but remained just out of his field of vision—until they pounced. One grabbed him from behind and reached into his pocket as he kicked, twisted, and struggled; the second grabbed his legs and lifted him up so he was parallel with the ground. Then they dropped him and ran.

But the cameras then tracked the men in orange from street to street. First they ran, and then, after a few blocks, they slowed to a trot and discarded their orange caps and overshirts. When they ducked down a side street, the cameras lost them—that particular corner didn't have an ECU-linked camera. But by then, a police car was coming toward them from one direction, and a police motorcycle from another. A couple of minutes later, the two men were being dragged away in handcuffs.

On another day, the cameras caught a woman standing on the side of a highway bridge. She was holding on to the railing and slowly rocking back and forth as cars drove past. She was clearly in distress. After a few minutes, a police car drove up, and the officers approached, coaxed her into the car, and drove away with her. The guide told me (I could not independently verify this) that they brought her to a psychologist at the police station, then released her into her family's care.

In a third scene, the cameras recorded a man running down a street. The guide told me he had just killed someone. They followed him as he crossed another street and boarded a bus, whereupon the bus camera flicked on. The bus drove away, and after a short time police boarded it and dragged the suspect away.

◉

Later that afternoon I visited Maria Paula Romo, Ecuador's interior minister. She's young, savvy, competent, and ambitious; one source told me that the US State Department's Latin America watchers consider her presidential material.

Romo's ministry oversees Ecuador's police and internal security service, and she is on ECU911's board of directors. Although the system was a pet project of the previous government, she talks it up, saying it has helped reduce response times to emergencies and natural disasters, as intended. She told me that ECU911 centers become "operations centers" after natural disasters: all officials in an affected province head to the ECU911 center so they can see how their region has been affected. A provincial transport minister can see the region's roads; education ministers can see its schools. This, says Romo, lets them make better, more informed decisions.

And it is popular. A few mayoral candidates recently campaigned on promises to build ECU911 response centers in their cities (an impossible promise, as it happens: the system is highly centralized, and mayors cannot unilaterally open a building and demand the feeds).

"People see it as a system that has had success," Romo told me. "In fact, the system probably has a better reputation than the police themselves." In Ecuador, that is a low bar. Among Quiteños, a dark joke prevails: If you find yourself witness to or victim of a serious crime, call the police and tell them the neighbors are playing music too loud; they will rush over. Tell them you've been robbed, beaten, or worse, and you will grow old waiting.

The system in Ecuador has conceptual and practical advantages. Ask a cop in London or New York about security cameras, and prepare to hear a torrent of frustration: cameras have different formats; they record for different amounts of time; some do not record at all. After a crime, sorting through all the footage takes hours, sometimes days. So, if you were the victim of a crime, wouldn't you prefer that the police had video quickly—even in real time, as ECU911 allows?

But, as with other kinds of surveillance technology, the question is never just whether they can do some good. They always can. Bodycams can catch misconduct; facial recognition can bring criminals to light; and automatic license plate readers can track malefactors' cars. Public safety success, however, is always just half the story.

The other half can be found in Ecuador's domestic intelligence agency. Although the current president, Lenín Moreno, shuttered the National Intelligence Secretariat (SENAIN)—which was feared by many for the abuses it was responsible for under former president Correa, who had used it to hound and harass journalists, activists, environmentalists, and his political opponents—when I met with her

Romo confirmed that its successor agency still received ECU911's camera feeds.

When I asked who precisely was authorized to access them, she said, "We don't know." She noted that as a result of an outstanding *New York Times* article on ECU911 that had run a couple of months before my visit, the government was "working on protocols," but precisely what that meant was unclear.[7] Her answer was disturbing enough if it was true. It meant that the government had bought and deployed a nationwide surveillance network before fully thinking through the rules surrounding its use.

But, of course, she could be lying. Or she could be misinformed, perhaps deliberately, by those who have access. Or she could be partially informed—meaning she may know some of the people permitted to access it, but suspects that others, whom she does not know, can also see the feeds. In any case, it seems clear that the Ecuadorian government cares far more about gathering information on their citizens than about safeguarding their civil liberties.

Both Romo and my ECU911 guides claimed that the system has neither facial nor voice recognition (though, said Romo, "ideally they should"). According to my ECU911 guide, the system can only monitor license plates by pausing and zooming in.

But ECU911's website boasts that the system "includes thermal cameras for monitoring volcanic activity, vehicle license plate readers, mass concentration events monitoring, facial recognition, drones, tools used to perform monitoring tasks, fire control, video surveillance of inaccessible places, rescue, prevention and actions of timely response to incidents" (awkward translation courtesy of Google Translate, from a now-outdated ECU911 webpage).

That dull-sounding phrase—"mass concentration events monitoring"—seems to give the game away. One person I spoke with in Quito recalled seeing government agents controlling drones that flew over an antigovernment demonstration in 2016, and told me the government had bought voice-recognition software nearly a decade ago. Another particularly well-connected source called the emergency response side of ECU911 "a glorified call center" and said that when it was first proposed, "the idea was always to have a link to intelligence," which "definitely has" analytics, including facial and voice recognition. (If that's the case, it would make Romo's statement technically true, but misleading.) In July 2019, the government mooted the idea of going one step further, and installing facial-recognition-equipped cameras on public buses. As usual, the government talked up the public safety benefits and said nothing about data protection.

This ambiguity may not be deliberate, but it still provides the government a strategic advantage: people who are unsure whether they are being monitored, particularly in a country with a track record of surveilling and harassing its enemies, will tend to self-censor. The efficacy of a surveillance network does not entirely depend on the efficacy of its tech. China's facial-recognition glasses, for instance, may work less well than the manufacturers and government want them to, but as long as people believe they work and act accordingly (i.e., by toeing the political line), then they have achieved their objective.

But in Ecuador, as in China, sometimes force helps. In the summer of 2015, protests roiled the country. President Correa had entered office eight years earlier, and during his tenure, oil prices collapsed. That left Ecuador, a major exporter, with some budgetary holes to fill. Correa's ambitious social programs looked less feasible. The government had to cut spending, as well as some government wages, and raise taxes, which of course sparked popular discontent. Protesters also opposed Correa's efforts to end presidential term limits (Ecuador reinstated them in 2018, a year after he left office). Over time, as often happens, different groups of people took to the streets with a range of grievances, upset about austerity measures, corruption, and oil projects.

One morning in downtown Quito, I met someone who had worked during this period—the late Correa era—in the Interior Ministry (this was well before Maria Romo assumed her post). This person, whom I will call T, told me the following story. A word of caution: the former interior secretary did not respond to an interview request, and I was unable to independently verify every detail of what T said took place inside the ministry.

President Correa, said T, hired a lot of journalists to do PR: not only to write press releases, edit videos, and get ministers in the news, as PR people normally do, but also to staff "troll factories," to boost Correa, and to attack his opponents online. T said that every ministry had its own "meme generators," people tasked with creating catchy images for their minister that might go viral online.

T had worked for a pro-government newspaper for a time, where T says salaries were triple the level of independent outlets. T also got other perks unavailable elsewhere, including hefty travel budgets and extra pay for weekend work. The top salaries, said T, went to those who worked in President Correa's office, either doing advance preparation or helping on his weekly television show, *Citizen Link*. The show was broadcast on Saturday mornings and lasted, as one Quiteño told me, "for around three hours, or until his voice got tired."

That summer, T had just graduated from college and applied to work in the Interior Ministry's press room. They hired T, surprisingly, without even asking to see a diploma. T arrived at work to find that the ministry's press office "wasn't focused on reporting or coverage." Instead, it was "a war room," and the demonstrators protesting the president's policies were the enemy.

On the wall was "a map of the demonstrations, city by city," alongside photographs of the demonstration leaders as identified by members of the ministry's media team. When the demonstrations were active, "the war room at the ministry would ask ECU911 for information: where the demonstration had come from and where it was heading," said T. "Any cabinet minister in an app chat with the ministry's press office could ask ECU911 for information. ECU911 was created to provide strategic information to the government; it was someone's job at ECU911 to be a liaison to the rest of the government."

According to T, the Interior Ministry had a pair of large televisions that showed the ECU911 feed. The deputy minister could demand footage from ECU911. There were both police and military officials in the room, even though Ecuador's 2008 constitution maintains a separation in their duties. Whereas "internal protection and uphold-ing law and order" are supposed to be "exclusive duties of . . . the national police force," the military is tasked with "defense of the coun-try's sovereignty and territorial integrity."

Correa himself would show up daily during this period to watch ECU911's feed (the ministry and the presidential palace are con-nected). Orders would come from the war room to dispatch police based on ECU911's footage.

Ecuadorian demonstrations, one friend told me, tend to be peace-ful. "It's not like Germany or France," he explained. "People will drive to the demos, leave their cars there, and at the end there won't be a scratch on them." By contrast, T said, the ministry staff used ECU911 footage to target demonstrators for assault by paid pro-government thugs. "The cameras would zoom in on individuals, especially on in-digenous people. [A ministry official] would tell the cameras where to point, and would give the order to grab a protester and beat him so he looked bad. They were laughing in the office."

The official told his trolls to make memes of one particularly prominent demonstrator whom pro-government forces had worked over. "It worked," said T. The beaten protester "became a figure of fun. People said he dirtied his own face." T also said that police, us-ing ECU911 footage, had tracked down the foreign-born wife of an indigenous protester and had her deported. For T that was the last straw. T left the Interior Ministry soon afterward. For some time after that, people T assumed worked for the domestic intelligence agency would call T at night and describe precisely what route T had taken to get home.

◉

Mario Pazmino has similar stories of being targeted by ECU911's cameras. Once he was a military-intelligence bigwig; his card now says he's a "consultor internacional" in defense and security. He is a genial, gregarious, heavyset man. His modest office, just behind a shopping center in central Quito, was decorated in a sort of Rococo Small Arms style: It was filled with trophies and decorations from his long military career. Diplomas from various military academies festooned the walls. Sheathed swords and knives sat mounted on display on desks, and mounted on the back wall were a pair of M-16s. When I asked him about them, he got a gleam in his eye, then ducked behind his desk and pulled out a Beretta M9—a replica, he said, just after he handed it to me, barrel first. As we spoke, an intricately decorated and bejeweled skull grinned at me over his shoulder.

Pazmino showed me photographs of the monitors trained on his house: along with a 360-degree camera right outside, there's a parabolic listening device on a building across the street. He says that Correa accused him of working for Mossad and the CIA after he began to criticize the government. While Correa was in office, there were two attempts on Pazmino's life. Correa's government, he claimed, wanted him to flee to the United States, "so it would look like I'm begging the gringos for protection": "But I'm still here," he added. "My wife and kids are here. My dogs are here."

Pazmino is deeply cynical about ECU911: "It was a cover-up operation sold to society to give them a feeling that the police were going to address drug trafficking, robberies, and violent crime." And it could do that, he said, "if it didn't have a false bottom." The technology is there, but "it can also be used to catch people in society, to control their actions. This was a propaganda tool to legitimize public spending in this area." The government got its surveillance tool, and it got closer ties with China—Xi Jinping even visited Quito's ECU911 center in 2016—while China got market access and a showpiece that it can use to promote its wares to other nervous leaders in the region.

Pazmino is equally cynical about Lenín Moreno, Correa's successor. "He can say he's suspending" the use of ECU911 by domestic intelligence, he said, "but the technological capacity is still there. He can also say he has suspended it and then not do it. And the intelligence chief has autonomy. He can say, 'We need to know what this guy is doing in Ecuador'"—he pointed to me—"and the president would never know." This is true of surveillance technology more broadly. One political leader can order it built with benevolent intent, and another can use it malevolently. It echoes Matt Cagle's concerns about building facial-recognition databases: even if the police chiefs who set them up do so with the best intentions, and are scrupulous about using them only in the limited, lead-seeking way they publicly promised, that capacity is still there for a less scrupulous successor to abuse. This highlights the need for strict, enforceable rules around the use of such systems as well as regular audits to ensure that those rules are followed and there are penalties for those who violate them.

I don't think I was followed or spied on while in Ecuador. But at the gate of my flight home, a plainclothes policeman approached for what he said was a "standard screening." I didn't see him approach anyone else. He asked how long I had been in Ecuador and what the purpose of my visit was. I said something bland, and after a cursory flip through my passport, he left. It may indeed have just been a standard screening. But surveillance states thrive on opacity and ambiguity. I returned home safely.

That may not have been true had I tried to report this story from China. Its surveillance state is of a different order from Ecuador's: larger, less covert, more brutal, and aimed less at monitoring, responding, and deterring than at repressing and controlling. I had considered trying to get into Xinjiang, but people far more familiar with China than I dissuaded me. Getting a visa to do real, independent reporting from Xinjiang would have been difficult, if not impossible. I speak little Chinese, and I have no sources in China. If I had actually managed to bluff my way there, ordinary Uyghurs would have probably ignored me—or, if they had spoken to me, even in passing, they quite possibly may have found themselves detained for questioning. Ultimately, I decided that the risks—to them and to me—outweighed any benefit I might have obtained from a week or two on the ground. For that reason, in the following section I rely on the work of others, whom I credit where possible.

For centuries, the region of Xinjiang, in China's far west, was a Silk Road hub. Here, cultures and empires met, fought, and traded. An old Chinese proverb, "The mountains are high, and the emperor far away," suits the region perfectly: peripheral for centuries, it resisted state control. Though Chinese rulers long considered it a backwater, it has become increasingly important to China's Belt-and-Road ambitions—an initiative to partner with different countries in trade and infrastructure projects. It is rich in resources and strategically located—it borders eight countries.

Before 1949, Xinjiang was divided between the Soviet-backed East Turkestan Republic in the province's northwestern corner and Kuomintang rule everywhere else. Chiang Kai-shek's Kuomintang, the Nationalist Party, was defeated by Mao Zedong in 1949, and China subsumed the region. Until recently, the population was overwhelmingly made up of Uyghur Muslims. The members of this ethnic group, culturally and linguistically Turkic, have more in common with the populations of the rest of Central Asia and Greater Persia than with Han Chinese.

But a concerted effort to encourage Han migration westward has cut their share markedly. Precise figures vary. According to Amnesty International, as of the autumn of 2018, roughly 11.3 million of Xinjiang's 22 million people were Uyghurs. Other sources put the province's Uyghur population at a slim plurality rather than a majority, making up around 45 percent of the population compared with 40 percent Han (the remainder are a hodge-podge of other ethnic minorities, mostly ethnic Kazakhs). But those numbers understate the extent of Han political and economic dominance.[8]

China's government grew nervous when the Soviet Union collapsed, birthing Uzbekistan, Tajikistan, Kyrgyzstan, Kazakhstan, and Turkmenistan—all newly independent states with Turkic-speaking Muslim majorities. China worried that Uyghurs would begin agitating for their own independence, as indeed many have. Tensions rose throughout the 1990s, a vicious cycle of demonstrations breeding repression breeding resentment breeding demonstrations.

After the attacks of September 11, 2001, China branded the East Turkestan Independence Movement, a tiny militant group with little popular support, a terrorist group. In 2013 and 2014, a spate of attacks that China's government blamed on Xinjiang separatists killed hundreds. China contends that thousands of Uyghurs went to fight with ISIS in Syria; the United States and Europe have designated the Turkestan Islamic Party, a particularly violent Uyghur separatist group, a terrorist organization. So China's fear of violent separatism is neither paranoid nor entirely without merit, but neither does it justify a crackdown in Xinjiang that is now broader, longer lasting, and more tech-dependent than any previous wave of repression.

In 2016, Chen Quanguo was appointed party secretary in Xinjiang, having served in the same position in Tibet. This makes him the de facto regional leader. Adrian Zenz, an anthropologist who studies China's ethnic policies, argues that Chen has imported to Xinjiang the same policing and control strategy he used in Tibet, known as "grid-control social management."[9]

Chen opened thousands of small concrete-block "convenience police stations" around Tibet. Zenz, writing about Chen's first year in power, reported that 161 of these structures appeared in Lhasa, Tibet's capital, often with no more than half a kilometer between them. By 2016 there were at least 700 of them spread across Tibet's urban and semi-urban centers. Each of these stations keeps tabs on its surrounding square of the city's grid, using whatever technology the government deems helpful.

In Chen's first year in Xinjiang, 7,000 of these stations opened across the province, each staffed, according to Zenz, by between six and thirty security personnel. Needless to say, the region is now heavily policed. Zenz found that in 2010, fewer than 5,000 security-related jobs in Xinjiang were advertised, compared with over 60,000 in just the first eight months of 2017. Between the summers of 2016 and 2017, almost 90,000 new officers were recruited, twelve times as many as in 2009.

A colleague of mine at *The Economist* who spent time in China in 2018 reported that in Hotan, a modestly sized city in southwestern Xinjiang, one of these stations appeared roughly every 300 meters. Meanwhile, poles bristling with eight to ten video cameras were placed on every street at intervals of 100 or 200 meters.[10]

Many of those cameras are equipped with automatic license plate readers and facial recognition. A public security official told my colleague that together they can match drivers' faces to their car registrations, and anyone found driving a car for which they are not the registered owner will be arrested. A report from Radio Free Asia found facial-recognition cameras used even in rural villages; one policeman, in Siyek township, said they use the cameras "to inspect anyone entering the village."[11]

Security services in Xinjiang have a much broader and more intrusive mandate than police in the West. Under a program called "Becoming Kin," Uyghur families "adopt" Chinese officials; the officials visit their "adopted" families regularly, even living with them from time to time, teaching the family Mandarin and bringing gifts for the children. According to a 2018 report cited by my colleague, more than 1 million officials have been placed with 1.6 million local families.

Another initiative of Chen's, the "Uyghur-Chinese One Relative" policy, assigns Han "relatives" to Uyghurs. The government also encourages assimilation through intermarriage, offering 10,000 yuan (around $1,440 in 2018 US dollars) to Uyghur-Han couples who marry. China has banned men from growing "abnormal beards," women from wearing the veil in public, and parents from giving children names it deems too religious, including Muhammad, Arafat, Fatima, and Muslime.

Security services feed information on locals into the Integrated Joint Operations Platform (IJOP), a data-aggregation tool that China's security personnel use to identify people whom they deem potential threats. Human Rights Watch reverse-engineered the IJOP app, which is carried by officials on their smartphones, and found that it helps authorities gather an alarming amount of information: not just names, addresses, and identification numbers, but also ethnicities, blood types, education levels, and political affiliations of people living in Xinjiang; the numbers on their electricity and water meters; whether and why their households might have exhibited an "unusual use of electricity"; whether a person who buys gas for a car is the registered owner; and whether a person has taken suspiciously long trips abroad (and what reasons that person and his or her relatives gave for the travel). Authorities also collect Uyghurs' biometric identifiers, including DNA samples, fingerprints, iris scans, and voice samples.

Human Rights Watch also found that having any one of dozens of apps on one's phone—particularly VPNs and encrypted but common messaging services, such as Viber and WhatsApp—is cause for suspicion, as are a range of other innocuous activities, including "not socializing with neighbors, often avoiding using the front door," and donating to mosques. Fasting during Ramadan, praying regularly, and avoiding alcohol are also potential "signs of extremism."[12]

One Chinese Muslim told the Australian Broadcasting Corporation that having prayer mats or religious books in one's home was often cause for detention.[13] Police keep tabs on people's phones through spyware, which is mandatory to install. Human Rights Watch noted that Chinese authorities describe the networked information provided by IJOP, through both physical and virtual surveillance, as "a series of 'filters' or 'sieves' throughout the region, sifting out undesirable elements."

Once they're filtered out, those "undesirable elements" can end up in one of the numerous reeducation camps that have opened across Xinjiang over the past several years. (Nobody knows precisely how many; estimates range from 27 to 1,200.) Adrian Zenz estimated that as many as 1.5 million people—or around one in six adult Muslims in Xinjiang—are being (or have been) detained in such camps. For the most part, detainees have not been charged with crimes; nor can they challenge their detention. At a party conference in March 2019, a Chinese official said they were "educational training centers . . . like boarding schools where students eat and live for free."[14]

Former detainees have painted a much darker picture—of being forced to stand for hours and chant "Long live Xi Jinping" before being allowed to eat, of sleep and food deprivation as punishment for failing to learn Chinese quickly enough, of beatings and being forced into stress positions.

A Kazakh Muslim woman who escaped the camps told *Haaretz*, an Israeli newspaper, that women in the camps were repeatedly raped. She said that inmates were forced to confess "their sins," which could include failing to know Chinese well enough. They were also, she said, forced to eat pork, beaten with electric truncheons, and forced to sit "on a chair of nails"; some were subjected to forced medical experimentation and abortions. Their families often did not know where they had gone or when they would be released; detainees have said that on their return home, people were often frightened to approach them. Knowing a detainee can increase your chances of becoming one.[15]

And release is no guarantee of a life free of harassment. One Uyghur told Human Rights Watch that after serving several weeks in a detention center for "disturbing social order," he triggered an alarm while trying to enter a shopping mall. Police brought him to the station and told him to stay away from public places. He told them, "I was in a detention center and you guys released me because I was innocent. . . . What do I do now? Just stay home?" He said the police told him, "Yes. That's better than this, right?"

It would be frightening enough if Xinjiang were an isolated case of Chinese repression. It is not; it is just the most extreme incarnation of China's surveillance state. Other facets include the state's social credit system, in which citizens' "trustworthiness"—in essence, their financial and political reliability—is scored and ranked, in much the same way Westerners' financial creditworthiness is scored by private companies. This is not yet a national program, but that seems to be the ambition, and it rests on inputs from numerous sources, including banks; online shopping and browsing habits; activity on WeChat and Weibo, China's instant-messaging services; and, of course, police and court records.

Citizens with low social credit may find it harder to travel outside of China, buy airplane or high-speed rail tickets, or send their children to private schools. Before American readers shake their heads at the remote unfairness of such a system, consider the collateral consequences of a criminal record at home. In the United States, ex-felons, often no matter the crime or how long ago it was committed, may be barred from public housing, voting, welfare benefits, and job training. They may find it harder, for the rest of their lives, to find work—especially work that pays a living wage.

China's surveillance state also includes relentless monitoring of its citizens' online habits and a vast CCTV network. According to a report from the Brookings Institution released in July 2019, more than sixty agencies police Chinese Internet use. The report, "Exporting

Digital Authoritarianism," also noted the Chinese government's desire for constantly monitored public spaces, in order to create an "omnipresent, fully networked, always working and fully controllable" surveillance system (the quote is from a Chinese government commission).[16]

Paul Mozur, a Shanghai-based tech reporter for the *New York Times*, reported that as of July 2018, China had around two hundred million CCTV cameras, around four times as many as the United States.[17] Between the time Mozur wrote that sentence and the time you're reading this one, the government will have probably installed millions more. And while most American cameras are privately owned and monitored, Chinese cameras are overwhelmingly owned by the government. Mozur reported that billboards depict the names, faces, and government ID numbers of jaywalkers and drivers who exceed the speed limit. Police officers wear facial-recognition-enabled glasses. This vast on- and offline surveillance system allows the government to document and retain records of citizens' activity in frighteningly granular detail.

During the Hong Kong protests in the summer of 2019, protesters shielded their faces with umbrellas to evade CCTV tracking. An Italian freelance journalist tweeted remarkable footage of protesters deploying lasers against tracking cameras. Some have cut down lampposts on which they believe facial-recognition-enabled cameras and audio-surveillance equipment were mounted.

At this point, perhaps you're rethinking that hiking vacation in Yunnan, or your planned pilgrimage to see the terracotta soldiers in Xi'an. Perhaps you're telling yourself: I'll be fine if I just stay out of China. But it's not that simple. Huawei, Hikvision, Tiandy, Dahua, and other big surveillance-tech firms do a thriving business selling their goods to nervous companies and governments outside of China.

The Brookings Institution's report details how surveillance tech from Chinese firms gets used in countries across Southeast Asia, sub-Saharan Africa, and Latin America: there are networks of street cameras in Singapore, cameras spy on journalists in Ethiopia, and Venezuela is building a vast database of citizens' activities. Chinese surveillance tech is generally well made, cost competitive, and easy to use, and it's leading to a bristling globe of plug-and-play surveillance states.

So far, the more frightening aspects of China's exported surveillance state have appeared in countries with weak institutions, many of which have a long history of hostility toward civil liberties. Chinese surveillance did not make Ethiopia, for instance, a dangerous place to be an independent journalist; it just ensured that as technology made new forms of communication and data storage available, the state could pick the locks. And it's not as though Ecuador would have been a haven for civil liberties, with strong due-process rights and a reliably independent judiciary, but for Chinese technology.

Western readers may at this point be tempted to sigh with relief. After all, we do not punish people for practicing their faith. We don't tell people what to name their children; we imprison people only after convicting them in open court, not on the dictum of police or a government official; and our jailers do not deny people food if they fail to wish long life to our countries' leaders. The counterintelligence program to illegally surveil and discredit political dissidents during J. Edgar Hoover's years of running the FBI notwithstanding, Western police do not make a habit of harassing and surveilling their bosses' political opponents; nor do they use CCTV cameras to track protesters before sending goons to beat them bloody. By and large, Western institutions are stronger and more resilient than Venezuela's or Ethiopia's, and our governments, while far from perfect, are not nearly as paranoid, control-obsessed, and hostile to the civil liberties of their citizens as China's.

That is false comfort. Chinese technology is not limited to the developing world. Chinese firms make one in every three smartphones in Europe, and they are helping to develop 5G networks across the continent.[18] Hikvision and Dahua cameras dot Pittsburgh's south side. The geopolitical risk there is less that Pittsburgh's mayor is about to start keeping tabs on every yinzer (absent strong usage policies, he could do that with cameras manufactured anywhere); it's that the cameras could well be transmitting data back to the Chinese government without Pittsburgh realizing it.

More importantly, our institutions are only as strong as we make them. They aren't looking all that strong in Europe and the United States these days. If we want to preserve some semblance of privacy in public, if we want to keep our spaces for disobedience alive—if we just want to ensure a future in which our children won't be tracked everywhere they go—then we need to start speaking up and taking a more active role in how we are policed.

10

THE OAKLAND SOLUTION

"We just started showing up."

AMONG THE MORE FRIGHTENING ASPECTS OF CHINA'S SURVEILLANCE state is how feasible and comprehensible it is. Any rich state could replicate it. But it is more an artifact of politics than technology, and it is not inevitable. It had to be imagined, argued for, planned, paid for, constructed, maintained, and expanded. Each of those is at root a political decision, which is why Catherine Crump's question— "What democratic practices do we need to not become China?"—is so crucial. Fortunately, that question has an answer. It begins in Oakland, California, nearly a decade ago.

The lead article in *The Guardian* on June 6, 2013, had the headline "NSA Collecting Phone Records of Millions of Verizon Customers Daily."[1] It revealed that an order from America's Foreign Intelligence Surveillance Court, which operates in secret, had directed Verizon to provide information to the National Security Agency "on an ongoing, daily basis" about all the calls made on its network, both within and outside the United States. Though the calls themselves were neither recorded nor monitored under the court order's terms, the NSA had collected the calls' metadata: which number called which number, when, how long the call lasted, and where the two phones were located at the time of each call.

Further revelations followed over the next few days. The *Washington Post* reported that the NSA and FBI were hoovering up data directly from the servers of nine Internet companies, including Facebook, Google, Yahoo, and Apple.[2] *The Guardian* reported that GCHQ, Britain's version of NSA, was doing the same thing.[3] *The Guardian* reported that Barack Obama ordered senior intelligence officials to come up with an extensive list of overseas targets for cyberattacks.[4]

On June 10, the source of this information gave a public interview. He was a government contractor upset with the sprawl of America's surveillance state. Barack Obama, reelected just months earlier, had "advanced the very policies that I thought would be reined in," he said.[5] The young man's name, of course, was Edward Snowden. He gave the interview in Hong Kong shortly before boarding a plane to Moscow, where he remains to this day.

At that same time, Oakland was worried about the security of its port—one of America's ten biggest. Using some grant money from the Department of Homeland Security, the city created a single monitoring system that wove together disparate sources of information—security cameras, sensors on fences, perimeter detection systems, vehicle management systems, and the like.

Joe DeVries, Oakland's assistant city manager, explained to me in early 2018 that the city then wanted to expand that system: "Someone said, 'Instead of a port awareness center, why don't we make it a whole Domain Awareness Center [DAC], and link up systems throughout the city?'" So the city council unanimously approved spending $2 million of Homeland Security funds on a citywide system to be built by a firm that provided technical and engineering support to various federal agencies, including the Defense Department and the intelligence agencies.[6]

The DAC would have linked together data streams and video feeds from sources across the city: all the feeds at the port, along with around seven hundred cameras in schools; license plate readers mounted on police cars, plus highway cameras; data feeds from the National Weather Service and the federal terrorism task force in Northern California; as well as seismic monitoring, plans from the city's building department, and so on.

At first, nobody batted an eye. City officials saw it as a way to make their network smarter and more efficient. Police could respond instantly to a school shooter. Firemen rushing into a burning building could see where the gas mains were. First responders after a natural disaster could have eyes all over the city. The more city officials knew during an emergency, the better they could direct their resources. "There was this concept," explained DeVries, "that if we kind of wire everything up, and we can see it all, merged in one spot, at the Emergency Operations Center, just think what we could do for public safety."

The council's Public Safety Committee approved the DAC unanimously, and it was slated for approval by the full council on July 16. It followed the usual public process for approval, but as with most local government processes, not many people paid attention. As DeVries noted, "Council meetings are long, agendas can go for several hours, and no one from the advocacy community flagged this for attention."

But then the Snowden revelations broke. Oakland—a community with "activism in its DNA," in DeVries's words—learned that the federal government had been spying on as many people as it could with as little oversight as possible. Suddenly, building a massive, interlinked data system using federal grant money did not seem so benign.

By July 16, many more people than usually care about the intricacies of city government were paying attention. The council meeting was packed. One by one, citizens approached the microphone and voiced perfectly reasonable concerns (except for the guy in a red bandanna, intently wielding a guitar, who sang "Everybody Must Get Droned"; he told the city council members that they were "just pieces of meat with mouths, like those newscasters"). One speaker worried about police militarization. Another wanted to know which other law enforcement agencies would have access to information gathered through the DAC, and bemoaned the lack of guidelines regarding data use and storage.

The protests had their intended effect: the city council put the brakes on. Larry Reid, a twenty-year council veteran, noted, "We can't even get our freakin' phones to work for police officers," so perhaps a sprawling, citywide surveillance network that could track anyone, anywhere, and had no rules yet about what the city did with the data it collected, was a bit too ambitious to simply approve without thinking harder. The council postponed making a decision until the next meeting, two weeks later.

On July 30, more than fifty people signed up to speak at a meeting that lasted long into the night. Their appeals failed: the council approved the DAC 6–0. But they were not entirely unsuccessful: the council vowed not to activate the system until the city came up with privacy guidelines and data-retention policies. So the councilors formed an ad hoc committee to create such policies and guidelines.

Among those who began speaking out against the DAC was Brian Hofer, a good-humored, nimble-minded attorney, originally from rural Northern California but long a resident in Oakland. He was not a gadfly or a serial activist; he was just an ordinary citizen worried about what information such an extensive system could glean, and about the lack of oversight and guidelines on what the city could do with that information.

Those are linked but discrete concerns. The former, which is largely a question of technological capacity, often gets more attention than the latter, thornier concern, which is ultimately more important. A local police force using license plate readers, for instance, can build a complete portrait of a citizen's movements. But if the police store that data on a well-secured server, and discard it after a day for all license plates not involved in a crime, the opportunities for abuse or leaks are far fewer than if they retained that data for as long as they liked, sharing it at will with private firms or other law enforcement agencies.

Hofer began attending meetings of what was then known as the Oakland Privacy Working Group. Activists from the Occupy movement and elsewhere constituted a large share of attendees; Hofer said that many of them assumed he was a cop. It was not a difficult mistake to make: Hofer was probably a good deal older than the average Occupy activist. He has close-cropped hair; a wry, watchful manner; and a lawyerly dress sense.

Hofer proved skillful at navigating city politics and raising public awareness. "We just started showing up and educating the council on the risks of this equipment," Hofer explained. "We really had no privacy policy at all, but with the Snowden revelations we had a spark that ignited enough of the public to be concerned, to come out to City Hall and mobilize against [the DAC]."

Still, the city's plans kept creeping forward. On March 4, 2014, the city council voted to limit the DAC to just the port, and to create a privacy policy for its use. Two months later it announced the creation of a citizen-staffed ad hoc committee to advise on the policy. Brian Hofer led it.

"I'm the lucky guy that got assigned to work with them," said Joe DeVries. DeVries is a wiry, energetic, almost fervently agreeable guy; one can imagine him working equally with anybody. In addition to the activists on the committee, he pulled together representatives from the city's police and fire departments, as well as the city attorney's office, the city clerk's office, the port, and the city's IT department.

"We all got in a room," he remembered, "and everyone screamed and shouted about their fears about the thing. Then we got IT to explain what the thing actually was, because we realized that people didn't really understand what the DAC was. Once we got all that done, the people in the room said, 'Let's look at the privacy policy that the staff wrote.' And [different agencies and others on the committee] said [to each other], 'Well that's pretty good on that note, but you forgot about this.'"

As the parties were working on creating a privacy policy for the DAC, the Port of Oakland quit the project and withdrew funding. That effectively killed it; the DAC exists today as a purely legal entity on paper, but no part of it has been built. Elected officials have shied away from reviving it. The port developed its own, more limited security system.

That means that the DAC's most lasting achievement is not a security system. It is the process of hashing out a privacy policy, which brought parties with opposing views—and probably a relatively high amount of distrust for each other—together to work productively.

Nearly two years later, in early 2016, privacy activists notched a greater victory by pushing the council to pass an ordinance that created a permanent statutory Privacy Advisory Commission. The commission has nine members: one from each of the city's seven city-council districts, one appointed by the mayor, and an at-large member.

The ordinance assigned the Privacy Advisory Commission six tasks. The first was to advise the council on how to protect citizens' rights "in connection with the City's purchase and use of surveillance equipment and other technology that collects or stores citizen data." That wording obviously risks overreach. Copying machines, for instance, usually require employees to enter a code whenever they want to use them. Does the city council really need to debate why Linda from purchasing made 8 percent more copies in October than she did in the previous three months—or why security cameras show that Pete from accounts payable makes 1.7 times more trips to the water cooler per quarter than the average employee?

Yet, by all accounts, Oakland has avoided such pettiness. As Joe DeVries said, the basic idea of the ordinance is to ensure that governments "use the data the way you intended [them] to use it. Tell people how you're going to use it. Have a system to make sure you're using it the way you're supposed to be using it. And have consequences if you don't use it that way."

Second, the advisory commission drafts model legislation "relevant to privacy and data protection." In that goal the commissioners have had help from the American Civil Liberties Union. Soon after the commission was created, the ACLU came out with its Community Control Over Police Surveillance (CCOPS) initiative, which has as its principal goal encouraging local communities to oversee police use of surveillance technology.[7]

As of early 2020, more than thirty cities and counties had passed or were working on CCOPS legislation derived from a model bill created by the ACLU. The bill is thoughtful, detailed, and maximal; at root, it is designed to ensure that citizens, rather than police, have the final say over the type of technology the police use and how they use it. It calls for city councils to approve the purchase, acquisition, and deployment of any military or surveillance technology by any city agency. Usually, that will be municipal police forces, but it can also be fire departments (sensors and cameras to detect fires at landfills, for instance) or municipal transit services (which often install cameras on buses and trains and use data to record and track commuting and travel patterns).

Third, it mandates that agencies create usage policies for their technology, regularly report on how they adhere to those policies, and make those reports public. That need not mean that agencies are left without the tools they need, or required to seek approval every time they want to deploy any sort of technology. Oakland, for instance, has an "exigent circumstances" exception that has allowed the police department to quickly deploy drones—for example, to find someone suspected of shooting at a police officer—and to deploy them for large public events, such as a victory parade for the city's basketball team, the Golden State Warriors, which drew about a million people onto city streets in one afternoon.

So police departments can use whatever technology they need to use, when they need to use it; they just have to report what they used, as well as why and how, soon afterward. This exemption obviously creates an immense loophole in usage policies. But without it, departments would be hamstrung—and probably more reluctant to agree to worthwhile oversight. My feeling is that it's better to have agency buy-in with this loophole than to have no agreement at all. It is open to being abused, of course, but regular audits should mitigate persistent or systemic abuse.

The model bill makes misusing surveillance equipment a misdemeanor punishable by a $2,500 fine and/or six months' imprisonment. That plank, said DeVries, proved unacceptable to police unions. "I had to go to the labor unions and say, 'Look, guys, the goal is not to punish you. It's to make sure there are consequences and people take this seriously.' Then I had to go back to the privacy commission, and say, 'Guys, you can't tell every employee that they can go to jail for doing their job if they fail to file a report on a piece of surveillance tech.'"

That almost scuttled the deal. Activists felt, rightly, that without an effective enforcement mechanism ensuring consequences for failing to follow the rules, the privacy ordinance would have been hollow. But police and other city employees, also rightly, were worried that they could be fined or sent to jail for an innocent mistake. Eventually,

Oakland settled on a set of progressive penalties that started with extra training for the first violation and increased from there, up to suspension for repeated violations. Although violating a city ordinance is technically a misdemeanor, the ordinance did not mention criminal penalties.

That process may have left people on both sides feeling slighted. A police officer warned DeVries that passing the privacy ordinance would cause the murder rate to spike. Some activists no doubt wanted more serious penalties and enforcement, and some city employees no doubt wanted none at all. But crafting effective legislation is a process of compromise. At its best, this process acknowledges the fringes and ensures that they are heard—and that they feel heard—but does not cede the debate to them.

The commission's last four responsibilities are administrative. It must conduct hearings and make recommendations to the city council; keep abreast of and make recommendations to the city council about other federal, state, and local legislation dealing with surveillance technology; submit annual reports detailing how the city has used surveillance technology in the past year, and, in light of such use, whether the city needs to amend its usage and data-retention policies; and, in an elegant nod to its now vestigial origins, review and make recommendations to the council about any proposed changes to the DAC.

The commission began its work by crafting usage policies for technology that the police already had: bodycams, Stingrays, and the like. That work is still ongoing. For every tool or piece of technology the city uses that collects and stores citizen data, the commission's job is to ask the agency using it basic but essential questions: What is this technology used for? Why is it necessary? What data does it gather? How long do you store it? Who has access to the server where it's stored?

When I first heard about this process, I expected to find an antagonistic relationship between the commission and the police. I found the opposite. Tim Birch, then the Oakland Police Department's liaison to the commission, said that working with the commission "encourages us to think about what technology is really needed."[8]

Thinking through usage policies and making them public before implementing a new type of technology has two benefits. First, it promotes transparency, which boosts public confidence in the police. The Oakland commission holds the police accountable—and not just to the mayor or elected officials, as is the case in many other cities, but to the citizens who are on the commission.

Oakland's citizenry has historically had a rocky relationship with law enforcement. Bobby Seale and Huey Newton founded the Black Panther Party in Oakland in 1966—in large part because, as one point of the party's Ten Point Program explained, "We believe we can end police brutality in our Black community by organizing Black self-defense groups that are dedicated to defending our Black community from racist police oppression and brutality."

The FBI had a counterintelligence program (COINTELPRO) from 1956 to 1971 that involved clandestine, often illegal surveillance and infiltration of activist groups. The groups surveilled were the ones whose politics J. Edgar Hoover, the FBI director, happened to dislike—and he zealously targeted the Black Panther Party, with harassment, intimidation, and worse. Forged letters sent by the FBI fomented battles between the Black Panthers and another organization in California that left four Panthers dead. Fred Hampton, the leader of the Panthers in Chicago, was shot dead during an FBI raid on his house.

To many Oaklanders—even those born long after the Panthers' heyday—COINTELPRO remains living history and an object lesson in what law enforcement is capable of without adequate oversight. On a long ride through the East Bay, my Uber driver—a visual artist who could not have been more than thirty years old—gave me chapter and verse on how the legacy of COINTELPRO continues to poison relations between Oakland's citizenry and police. Raymundo Jacquez III, the youngest member of the Privacy Advisory Commission (he graduated law school in 2014) cited COINTELPRO as one of the reasons he joined the commission.

Another member of the commission, Robert Oliver, spent eight years as an Oakland police officer and several more in the army. He also majored in computer science with a minor in math at Grambling

State University. His wife is still an Oakland police officer. If you lab-designed the perfect person to work in city government at the cross-section of technology and policing, you would have a hard time doing better than Oliver.

Oliver spoke proudly of his time on the force, even though, as he explained, "as a black man, you get one of two positions from your community when you're actually trying to police your community. Either you're too blue for your community, or you're too black for the badge. I never felt I had to pick. I'm from this community, I've policed this community. I've arrested high school friends. I've arrested relatives. I did that for eight years. My children were born here in Oakland. I attend church in Oakland, I shop in Oakland. I don't have to worry about anyone coming to get me or my wife, or having any ill feelings toward me, because I was able to play it straight across the board.

"I have friends, I went one way and they went another way. Going in the academy I had friends in that life. They said, 'Look Rob, you're going to do this police thing, we understand. All we ask is be fair about it. Write what is right. Don't make up stuff and use your badge and be dirty with it. Don't come break up the dice game and steal all the money. Don't bust someone for narcotics and only one-quarter of the money shows up in evidence.'"

To Oliver, doing his job honestly and honorably was one way to help build trust between police and the policed. It's not transparency on a citywide scale, like the Privacy Advisory Commission, but on an intimate level, building trust person by person, interaction by interaction. Such trust is hard to come by. Oakland, Oliver explained, "is the home of the Panthers, of COINTELPRO. Now, that stuff has some years on it, but it's still very fresh in the minds of a lot of people. Trust and police don't go in the same sentence anywhere, unfortunately. I'm not saying it always needs to be like that, but that's the current state of affairs right now."

To Oliver, the commission not only keeps city agencies honest, but also helps to ensure equity for the city's residents. Like the rest of us, they generate usable data as they go about their daily lives, through their cellphone trails, their shopping habits, and their transit patterns. "The general problem we have as a city," he believes, "is that we're still dealing with too many third-party entities. . . . If the private sector figured out a way to monetize [consumer data], so can we. . . . If we have all of these mountains of data, maybe the city should look at whose data it is. If it's the taxpayer, and I'm giving away all of this data for free, it would be good if something came back to me. You can't just leave it to private industry; they'll take the lion's share and leave just a small amount for the rest of us."

Oliver's main concern about surveillance technology—the risk of private-sector profiteering at the expense of locals—may not be the main concern of the other eight commissioners. But after everything we have learned about how social media companies use and monetize our data without our fully informed consent, and how often and easily data storage has been breached at private companies, some skepticism about the private sector's civic-mindedness when it comes to consumer data is more than warranted.

Similarly, not everyone on the commission in Oakland may be as well informed about COINTELPRO as Robert Oliver and Raymundo Jacquez. Not everyone may have the same concerns. A nine-member body allows for a diverse range of viewpoints, which makes it likelier that Oaklanders will find their own views and concerns represented by someone on the commission.

Now, obviously, if police-community relations have been sour for decades, one municipal advisory body will not fix them overnight. But overnight fixes to complex problems do not exist anywhere, ever. Improving police-community relations takes years of grinding, incremental progress, with inevitable setbacks and suspicion. But by institutionalizing a place for that sort of work to happen, and for citizens to have their voices heard, Oakland lessens the risk of collapse, and it lessens the risk that extreme voices on either side—people who want the police to function without oversight, and others who do not want the police to function at all—will hijack and sabotage the process.

Another benefit of a governmental body that compels city agencies to think through technology before they use it is that it lessens the chances that those agencies will waste money on cool-looking gadgets that they do not need. For the most part, explained Andrew

Ferguson, a law professor at the University of the District of Columbia and author of *The Rise of Big Data Policing*, police departments do not decide what tech they lack and then set out to find it. "It's not about chiefs sitting around strategizing," Ferguson told me. "It's tech companies selling them cool stuff, and then charging departments for storage. Or [predictive-policing firms] saying we can help you solve more crimes with our cool tech. This all takes place in the procurement process: companies give police departments 'free tech' to solve problems, but they don't realize they're the product"—because by using the product they provide the data on which these companies depend.

Joe DeVries would agree. "We had these guys try to sell us these wacky cameras that you put on top of streetlights," he said. "They said, 'You let us put these up all over the city and you'll have free Wi-Fi everywhere. And better cell service. And we can see a flea sneeze and it has a listening device so we can hear it.' I said, 'Why would we want that on every pole in the city?' 'Well, free Internet.' No. It's not free. There's a cost."

One of DeVries's colleagues who was sitting in on our conversation chimed in: "People have discovered that government is a great sector for technology. It's big business, and government technologists have often not been very savvy. So government agencies have made decisions about handing over massive contracts to vendors without really understanding what they're buying or how to use it."

As a result, data collected by public agencies can end up in the hands of private companies. That is not an inherently bad thing, provided government agencies negotiate the right data-retention, sharing, and access policies. But public agencies operate for public benefit, whereas private firms operate to maximize profit. That is as it should be; there is nothing wrong with profit or success. But that is not the same thing as providing a public service. People should have the right to know who is using and buying their data.

Vendors, warned Dave Maass of the Electronic Frontier Foundation, can exert a surprisingly large influence over how police departments operate. Companies "make their products free to agencies to get them hooked, or get them so bought in they can't live without them," he told me. "[Agencies] sign contracts that give [companies] control over certain arrangements: we'll give you these things free or at a discount, but you have to prove you made this many stops, or provide us with details so we can use them in our marketing details.

"In other contracts, agencies are prevented from saying anything bad about the company without written permission. So officers can't talk about tech not working. Agencies can't reveal anything without permission. . . . You can't give interviews to the press about the tech. I've done public-records requests—things have been redacted to comply. That's not how the law works."

Making sure police think about what tech they want to use and how they want to use it before they take it out of the box (or even agree to accept the box) lessens the odds that they will find themselves taken advantage of by a vendor whose goals they do not share.

Brian Hofer has a blunter assessment of the Privacy Advisory Commission's main advantage: "The police are aware that they have to behave differently because somebody is watching." But he is not a Luddite, or anti-police; nor does he view his job as simply saying no. In fact, the commission has never recommended that the city council block the police from acquiring the technology they say they need. That stems not from acquiescence, but from the presence of a governmental body that promotes police forethought. "Technology itself isn't good or bad," explained Hofer, "as long as they tighten up their usage policies."

That doesn't mean that the commissioners and the police end each hearing by singing "Kumbaya" or going out for beers together. No doubt there are plenty of officers who roll their eyes at the sort of nosy questions the commission asks—just as there are probably plenty of privacy activists who take a reflexively dim view of the police, both in practice and as an institution.

But a functional privacy commission keeps those views on the margin. "What was beautiful" about creating the commission, said DeVries, "was that when you got the police personnel and the emergency responders and the fire personnel and the port security expert in the room with the ACLU attorney, and the Electronic Frontier Foundation advocate, and the average Oakland resident who just cares, and you talked it out, you suddenly realize it wasn't really that hard to come up with a policy that everyone could agree to, that would neither infringe on our civil liberties nor impede public safety response. And there it is. You don't really need to have a tradeoff.

"There could be all the rhetoric from law enforcement and emergency responders: 'Don't get in our way or lives will be lost.' And you can have all the rhetoric from the advocates that say anything you do is going to strip people of their rights, but when you take that rhetoric away and actually boil it down to the functionality of the machinery, it's just like, 'Come on, guys. We can get on the same page here.' And we did."

◉

Oakland's model—an advisory commission attached to the city council that holds hearings, keeps abreast of relevant state and federal legislation, and provides annual reports—is far from the only one available to citizens who want to help their local governments take a more active role in protecting their data. The same system will not work everywhere. Oakland has a mix of characteristics—a deep-seated suspicion of law enforcement, a history of activist politics, and a tech-savvy populace—that exist in few places off the West Coast.

But at least seventeen states, cities, and counties have chief privacy officers, including solidly Republican states, such as West Virginia, Tennessee, and Arkansas, as well as Maricopa County, Arizona—home of the disgraced (and, unfortunately, pardoned) sheriff Joe Arpaio. Their precise duties vary, but broadly, they ensure that state agencies protect their citizens' private data.

One suspects that at least some states created these roles not in response to public outcry, as Oakland did, but out of liability concerns (data breaches, as the private sector has learned, can lead to hefty lawsuits). That is not a reason to denigrate or dismiss them, but only to note that their existence does not obviate the need for bodies like Oakland's Privacy Advisory Commission.

Just as the ACLU created a blueprint for surveillance ordinances with its CCOPS legislation, Brian Hofer and his colleagues created a blueprint for durable, effective citizen engagement. The grinding,

unglamorous work of attending public hearings and poring over police reports may be less emotionally satisfying than marching and
shouting slogans. But if your goal is building trust between police
and the policed, and ensuring effective citizen oversight over those
whom taxpayers pay and empower to use force in their name, it is
also more effective.

CONCLUSION

The case for optimism

————————

BACK IN NEWARK, THE DAY'S GOLDEN LIGHT HAS STARTED TO FADE. IT'S not yet nighttime, but the shadows are going from long and loping to ghostly and street-lit. The scene that Shotspotter directed us to has petered out: no victim, nobody running, no shell casings.

Maybe Shotspotter mistook the sound. Maybe the shooter wasn't in the cemetery. Maybe he was a bad enough shot to miss seven times, smart enough to pick up the casings, fast enough to run away, and savvy enough to know how to elude the police. Maybe someone was firing into the air. Maybe he was driving past and firing erratically from his car, in which case nobody would be hit, and the casings would have ejected back into the car.

After another few minutes of scanning the area and talking to other officers doing the same, we roll out as we arrived, with Leo Carrillo driving, me in the passenger seat, and Mark DiIonno in back. Along the side streets people are hanging out, laughing, flirting. A few minutes later we're at a stop sign. The car windows are open; it's a beautiful early-summer evening.

Leo and Mark are trading Newark war stories. They talk about a young girl who was shot taking out the trash on Christmas morning, and I'm briefly lost in thought when I hear two pops from Leo's side of the car. The sound is unmistakable.

Leo again shifts, in an instant, from a smiling, expansive raconteur to a bloodhound catching a scent. He flips the radio to the precinct channel, checks the dispatch computer on his dashboard, and starts talking about where we heard the shots, how far, what's the best way to get there. I've been on a lot of ride-alongs, but never one on which I heard nine bullets fired in two separate shootings in the space of thirty minutes. If you're a police officer reading this, I know it makes me sound breathless and green, but I didn't grow up around guns. Aside from an occasional visit to a range with a friend (I enjoy shooting but don't own any firearms), guns play no part in my life. Hearing gunshots and not knowing where they came from is unnerving.

Shotspotter has picked nothing up (its coverage extends across some but not all of Newark), so Leo estimates where the shots might have been fired. We drive in that direction, up and down side streets for a while, but see nothing amiss. No calls for service come in. We turn back onto a broad street, quiet in the early evening—a lull in activity between the workday and the coming night.

As we're heading back to the precinct house, a man in a black cap, sweats, and a black tank top flags us down. "She's on something, I think; she's about to fall over."

He points down the side street behind him. A woman pirouettes and lists dangerously down the middle of the street, across the double yellow line. She wears a fuchsia jumpsuit, mismatched socks, and flip-flops; a round belly protrudes beneath her top. We pull to a stop. Leo gets out and walks over to her, his demeanor gentle and smiling, and asks her name. She keeps saying, "I'm all right, I'm all right." Then she stumbles.

"I know you are, but just come on over to the side of the street with me," he tells her. "You're going to be okay." Gently, he helps her to a seat on the curb. A passing black SUV slows, and the young man with cornrows behind the wheel asks if she's okay.

"You know her family?" Leo asks. The young man nods. "Please can I ask you a favor? You mind asking some of them to come over here?"

He nods again.

The woman in the jumpsuit falls suddenly on her side, her eyes closed. I wonder if she might be drunk, but I can't smell any alcohol. If she's high, this is different: she hadn't really been slurring her speech; she was just awake and erratic one minute, out the next. Leo calls for an ambulance.

A teenage girl in a gray T-shirt and black sweats arrives. Leo asks if she knows the woman.

"She's kind of like my aunt," the girl says. She tells us the woman's name. It was distinctive enough that I don't want to cause her any embarrassment by repeating it here. Let's call her Jane.

The girl in gray says that twenty minutes ago, Jane had given her a hug and told her that she loved her. She had seemed fine.

Leo asks if she's been like this before. The girl shrugs and looks down—a tacit admission.

Other family members and friends steadily arrive. A wiry, emphatic older woman in braids and a ballcap is especially distraught: apparently, this is not unusual for Jane.

Others call her name, ask how long she's been here, whether they should call for an ambulance—Leo tells her one is on its way; he called for it right when he arrived.

He asks the woman in the pink jumpsuit her name again; she groans a response. She is breathing heavily and regularly, her eyes closed.

Another police car arrives; handshakes and appraisals follow.

One of Jane's younger relatives, a whip-thin woman with long, tight dreads, a sharp and multiply-pierced nose, and extraordinary, appraising eyes, is dressed for a night out. She walks, stands, moves with leonine grace and economy. She lights up when she catches sight of one of the arriving cops. She has seen him around. "How you get everywhere so quickly?" she asks. "They thinking of making you Cop of the Year?"

He tries to hold her gaze—a formidable challenge—then smiles shyly. "I wish," he says.

Leo leans over and talks to the other cop briefly, then claps him on the shoulder and walks back toward us.

The ambulance is bringing a body to the morgue, he tells us, and that's probably why it hasn't gotten here yet.

From the dozen or so family members and friends crowded around Jane, looking at her with concern and frustration, a consensus emerges: she smoked "wet"—a joint dipped into formaldehyde or embalming fluid laced with PCP.

I mention this a couple of days later to a friend from another force who has worked a lot of drug cases. He says Jane's reaction is typical. The effects are immediate but very brief. Sometimes, he says, people get "stuck"—they pause in the middle of some routine physical task, unable to move: standing for minutes in the middle of the street with one foot raised midstride, pausing in conversation in the middle of a word. Sometimes they're just dead to the world. They don't react to pain, he tells me, and appear not to remember being high after they come down.

The ambulance arrives. One of the EMTs gets out, his eyebrows raised, and subtly, quickly, moves his hand across his throat. Leo says no, she's breathing. Just after he says that, she manages to sit up. Her eyes scan the crowd. Some of those standing in the loose semicircle around her smile, others glare and shake their heads.

The EMTs put her on a stretcher—really, they just lead her to the stretcher; she can walk by now—and load her into the back. The other units disperse, with one staying to direct traffic and tidy up. We climb back into the cruiser and take off.

◉

This is the essence of what policing should be: taking care of those in need, with the help and goodwill of the community. The advanced technologies that I've discussed in this book played no part in the interaction—not even to guide us to the scene.

At the heart of policing is talking, watching, persuading. At the Compstat meeting, Mark introduced me to a senior officer, one of the crime-unit heads, a fireplug of a guy in a gray suit. Mark told him why I was there and what my book was about.

Unprompted, the officer took a half-step closer to me. "I don't care what it is," he said, his finger wagging. "Technology can never replace boots on the ground." Over the time I spent reporting this book, I heard statements like that often—from cops, of course, but also from other people. They used different phrasing, but they agreed on one thing: technology can assume some responsibilities that were once the exclusive domain of humans, but for the foreseeable future, policing will remain a deeply human endeavor.

Around five years before that summer night, back in 2014, Newark's police department entered into a consent decree with the federal government. It wasn't the first department to do so, and—although Donald Trump's first attorney general, Jeff Sessions, strictly limited their use—it won't be the last.

Consent decrees are agreements between two parties to resolve a lawsuit without a formal admission of guilt. Local police departments may enter into consent decrees after the Justice Department sues them for violating the law—the phrase is usually "a pattern and practice of unconstitutional policing." The department being sued and the Justice Department come up with a set of reforms, and a monitor appointed by the court makes sure those reforms are implemented.

In essence, a consent decree lets a police department rethink, and change, its habits and behaviors. Some departments struggle with the changes. Others seize the opportunity to, in effect, rewrite the rules of the relationship between police and policed. When that happens, both the department and the city they police tend to emerge better for it.

Collectively, the technologies that I have discussed in this book offer the same opportunity to rethink how the police and the communities they police relate to each other. As the widespread protests following George Floyd's killing in 2020 showed, this relationship has broken down in too many cities. There are exceptions, of course—but in communities across America and the world, mutual contempt and mistrust have been allowed to fester. That must end. In cities where police forces have successfully come through a consent decree, such as Los Angeles and Seattle, police are more effective, crime is lower, and the relationship between police and the policed is better. That's because police were given the chance to reassess long-standing habits and practices. The process of publicly justifying and assessing the use of new technology provides much the same opportunity: citizens talk while police listen; police talk while citizens listen. Through that process comes mutual respect, understanding, and negotiation—through that process, democracy is renewed.

Eventually, many of the technologies I've discussed will find their way into regular use. Some places will hold out longer than others, but facial recognition will get better, and bodycams will eventually be as standard a piece of police equipment as a flashlight and gun. Some degree of algorithmic processing and decision-making seems inevitable, given how much data we generate. But because they pose an unprecedented risk to our civil liberties and privacy, we cannot passively accept them, as we have done too often with previous technologies.

This is not because the police are bad people who just want to monitor and control everyone all the time. They are not; they do a hard, dangerous, necessary job. Most of them, in my experience, do this job because they feel compelled to. They are their brothers' keepers, and they genuinely care about public safety. But that doesn't mean they should be free of any civilian oversight.

All of us, as citizens of liberal democracies that we want to keep free and open, must speak up. The use of surveillance technologies may be inevitable, but the terms of their use should be ours to determine. We need to do what those citizens in Oakland did in 2014: we need to show up at city council meetings, start asking questions, and not stop until the answers satisfy us.

What happens when we do that—when we compel police departments to think about and justify how they use technology? Well, those initial conversations might be uncomfortable, especially in places with little or no functional civilian oversight of police. But the alternative is to permit the state to gather and hold vast amounts of information about us, all the time, when we've never been convicted or even suspected of any crime, with minimal rules and oversight. That is unacceptable; that way China lies.

But after those first awkward encounters—after the police understand that citizens concerned about privacy aren't anti-police radicals, just ordinary people out to safeguard everyone's civil liberties, including, of course, those of off-duty and retired police officers; and the citizens understand that police, for the most part, aren't interested in using technology to surveil and build databases on innocent citizens, and that they, too, share many of the citizens' concerns—I'm willing to bet that the conversation grows steadily more productive. As that happens, relations between the police and policed improve. Perhaps not immediately, but real change is rarely immediate. Good things happen when opposing sides listen to and learn from each other.

I know that in today's polarized environment, that sort of sentiment elicits eye rolls, but better policy through mutual understanding is a goal worth pursuing. Not every community will come up with the same set of rules; nor should they. Not every community has the same history or concerns. But citizens, police, and elected officials in every community, working together, can come up with a set of policies that suit its needs. Tailored guidelines are needed, developed with citizen participation.

Perhaps people want to live in a world in which facial-recognition-enabled cameras and voice-activated microphones are everywhere, transmitting everything they record to the police. If they do not—if we do not—then we must speak up: forcefully, and now.

ACKNOWLEDGMENTS

THIS BOOK BEGAN AS A SERIES OF ARTICLES PUBLISHED IN *THE ECONOMIST* in May 2018. I am grateful to Zanny Minton Beddoes for assigning them to me, for her permission to repurpose my research and writing for this book, and for her consistently sound editorial judgment.

Oliver Morton edited that series, and I am deeply indebted to his patience and imagination. His perceptive questions shaped my initial series, and his enthusiasm for the subject made me feel it was important and engaging enough to merit a book. He also championed the graphic short story that ran alongside my initial series, which Simon Myers illustrated brilliantly. In addition to showing how these technologies might work in practice, collaborating with Simon, Oliver, and Rob Gifford, who ably shepherded my series through the editing and production process, was tremendously rewarding.

The Economist has been my home for the past seventeen years—with many more to come, I hope. It is a dream job: to grapple with the world on its own terms, week after week, trying to make sense of it as best we can. To say that it is the people—my colleagues—who make my work so meaningful, enjoyable, and rewarding is in this case not a truism; it is just true. I am grateful to you all.

Special thanks are due to Robert Guest and the late Peter David for encouraging me, more than a decade ago now, to return to beat reporting, my first love as a writer; to John Prideaux for his unflappable good cheer and brilliant editing; to James Astill, Ryan Avent, Rachel Horwood, Idrees Kahloon, Soumaya Keynes, G. Elliott Morris, David Rennie, and Mian Ridge for making the Washington office such a delightful place to work; to Alexandra Suich Bass and Tim Cross for generosity with their insight, and for always being ready to engage and ask the right questions, on the subjects of technology and surveillance; and to Andrew Miller for a steady stream of unturndownably compelling commissions and, more importantly, his steadfast and sustaining friendship.

John Mahaney approached me shortly after my articles were first published and inquired whether I might want to turn them into a book. I am grateful for his interest, counsel, and confidence as well as to the rest of the PublicAffairs team for their dedication and professionalism.

Nick Joseph, *il miglior fabbro*, has been a dear and trusted friend for more than thirty years. His careful reading of an early draft of this book improved it immeasurably, saving me from more errors and solecisms than I would care to admit. Any mistakes that remain are, of course, entirely my fault.

I am immensely grateful to everyone who spoke with me over the course of researching and writing this book and the articles that inspired it—those I have quoted by name, those I haven't, and those I could not. I owe particular thanks to Adam Ghetti, for patiently explaining complex subjects until they penetrated my thick skull; to Dave Maass and his colleagues at the Electronic Frontier Foundation, Matt Cagle and his colleagues at the ACLU, and Clare Garvie and her colleagues at the Center for Privacy and Technology at Georgetown Law, for tirelessly fighting for all of our civil liberties; to Catherine Crump, for asking the question that powered this book; and to Brian Hofer, Raymundo Jacquez, Robert Oliver, and their fellow members of the Oakland Privacy Commission, for reminding us how to be responsible, committed citizens of a democracy.

In addition to showing up at town, city, and county council meetings, I would strongly urge citizens concerned about the issues I discuss in this book to donate to groups who defend our liberties.

In America, that includes the American Civil Liberties Union, the Electronic Frontier Foundation, the Center for Democracy and Technology, the Electronic Privacy Information Center, the Leadership Conference on Civil and Human Rights, and Human Rights Watch—among many others.

Like all citizens of liberal democracies, I owe a great deal to privacy activists, lawyers, and nonprofits dedicated to protecting civil liberties, as well as to law enforcement officers. These groups may—and should—at times be at odds with each other, but they all do essential work, and our societies would be immeasurably poorer without them.

I have dedicated this book to two men whose influence on me has been incalculable. George Krimsky was a renowned journalist, an ardent fighter for press freedoms and freedom of expression, and a world-class storyteller. He was skeptical of power, idealistic, and instinctively devoted to the underdog.

I met him because I married his daughter, which means I also came to know him as a dedicated husband, loving father, doting grandfather, ideal father-in-law, and reliable friend. He has been gone for three years, and yet I've never shaken the sense that I'm collecting stories for him. I still mentally file away comments or anecdotes that I know he'll like. A large share of them make it into print. He always did know the right word.

Sidney Metzger was my mother's father. He was not a writer or journalist; he was an engineer. But he had a quality essential to any journalist: an insatiable, constant curiosity about the world around him—a trait I have tried to emulate and pass on to my children. He was diligent, patient, devoted to his family, and the most honest person I've ever met. I miss him and George terribly, and I hope this book would have made them both proud.

Finally, the burden of this book fell heaviest on my family—on Leo, Zephyr, and especially Alissa, from whom I was often absent, mentally and physically. I cannot begin to express what I owe them, or what they mean to me. Here, too, I am lucky beyond measure.

NOTES

PROLOGUE

1. Kashmir Hill, "The Secretive Company That Might End Privacy as We Know It," *New York Times*, January 18, 2020, www.nytimes.com/2020/01/18/technology/clearview -privacy-facial-recognition.html.

2. Kashmir Hill, "Before Clearview Became a Police Tool, It Was a Secret Plaything of the Rich," *New York Times*, March 5, 2020, www.nytimes.com/2020/03/05/technology /clearview-investors.html.

3. Hill, "Secretive Company."

4. John Fasman, "Data Detectives," *The Economist*, Technology Quarterly: Justice, June 2, 2018.

CHAPTER 1: TECHNOLOGY AND DEMOCRACY

1. Philip Roth, *The Counterlife* (New York: Farrar, Straus and Giroux, 1986), 237.

2. Shotspotter, 2020 Annual Report, available at https://ir.shotspotter.com/annual -reports.

3. It is not unconstitutional for a police officer to stop and frisk someone without probable cause for arrest, provided the officer has reasonable suspicion that a person has committed, is committing, or is about to commit a crime. But, as Judge Shira Scheindlin of the United States District Court for the Southern District of New York explained, in Floyd v. City of New York, 959 F. Supp. 2d 540 (2013), "in practice, the policy encourages the targeting of young black and Hispanic men based on their prevalence in local crime complaints. This is a form of racial profiling," and therefore unconstitutional.

4. Monte Reel, "Secret Cameras Record Baltimore's Every Move from Above," *Bloomberg Businessweek*, August 23, 2016, www.bloomberg.com/features/2016-baltimore -secret-surveillance.

5. Jay Stanley, "Baltimore Aerial Surveillance Program Retained Data Despite 45-Day Privacy Policy Limit," American Civil Liberties Union, October 25, 2016, www.aclu.org/blog/privacy-technology/surveillance-technologies/baltimore-aerial-surveillance-program-retained.

6. Lawfare, a blog focused on thorny national security questions, offers a characteristically outstanding discussion of the third-party doctrine at Michael Bahar, David Cook, Varun Shingari, and Curtis Arnold, "Third-Party Party-Crashing? The Fate of the Third-Party Doctrine," October 19, 2017, www.lawfareblog.com/third-party-party-crashing-fate-third-party-doctrine.

7. ACLU v. USDOJ, Civil Action 19-cv-00920-EMC, filed in United States District Court for the Northern District of California (San Francisco), September 6, 2019.

8. Clare Garvie, Alvaro Bedoya, and Jonathan Frankle, "The Perpetual Line-Up: Unregulated Police Facial Recognition in America," Georgetown Law, Center on Privacy and Technology, October 18, 2016, www.perpetuallineup.org.

9. Jan Ransom and Ashley Southall, "NYPD Detectives Gave a Boy, 12, a Soda. He Landed in a DNA Database," *New York Times*, August 15, 2019, www.nytimes.com/2019/08/15/nyregion/nypd-dna-database.html.

10. From PredPol's primer, www.predpol.com/how-predictive-policing-works.

11. Shotspotter Missions FAQ, www.shotspotter.com/wp-content/uploads/2019/08/Missions-FAQ-External-website-FAQ-9-1-19.pdf.

12. Jacob Snow, "Amazon's Face Recognition Falsely Matched 28 Members of Congress with Mugshots," American Civil Liberties Union, July 26, 2018, www.aclu.org/blog/privacy-technology/surveillance-technologies/amazons-face-recognition-falsely-matched-28.

CHAPTER 2: EXPANDING THE PLATFORM

1. Taylor Tiamoyo Harris, "Everyone Can Now Patrol This City's Streets for Crime. ACLU Says That's a Bad Idea," NJ.com, January 30, 2019, www.nj.com/essex/2018/05/newark_the_world_is_watching_you.html.

2. Bill Budington, "Ring Doorbell App Packed with Third Party Trackers," Electronic Frontier Foundation, January 27, 2020, www.eff.org/deeplinks/2020/01/ring-doorbell-app-packed-third-party-trackers.

3. Alfred Ng, "Amazon's Helping Police Build a Surveillance Network with Ring Doorbells," CNET, June 5, 2019, www.cnet.com/features/amazons-helping-police-build-a-surveillance-network-with-ring-doorbells.

4. Jacob Snow, "Amazon's Disturbing Plan to Add Face Surveillance to Your Front Door," American Civil Liberties Union, December 12, 2018, www.aclu.org/blog/privacy-technology/surveillance-technologies/amazons-disturbing-plan-add-face-surveillance-your.

5. Jerry Ratcliffe, "Video Surveillance of Public Places," Response Guide No. 4, Arizona State University, Center for Problem-Oriented Policing, 2006, https://popcenter.asu.edu/content/video-surveillance-public-places-2.

6. "Automated License Plate Readers: To Better Protect Individuals' Privacy, Law Enforcement Must Increase Its Safeguards for the Data It Collects," California State Auditor, Report 2019-118, February 2020, www.auditor.ca.gov/reports/2019-118/index.html.

7. The ACLU wrote an excellent primer on the NYPD's Muslim surveillance program. See "Factsheet: The NYPD Muslim Surveillance Program," American Civil Liberties Union, n.d., www.aclu.org/other/factsheet-nypd-muslim-surveillance-program.

8. "Privacy Impact Assessment Report for the Utilization of License-Plate Readers," International Association of Chiefs of Police, September 2009, www.theiacp.org/sites/default/files/all/k-m/LPR_Privacy_Impact_Assessment.pdf, 15.

9. Dave Maass and Beryl Lipton, "Data Driven: Explore How Cops Are Collecting and Sharing Our Travel Patterns Using Automated License Plate Readers," Electronic Frontier Foundation, n.d., www.eff.org/pages/automated-license-plate-reader-dataset.

10. "Automatic License Plate Readers," American Civil Liberties Union of New York, n.d., www.nyclu.org/en/automatic-license-plate-readers.

11. "Automated License Plate Readers: State Statutes," National Council of State Legislatures, March 15, 2019, www.ncsl.org/research/telecommunications-and-information-technology/state-statutes-regulating-the-use-of-automated-license-plate-readers-alpr-or-alpr-data.aspx.

12. Kenneth Lipp, "License to Connive: Boston Still Tracks Vehicles, Lies About It, and Leaves Sensitive Resident Data Exposed Online," *Dig Boston*, September 8, 2015, https://digboston.com/license-to-connive-boston-still-tracks-vehicles-lies-about-it-and-leaves-sensitive-resident-data-exposed-online.

13. Zack Whittaker, "Police License Plate Readers Are Still Exposed on the Internet," *Tech Crunch*, January 22, 2019, https://techcrunch.com/2019/01/22/police-alpr-license-plate-readers-accessible-internet.

14. Dave Maass and Beryl Lipton, "EFF and MuckRock Release Records and Data from 200 Law Enforcement Agencies' Automated License Plate Reader Programs," Electronic Frontier Foundation, November 15, 2018; Dave Maass, "EFF and MuckRock Are Filing a Thousand Public Records Requests About ALPR Data Sharing," Electronic Frontier Foundation, February 16, 2018, www.eff.org/deeplinks/2018/02/eff-and-muckrock-are-filing-thousand-public-records-requests-alpr-data-sharing.

15. Vasudha Talla, "Documents Reveal ICE Using Driver Location Data from Local Police for Deportations," American Civil Liberties Union, March 13, 2019, www.aclu.org/blog/immigrants-rights/ice-and-border-patrol-abuses/documents-reveal-ice-using-driver-location-data.

16. Todd C. Frankel, "The Surprising Return of the Repo Man," *Washington Post*, May 15, 2018, www.washingtonpost.com/business/economy/the-surprising-return-of-the-repo-man/2018/05/15/26fcd30e-4d5a-11e8-af46-b1d6dc0d9bfe_story.html.

17. Dave Maass and Jeremy Gillula, "What You Can Learn from Oakland's Raw ALPR Data," Electronic Frontier Foundation, January 21, 2015, www.eff.org/deeplinks/2015/01/what-we-learned-oakland-raw-alpr-data.

18. Jillian B. Carr and Jennifer L. Doleac, "The Geography, Incidence, and Underreporting of Gun Violence: New Evidence Using ShotSpotter Data," Brookings Institution, April 27, 2016, www.brookings.edu/research/the-geography-incidence-and-underreporting-of-gun-violence-new-evidence-using-shotspotter-data.

19. Aaron Karp, "Estimating Global Civilian-Held Firearms Numbers," Small Arms Survey, Briefing Paper, June 2018, www.smallarmssurvey.org/fileadmin/docs/T-Briefing-Papers/SAS-BP-Civilian-Firearms-Numbers.pdf.

20. Matt Drange, "ShotSpotter Alerts Police to Lots of Gunfire, but Produces Few Tangible Results," *Forbes*, November 17, 2016, www.forbes.com/sites/mattdrange/2016/11/17/shotspotter-alerts-police-to-lots-of-gunfire-but-produces-few-tangible-results/#c6dc0e5229ed.

21. "ShotSpotter Frequently Asked Questions," January 2018, www.shotspotter.com/system/content-uploads/SST_FAQ_January_2018.pdf.

CHAPTER 3: WATCHING EACH OTHER

1. Rick Smith, *The End of Killing: How Our Newest Technologies Can Solve Humanity's Oldest Problem* (Vancouver, BC: Page Two Books, 2019).

2. Axon 2019 Annual Report, available at https://investor.axon.com/financials /Annual-Reports-Proxies/default.aspx.

3. "Investigation of the Ferguson Police Department," US Department of Justice, Civil Rights Division, March 4, 2015, www.justice.gov/sites/default/files/opa/press-releases /attachments/2015/03/04/ferguson_police_department_report.pdf.

4. "Body-Worn Camera Program Fact Sheet," US Department of Justice, Bureau of Justice Assistance, n.d., https://bja.ojp.gov/sites/g/files/xyckuh186/files/bwc/pdfs /BWCPIP-Award-Fact-Sheet.pdf.

5. Kimberly Kindy, "Some U.S. Police Departments Dump Body-Camera Programs amid High Costs," *Washington Post*, January 21, 2019; "Body-Worn Cameras (BWCs)," US Department of Justice, Bureau of Justice Assistance, June 26, 2015, https://bja.ojp.gov /program/body-worn-cameras-bwcs/overview.

6. "Cost and Benefits of Body-Worn Camera Deployments," Police Executive Research Forum, April 2018, www.policeforum.org/assets/BWCCostBenefit.pdf.

7. H.R. 7028: DHS Body-Worn Camera Act of 2018, sponsored by Filemon Vela (D-TX) introduced October 2, 2018; Police CAMERA Act of 2019, sponsored by Steve Cohen, (D-TN), introduced January 3, 2019.

8. Vivian Hung, Steven Babin, and Jacqueline Coberly, "A Market Survey on Body Worn Camera Technologies," prepared by the Johns Hopkins Applied Physics Laboratory for the US Department of Justice, National Institute of Justice, 2016, www.ncjrs.gov/pdffiles1 /nij/grants/250381.pdf.

9. Elida S. Perez, "Police Union Pushes Back on Bodycams in El Paso," GovTech, December 11, 2017, www.govtech.com/public-safety/Police-Union-Pushes-Back-on-Body -Cameras-in-El-Paso-Texas.html.

10. Albert Fox Cahn, "How Bodycams Distort Real Life," *New York Times*, August 8, 2019, www.nytimes.com/2019/08/08/opinion/bodycams-privacy.html.

11. Emily Ekins, "Cato/YouGov Poll: 92% Support Police Body Cameras, 55% Willing to Pay More in Taxes to Equip Local Police," Cato at Liberty, January 5, 2016, www.cato .org/blog/catoyougov-poll-92-support-police-body-cameras-55-willing-pay-more-taxes -equip-local-police.

12. Katie Miller, "A Surprising Downside of Bodycams," *Slate*, May 3, 2019, https:// slate.com/technology/2019/05/body-worn-cameras-police-officers-discretion.html.

13. Lindsay Miller, Jessica Toliver, and Police Executive Research Forum, *Implementing a Body-Worn Camera Program: Recommendations and Lessons Learned* (Washington, DC: Office of Community Oriented Policing Services, 2014).

14. Alex S. Vitale, "Baltimore Body Camera Controversy Grows," *The Appeal*, September 19, 2017, https://theappeal.org/baltimore-body-camera-controversy-grows -9244fe2b211e.

15. Lily Hay Newman, "Police Bodycams Can Be Hacked to Doctor Footage," *Wired*, August 11, 2018, www.wired.com/story/police-body-camera-vulnerabilities.

16. Miller et al., *Implementing a Body-Worn Camera Program.*

17. "Cost and Benefits of Body-Worn Camera Deployments."

18. "Police Body-Worn Cameras: A Policy Scorecard," Upturn and the Leadership Conference on Civil Rights, updated November 2017, www.bwcscorecard.org.

19. David Yokum, Anita Ravishankar, and Alexander Coppock, "Evaluating the Effects of Police Body Worn Cameras: A Randomized Controlled Trial," The Lab @ DC, Working Paper, October 20, 2017, https://bwc.thelab.dc.gov/TheLabDC_MPD_BWC_Working _Paper_10.20.17.pdf.

20. Anthony Braga, James R. Coldren Jr., William Sousa, Denise Rodriguez, and Omer Alper, "The Benefits of Body-Worn Cameras: New Findings from a Randomized Controlled Trial at the Las Vegas Metropolitan Police Department," National Institute of Justice Document no. 251416, www.ncjrs.gov/pdffiles1/nij/grants/251416.pdf.

21. Ryan Stokes, Lee Rankin, and Tony Filler, "End-of-Program Evaluation and Recommendations: On-Officer Body Camera System," Mesa Police Department, Arizona, December 3, 2013, www.bwvsg.com/wp-content/uploads/2015/06/On-Officer_Body _Camera_Field_Study.pdf.

22. "Self-Awareness to Being Watched and Socially-Desirable Behavior: A Field Experiment on the Effect of Body Worn Cameras on Police Use-of-Force," National Police Foundation, March 2013, www.policefoundation.org/publication/self-awareness-to -being-watched-and-socially-desirable-behavior-a-field-experiment-on-the-effect-of-body -worn-cameras-on-police-use-of-force.

23. Barak Ariel, Alex Sutherland, Darren Henstock, Josh Young, Paul Drover, Jayne Sykes, Simon Megicks, and Ryan Henderson, "Report: Increases in Police Use of Force in the Presence of Body-Worn Cameras Are Driven by Officer Discretion: A Protocol-Based Subgroup Analysis of Ten Randomized Experiments," *Journal of Experimental Criminology* 12 (2016): 453–463.

24. Jeffrey Bellin and Shevarma Pemberton, "Policing the Admissibility of Body Camera Evidence," *Fordham Law Review* 87, no. 4 (2019): 1428, 1425.

25. Timothy Scott v. Victor Harris, 550 U.S. 372 (2007).

26. Plumhoff v. Rickard, 572 U.S. 765 (2014).

27. Blackston v. Alabama, 30 F.3d 117 (11th Cir. 1994).

28. Smith v. City of Cumming, 212 F.3d 1332 (11th Cir. 2000).

29. Glik v. Cunniffe, 655 F.3d 78 (1st Cir. 2011).

30. Am. Civil Liberties Union of IL v. Alvarez, No. 11-1286 (7th Cir. 2012).

31. Fields v. City of Philadelphia and Geraci v. City of Philadelphia, No. 16-1650 (3d Cir. 2017); Turner v. Driver, No. 16-10312 (5th Cir. 2017).

32. See "ACLU Apps to Record Police Conduct," American Civil Liberties Union, n.d., www.aclu.org/issues/criminal-law-reform/reforming-police/aclu-apps-record-police -conduct.

33. See www.raheem.ai.

34. Pierson v. Ray, 386 U.S. 547 (1967).

35. Jessop v. City of Fresno, 936 F.3d 937 (9th Cir. 2019).

36. Frank Edwards, Hedwig Lee, and Michael Esposito, "Risk of Being Killed by Police Use of Force in the United States by Age, Race-Ethnicity, and Sex," *Proceedings of the National Academy of Sciences of the United States of America*, August 20, 2019, www.pnas.org /content/116/34/16793.

37. "Race and the Drug War," Drug Policy Alliance, n.d., www.drugpolicy.org/issues /race-and-drug-war.

CHAPTER 4: MISSION CREEP

1. Order Compelling Apple, Inc., to Assist Agents in Search, Issued by US Magistrate Judge Sheri Pym, United States District Court for the Central District of California, February 16, 2016, available at US Department of Justice, United States Attorney's Office, Central District of California, www.justice.gov/usao-cdca/file/825001/download.

2. Tim Cook wrote his letter on the same day.

3. "A Special Inquiry Regarding the Accuracy of FBI Statements Concerning Its Capabilities to Exploit an iPhone Seized During the San Bernardino Terror Attack

Investigation," US Department of Justice, Office of the Inspector General, Oversight and Review Division 18-03, March 2018, https://oig.justice.gov/reports/2018/o1803.pdf.

4. Statement issued on March 28, 2016; see Alina Selyukh, "The FBI Has Successfully Unlocked the iPhone Without Apple's Help," NPR, March 28, 2016, www.npr.org/sections/thetwo-way/2016/03/28/472192080/the-fbi-has-successfully-unlocked-the-iphone-without-apples-help.

5. Joseph Bonneau, "A Technical Perspective on the Apple iPhone Case," Electronic Frontier Foundation, February 19, 2016, www.eff.org/deeplinks/2016/02/technical-perspective-apple-iphone-case.

6. Joseph Cox, "Here Are the Terms for Cellebrite's iPhone Unlocking Service," Vice, January 17, 2017, www.vice.com/en_us/article/78kadd/here-are-the-terms-for-cellebrites-iphone-unlocking-service.

7. Riley v. California, 573 U.S. 373 (2014).

8. For a thorough and thoughtful discussion of the border exception, see "The Border Search Muddle," Harvard Law Review, June 1, 2019, https://harvardlawreview.org/2019/06/the-border-search-muddle.

9. For a good explanation of Rigmaiden's case, including the drawings of a then hypothetical Stingray he made from his jail cell, see Rebecca McCray, "From Con Artist to Government Combatant: A Recluse Comes out of Hiding," Takepart, February 4, 2016, www.takepart.com/article/2016/02/04/daniel-rigmaiden-stingray-truth-and-power.

10. Kim Zetter, "U.S. Marshals Seize Cops' Spying Records to Keep Them from the ACLU," Wired, June 3, 2014, www.wired.com/2014/06/feds-seize-stingray-documents.

11. Adam Bates, "Stingrays: A New Frontier in Police Surveillance," Cato Institute, Policy Analysis No. 809, January 25, 2017, www.cato.org/publications/policy-analysis/stingray-new-frontier-police-surveillance.

12. The case was Rudenberg v. Chief Deputy Attorney General of the Delaware Department of Justice, N16A-02-006 RRC (Del. Super. Ct. 2016). For the relevant court filings, see "Rudenberg v. Delaware DOJ," American Civil Liberties Union of Delaware, www.aclu-de.org/en/cases/new-police-spying-documents-obtained-foia-lawsuit.

13. For the discussion that follows, I am especially indebted to Rachel Levinson-Waldman of the Brennan Center and to Dave Maass and Cooper Quinton of the Electronic Frontier Foundation, both for their outstanding work and for their time, patience, and insight; any errors are, of course, mine alone.

14. "Street-Level Surveillance: Cell-Site Simulators/IMSI Catchers," Electronic Frontier Foundation, n.d., www.eff.org/pages/cell-site-simulatorsimsi-catchers.

15. The system is called Seaglass; it's incredibly cool, and I'm grateful to its designer, Peter Ney, for describing it to me.

16. Jose Pagliery, "ICE in New York Has a Spy Tool to Hunt Undocumented Immigrants via Their Cell Phones," Univision, October 17, 2019, www.univision.com/local/nueva-york-wxtv/ice-in-new-york-has-a-spy-tool-to-hunt-undocumented-immigrants-via-their-cell-phones. In a letter dated August 17, 2017, Thomas Homan, then ICE's acting director, told Senator Wyden that ICE only uses Stingrays "in support of criminal investigations requiring judicial process, and not for administrative violations under the Immigration and Nationality Act." See Thomas D. Homan to The Honorable Ron Wyden, August 16, 2017, posted at DocumentCloud.org, https://assets.documentcloud.org/documents/3935329/88437-Signed-Response.pdf.

17. See Alexia Ramirez and Bobby Hodgson, "ICE and CBP Are Secretly Tracking Us Using Stingrays. We're Suing," American Civil Liberties Union, December 11, 2019, www.aclu.org/news/privacy-technology/ice-and-cbp-are-secretly-tracking-us-using-stingrays-were-suing.

18. Details of these cases available at "Street-Level Surveillance: Cell-Site Simulators/IMSI Catchers."

19. Bates, "Stingrays."

20. Policy announced on September 3, 2015.

21. The text of the letter is available at Senator Chuck Grassley's website; see "Leahy and Grassley Press Administration on Use of Cell Phone Tracking Program," December 31, 2014, www.grassley.senate.gov/news/news-releases/leahy-grassley-press-administration-use-cell-phone-tracking-program.

22. United States v. Jones, 565 U.S. 400 (2012).

23. Carpenter v. United States, 585 U.S. ___ (2018).

CHAPTER 5: THE END OF ANONYMITY

1. "Privacy Impact Assessment for the Traveler Verification Service," US Department of Homeland Security, DHS/CBP/PIA-056, November 14, 2018, www.dhs.gov/sites/default/files/publications/privacy-pia-cbp030-tvs-november2018_2.pdf.

2. The Justice Department's Inspector General's Office reviewed the FBI's handling of Mayfield's case. It makes for grim reading. See "A Review of the FBI's Handling of the Brandon Mayfield Case," US Department of Justice, Office of the Inspector General, Oversight and Review Division, March 2006, https://oig.justice.gov/special/s0601/final.pdf.

3. The California Innocence Project takes a dim view of bite-mark evidence, as does a Justice Department report. See "Relevant Cases: William Richards," California Innocence Project, n.d., https://californiainnocenceproject.org/issues-we-face/bite-mark-evidence; Committee on Identifying the Needs of the Forensic Science Community; Committee on Science, Technology, and Law Policy and Global Affairs; Committee on Applied and Theoretical Statistics Division on Engineering and Physical Sciences; and National Research Council of the National Academies, *Strengthening Forensic Science in the United States: A Path Forward* (Washington, DC: National Academies Press, 2009), available at www.ncjrs.gov/pdffiles1/nij/grants/228091.pdf.

4. Statement of Kimberly J. Del Greco before the House Committee on Oversight and Government Reform, March 22, 2017, www.fbi.gov/news/testimony/law-enforcements-use-of-facial-recognition-technology.

5. Matt Wood, "Thoughts on Machine Learning Accuracy," AWS News Blog, July 27, 2018, https://aws.amazon.com/blogs/aws/thoughts-on-machine-learning-accuracy.

6. Joy Buolamwini and Timrit Gebru, "Gender Shades: Intersectional Accuracy Disparities in Commercial Gender Classification," *Proceedings of Machine Learning Research* 81 (2018): 77–91.

7. "Diversity in Faces" dataset, released on January 29, 2019. See John R. Smith, "IBM Research Releases 'Diversity in Faces' Dataset to Advance Study of Fairness in Facial Recognition Systems," IBM, January 29, 2019, www.ibm.com/blogs/research/2019/01/diversity-in-faces.

8. Steve Lohr, "Facial Recognition Is Accurate, If You're a White Guy," *New York Times*, February 9, 2018, www.nytimes.com/2018/02/09/technology/facial-recognition-race-artificial-intelligence.html.

9. Patrick Grother, Mei Ngan, and Kayee Hanaoka, "Ongoing Face Recognition Vendor Test (FRVT). Part 2: Identification," NIST Interagency/Internal Report (NISTIR) 8238, National Institute of Standards and Technology, November 2018, https://nvlpubs.nist.gov/nistpubs/ir/2018/NIST.IR.8238.pdf.

10. Patrick Grother, Mei Ngan, and Kayee Hanaoka, "Face Recognition Vendor Test (FRVT). Part 3: Demographic Effects," NIST Interagency/Internal Report (NISTIR)

8280, National Institute of Standards and Technology, December 2019, https://nvlpubs .nist.gov/nistpubs/ir/2019/NIST.IR.8280.pdf.

11. "Using Facial Recognition Systems," Washington County Sheriff's Office (Oregon), Policy #808-R03, effective January 4, 2019, www.co.washington.or.us/Sheriff/Policies /800/upload/808-R03-FINAL-Using-Facial-Recognition-Systems-01-04-19.pdf.

12. James O'Neill, "How Facial Recognition Makes You Safer," *New York Times*, June 9, 2019; "Patrol Guide," New York City Police Department, March 12, 2020, www1.nyc.gov /assets/nypd/downloads/pdf/nypd-facial-recognition-patrol-guide.pdf.

13. Clare Garvie, "Garbage In, Garbage Out: Facial Recognition on Flawed Data," Georgetown Law, Center on Privacy and Technology, May 16, 2019, www.flawedface data.com.

14. Drew Harwell, "FBI, ICE Find State Driver's License Photos Are a Gold Mine for Facial-Recognition Searches," *Washington Post*, July 7, 2019, www.washington post.com/technology/2019/07/07/fbi-ice-find-state-drivers-license-photos-are-gold -mine-facial-recognition-searches.

15. Drew Harwell and Erin Cox, "ICE Has Run Facial-Recognition Searches on Millions of Maryland Drivers," *Washington Post*, February 26, 2020, www.washington post.com/technology/2020/02/26/ice-has-run-facial-recognition-searches-millions -maryland-drivers.

16. Clare Garvie, Alvaro Bedoya, and Jonathan Frankle, "The Perpetual Line-Up: Un- regulated Police Face Recognition in America," Georgetown Law, Center on Privacy and Technology, October 18, 2016, www.perpetuallineup.org.

17. "In Your Face: China's All-Seeing State," BBC, December 10, 2017, www.bbc.com /news/av/world-asia-china-42248056/in-your-face-china-s-all-seeing-state.

18. Clare Garvie and Laura M. Moy, "America Under Watch: Face Surveillance in the United States," Georgetown Law, Center on Privacy and Technology, May 16, 2019, www.americaunderwatch.com.

19. Dave Gershgorn, "Exclusive: Live Facial-Recognition Is Coming to U.S. Police Body Cameras," OneZero, March 4, 2020, https://onezero.medium.com/exclusive-live -facial-recognition-is-coming-to-u-s-police-body-cameras-bc9036918ae0.

20. Detroit Police Department, Directive 307.5, approved September 12, 2019.

21. Allie Gross and Ross Jones, "New Rules over Facial Recognition Approved, but Distrust and Confusion Remain," WXYZ News, September 20, 2019, www.wxyz .com/news/local-news/investigations/new-rules-over-facial-recognition-approved -but-distrust-and-confusion-remain.

22. Patel v. Facebook, Inc., No. 18-15982 (9th Cir. 2019).

23. Neutral Citation Number: [2019] EWHC 2341 (Admin), Case No.: CO/4085/2018, decided September 4, 2019.

24. Carpenter v. United States, No. 16-402, 585 U.S. ____ (2018).

25. Matt Cagle and Nicole Ozer, "Amazon Teams Up with Government to Deploy Dangerous New Facial Recognition Technology," American Civil Liberties Union, May 22, 2018, www.aclu.org/blog/privacy-technology/surveillance-technologies/amazon -teams-government-deploy-dangerous-new.

26. Michael Punke, "Some Thoughts on Facial Recognition Legislation," AWS Machine Learning Blog, February 7, 2019, https://aws.amazon.com/blogs/machine-learning /some-thoughts-on-facial-recognition-legislation.

27. "First Report of the Axon AI & Policing Technology Ethics Board," June 2019, https://static1.squarespace.com/static/58a33e881b631bc60d4f8b31/t/5d13d7e1990c 4f00014c0aeb/1561581540954/Axon_Ethics_Board_First_Report.pdf.

CHAPTER 6: EYES IN THE SKY

1. Robin Emmott, "Mexico's Ciudad Juarez, the World's Most Violent City?," Reuters, August 28, 2009, http://blogs.reuters.com/global/2009/08/28/violent-ciudad-juarez.

2. "Table 1: Number, Percentage, and Crude Rate of Homicides, by Sex, Race/ Ethnicity, and Age Group—National Vital Statistics System, United States, 2007 and 2009," in Morbidity and Mortality Weekly Report, "Homicides—United States, 2007 and 2009," Centers for Disease Control and Prevention, *Supplements* 62, no. 3 (November 22, 2013), www.cdc.gov/mmwr/preview/mmwrhtml/su6203a28.htm#Tab1; Francesca Mirabile and Daniel Nass, "What's the Homicide Capital of America? Murder Rates in U.S. Cities, Ranked," *The Trace*, October 1, 2019, www.thetrace.org/2018/04/highest-murder-rates-us-cities-list.

3. These biographical details, and much of the discussion that follows, come from my conversation with Ross McNutt.

4. Sarah Ryley, Jeremy Singer-Vine, and Sean Campbell, "Shoot Someone in a Major City, and Odds Are You'll Get Away with It," *The Trace*, January 24, 2019, www.thetrace.org/features/murder-solve-rate-gun-violence-baltimore-shootings.

5. Dan Gettinger, "Public Safety Drones, 3rd ed.," Center for the Study of the Drone at Bard College, March 2020, https://dronecenter.bard.edu/files/2020/03/CSD-Public-Safety-Drones-3rd-Edition-Web.pdf.

6. Federal Aviation Regulations, 14 CFR Part 107—Small Unmanned Aircraft Systems.

7. Florida v. Riley, 488 U.S. 445 (1989).

8. California v. Ciraolo, 476 U.S. 207 (1986).

9. United States v. Causby, 328 U.S. 256 (1946).

10. I attended this conference and saw Frazier's speech.

11. Maria Valdovinos, James Specht, Jennifer Zeunik, "Community Policing & Unmanned Aircraft Systems (UAS): Guidelines to Enhance Community Trust," National Police Foundation and US Department of Justice, Community Oriented Policing Service, 2016, www.policefoundation.org/publication/community-policing-unmanned-aircraft-systems-uas-guidelines-to-enhance-community-trust.

12. "Voluntary Best Practices for UAS Privacy, Transparency and Accountability," National Telecommunications and Information Administration (NTIA), May 18, 2016, www.ntia.doc.gov/files/ntia/publications/uas_privacy_best_practices_6-21-16.pdf.

13. "Drone Laws: Federal, State, and Local Drone Regulations," 911 Security, www.911security.com/learn/airspace-security/drone-laws-rules-and-regulations.

14. Arthur Holland Michel and Dan Gettinger, "Drone Incidents: A Survey of Legal Cases," Center for the Study of the Drone at Bard College, April 2017, https://dronecenter.bard.edu/drone-incidents.

15. Gregory McNeal, "Drones and Aerial Surveillance: Considerations for Legislatures," Brookings Institution, November 2014, www.brookings.edu/research/drones-and-aerial-surveillance-considerations-for-legislatures.

16. Kevin Rector, "Surveillance Company Wants Baltimore to Put Three of Its Planes over the City at Once," *Washington Post*, September 25, 2019, www.washingtonpost.com/local/legal-issues/surveillance-company-wants-baltimore-to-put-three-of-its-planes-over-the-city-at-once/2019/09/25/c8bdf4ae-dbfa-11e9-ac63-3016711543fe_story.html.

17. Louis Krauss, "In Baltimore, Complaints About the Sounds of Surveillance," *Baltimore Brew*, May 13, 2020, https://baltimorebrew.com/2020/05/13/in-baltimore-complaints-about-the-sounds-of-surveillance.

18. Justin Fenton and Talia Richman, "Baltimore Police Back Pilot Program for Surveillance Planes, Reviving Controversial Program," *Baltimore Sun*, December 20, 2019, www.baltimoresun.com/news/crime/bs-md-ci-cr-baltimore-police-support-surveillance

-plane-20191220-zfhd5ndtlbdurlj5xfr6xhoe2i-story.html; Emily Opilo, "ACLU Sues Baltimore Police over Contract for Private Planes to Survey City for Photographic Evidence of Crime," *Baltimore Sun*, April 9, 2020, www.baltimoresun.com/politics/bs-md -ci-baltimore-spy-plane-lawsuit-20200409-owedgyfulfhblgscuyv73ykd7y-story.html.

CHAPTER 7: WIDENING THE NET

1. Wendy Sawyer and Peter Wagner, "Mass Incarceration: The Whole Pie 2020," Prison Policy Initiative, March 24, 2020, www.prisonpolicy.org/reports/pie2020.html.

2. "Why We Need Pretrial Reform," Pretrial Justice Institute, n.d., www.pretrial.org /get-involved/learn-more/why-we-need-pretrial-reform.

3. Kilgord maintains a database of his writing on electronic monitoring. See "Challenging E-Carceration," www.challengingecarceration.org/author/jjincu.

4. Jan Bungerfeldt, "Old and New Uses of Electronic Monitoring in Sweden," Centre for Crime and Justice Studies, 2013, www.crimeandjustice.org.uk/sites/crimeandjustice .org.uk/files/09627251.2014.902193.pdf.

5. Rafael Di Tella and Ernesto Schargrodsky, "Criminal Recidivism After Prison and Electronic Monitoring," *Journal of Political Economy* 121, no. 1 (2013).

6. Told to me by David Feige. See also "Lorelei Laird, "The Bail Project Pays Defendants' Bail as Part of Plan to End Money Bail Entirely," *ABA Journal*, November 1, 2019, www.abajournal.com/magazine/article/the-bail-project-pays-defendants-bail-as-part-of-a -plan-to-end-money-bail-entirely.

7. Brice Cooke, Binta Zahra Diop, Alissa Fishbane, Jonathan Hayes, Aurelie Ouss, and Anuj Shah, "Using Behavioral Science to Improve Criminal Justice Outcomes: Preventing Failures to Appear in Court," University of Chicago Crime Lab, January 2018, www.court housenews.com/wp-content/uploads/2018/01/crim-just-report.pdf.

CHAPTER 8: THE BLACK BOX OF JUSTICE

1. Marie VanNostrand, "New Jersey Jail Population Analysis: Identifying Opportunities to Safely and Responsibly Reduce the Jail Population," Luminosity in Partnership with the Drug Policy Alliance, March 2013, www.drugpolicy.org/sites/default/files/New _Jersey_Jail_Population_Analysis_March_2013.pdf.

2. "The War on Marijuana in Black and White," American Civil Liberties Union, June 2013, www.aclu.org/report/report-war-marijuana-black-and-white.

3. Emma Pierson, Camelia Simoiu, Jan Overgoor, Sam Corbett-Davies, Daniel Jenson, Amy Shoemaker, Vignesh Ramachandran, et al., "A Large-Scale Analysis of Racial Disparities in Police Stops Across the United States," Stanford Computational Policy Lab, March 13, 2019.

4. David Arnold, Will Dobbie, and Crystal S. Yang, "Racial Bias in Bail Decisions," NBER Working Paper 23421, National Bureau of Economics, May 2017.

5. New York State Crime Report, September 2019.

6. George James, "New York Killings Set a Record, While Other Crimes Fell in 1990," *New York Times*, April 23, 1991.

7. "To Restore New York City; First, Reclaim the Streets," *New York Times*, December 30, 1990.

8. Much of what follows comes from "COMPSTAT: Its Origins, Evolution and Future in Law Enforcement Agencies," US Department of Justice, Bureau of Justice Assistance, and the Police Executive Research Forum, 2013, https://bja.ojp.gov/sites/g/files/xyckuh 186/files/Publications/PERF-Compstat.pdf.

9. "Race and the Drug War," Drug Policy Alliance, n.d., www.drugpolicy.org/issues/race-and-drug-war.

10. "Strategic Subject List," Chicago Data Portal, https://data.cityofchicago.org/Public-Safety/Strategic-Subject-List/4aki-r3np.

11. Jeff Asher and Rob Arthur, "Inside the Algorithm That Tries to Predict Gun Violence in Chicago," *New York Times*, June 13, 2017, www.nytimes.com/2017/06/13/upshot/what-an-algorithm-reveals-about-life-on-chicagos-high-risk-list.html; Brianna Posadas, "How Strategic Is Chicago's 'Strategic Subject List'? Upturn Investigates," *Medium*, June 22, 2017, https://medium.com/equal-future/how-strategic-is-chicagos-strategic-subjects-list-upturn-investigates-9e5b4b235a7c.

12. Stephanie Kollman, "An Enormous List of Names Does Nothing to Combat Chicago Crime," *Chicago Sun-Times*, May 16, 2017, https://chicago.suntimes.com/2017/5/16/18321160/an-enormous-list-of-names-does-nothing-to-combat-chicago-crime.

13. Yana Kunichoff and Patrick Sier, "The Contradictions of Chicago Police's Secretive List," *Chicago*, August 21, 2017, www.chicagomag.com/city-life/August-2017/Chicago-Police-Strategic-Subject-List.

14. Jeremy Gormer and Annie Sweeney, "For Years Chicago Police Rated the Risk of Tens of Thousands Being Caught Up in Violence. That Controversial Effort Has Quietly Been Ended," *Chicago Tribune*, January 24, 2020, www.chicagotribune.com/news/criminal-justice/ct-chicago-police-strategic-subject-list-ended-20200125-spn4kjmrxrh4tmktdjck htox4i-story.html.

15. For a good introduction to DMI, see "Drug Market Intervention," National Network for Safe Communities at John Jay College, n.d., https://nnscommunities.org/strategies/drug-market-intervention-2.

16. Jessica Saunders, Priscilla Hunt, and John S. Hollywood, "Predictions Put into Practice: A Quasi-Experimental Evaluation of Chicago's Predictive Policing Pilot," *Journal of Experimental Criminology* 12, no. 3 (2016): 347–371.

17. Julia Dressel and Hany Farid, "The Accuracy, Fairness and Limits of Predicting Recidivism," *Science Advances* 4, no. 1 (2018).

18. Julia Angwin, Jeff Larson, Surya Mattu, and Lauren Kirchner, "Machine Bias," ProPublica, May 23, 2016, www.propublica.org/article/machine-bias-risk-assessments-in-criminal-sentencing.

19. Cynthia Rudin, "Stop Explaining Black Box Machine Learning Models for High Stakes Decisions and Use Interpretable Models Instead," *Nature Machine Intelligence* 1 (2019): 206–215.

20. State v. Loomis, 881 N.W.2d 746 (2016).

21. Kristian Lum and William Isaac, "To Predict and Serve?," Royal Statistical Society, October 7, 2016.

22. Rashida Richardson, Jason Schultz, and Kate Crawford, "Dirty Data, Bad Predictions: How Civil Rights Violations Impact Police Data, Predictive Policing Systems and Justice," *New York University Law Review* 94, no. 192 (2019): 193–233.

23. Sandra G. Mayson, "Bias In, Bias Out," *Yale Law Journal* 128, no. 8 (2019): 2218–2300.

CHAPTER 9: THE CHINA PROBLEM

1. "Intentional Homicide Count and Rate per 100,000 Population, by Country/Territory (2000–2012)," United Nations Office on Drugs and Crime, www.insightcrime.org/images/PDFs/UNODChomicides.pdf.

2. Agnes Callamard, "El Salvador End of Mission Statement," United Nations Human Rights Office of the High Commissioner, February 5, 2018, www.ohchr.org/en/News Events/Pages/DisplayNews.aspx?NewsID=22634&LangID=E.

3. "United States Crime Rates, 1960–2018," The Disaster Center, www.disastercenter.com/crime/uscrime.htm.

4. China–Latin America Finance Database, The Dialogue, www.thedialogue.org/map_list.

5. Adrian Shahbaz, "The Rise of Digital Authoritarianism," Freedom House, Freedom on the Net series, 2018, https://freedomhouse.org/report/freedom-net/2018/rise-digital-authoritarianism.

6. Shahbaz, "Rise of Digital Authoritarianism."

7. Paul Mozur, Jonah M. Kessel, and Melissa Chan, "Made in China, Exported to the World: The Surveillance State," *New York Times*, April 24, 2019, www.nytimes.com/2019/04/24/technology/ecuador-surveillance-cameras-police-government.html.

8. "Xinjiang Uyghur Autonomous Region," Amnesty USA, www.amnestyusa.org/countries/china/xinjiang.

9. Adrian Zenz and James Leibold, "Chen Quanguo: The Strongman Behind Beijing's Securitization Strategy in Tibet and Xinjiang," Jamestown Foundation, *China Brief* 17, no. 12 (2017), https://jamestown.org/program/chen-quanguo-the-strongman-behind-beijings-securitization-strategy-in-tibet-and-xinjiang.

10. "China Has Turned Xinjiang into a Police State Like No Other," *The Economist*, May 31, 2018, www.economist.com/briefing/2018/05/31/china-has-turned-xinjiang-into-a-police-state-like-no-other.

11. "'Convenience Police Stations' to Closely Monitor Uyghurs," Radio Free Asia, n.d., www.rfa.org/english/news/special/uyghur-oppression/ChenPolicy1.html.

12. "China's Algorithms of Repression," Human Rights Watch, May 1, 2019, www.hrw.org/report/2019/05/01/chinas-algorithms-repression/reverse-engineering-xinjiang-police-mass-surveillance.

13. Tracy Shelton, "China Cracks Down on Ramadan Fasting, Prompting Activist Boycott of Chinese Products," ABC News, May 6, 2019, www.abc.net.au/news/2019-05-07/china-cracks-down-on-fasting-during-ramadan/11082244.

14. Stephanie Nebehay, "1.5 Million Muslims Could Be Detained in China's Xinjiang: Academic," *Reuters*, March 13, 2019, www.reuters.com/article/us-china-xinjiang-rights/15-million-muslims-could-be-detained-in-chinas-xinjiang-academic-idUSKCN1QU2MQ.

15. David Stavrou, "A Million People Are Jailed at China's Gulags. I Managed to Escape. Here's What Really Goes On Inside," *Haaretz*, October 17, 2019, www.haaretz.com/world-news/.premium.MAGAZINE-a-million-people-are-jailed-at-china-s-gulags-i-escaped-here-s-what-goes-on-inside-1.7994216.

16. Alina Polyakova and Chris Meserole, "Exporting Digital Authoritarianism: The Russian and Chinese Models," Brookings Institution, August 2019, www.brookings.edu/wp-content/uploads/2019/08/FP_20190827_digital_authoritarianism_polyakova_meserole.pdf.

17. Paul Mozur, "Inside China's Dystopian Dreams: A.I., Shame and Lots of Cameras," *New York Times*, July 8, 2018, www.nytimes.com/2018/07/08/business/china-surveillance-technology.html.

18. "Chinese Phones Now Account for a Third of the European Market, with Huawei Leading the Way," *The Verge*, February 14, 2019, www.theverge.com/2019/2/14/18224614/huawei-chinese-phones-europe-market-share-2018.

CHAPTER 10: THE OAKLAND SOLUTION

1. Glenn Greenwald, "NSA Collecting Phone Records of Millions of Verizon Customers Daily," *The Guardian*, June 6, 2013, www.theguardian.com/world/2013/jun/06/nsa-phone-records-verizon-court-order.

2. Barton Gellman, Aaron Blake, and Greg Miller, "Edward Snowden Comes Forward as Source of NSA Leaks," *Washington Post*, June 9, 2013, www.washingtonpost.com/politics/intelligence-leaders-push-back-on-leakers-media/2013/06/09/fff80160-d122-11e2-a73e-826d299ff459_story.html.

3. Ewen MacAskill, Julian Borger, Nick Hopkins, Nick Davies, and James Ball, "GCHQ Taps Fibre-Optic Cables for Secret Access to World's Communications," *The Guardian*, June 21, 2013, www.theguardian.com/uk/2013/jun/21/gchq-cables-secret-world-communications-nsa.

4. Glenn Greenwald and Ewen MacAskill, "Obama Orders US to Draw Up Overseas Target List for Cyber-Attacks," *The Guardian*, June 7, 2013, www.theguardian.com/world/2013/jun/07/obama-china-targets-cyber-overseas.

5. Mark Mazzetti and Michael S. Schmidt, "Ex-Worker at C.I.A. Says He Leaked Data on Surveillance," *New York Times*, June 9, 2013, www.nytimes.com/2013/06/10/us/former-cia-worker-says-he-leaked-surveillance-data.html.

6. Much of what follows comes from conversations with Joe DeVries, Matt Cagle, Brian Hofer, and from the information gathered at "Domain Awareness Center," Oakland Wiki, Local Wiki, https://localwiki.org/oakland/Domain_Awareness_Center.

7. For model legislation and information, see "Community Control over Police Surveillance," American Civil Liberties Union, www.aclu.org/issues/privacy-technology/surveillance-technologies/community-control-over-police-surveillance.

8. Birch was a sworn officer in Daly City, just across the bay, before coming to Oakland; he was the Oakland PD's head of research and planning for several years. He left that position shortly after I spoke with him in late March 2018.

INDEX

Jon Fasman is the Washington correspondent for *The Economist*, having previously been Southeast Asia bureau chief and Atlanta correspondent. In addition to his work for *The Economist*, he is the author of two novels, both published by Penguin Books: *The Geographer's Library* was a *New York Times* bestseller in 2005 and has been translated into more than a dozen languages, and *The Unpossessed City*, published in 2008, was a finalist for the New York Public Library's Young Lions Fiction Award.